Ecce Romani

A Latin Reading Program
Revised Edition

1
Meeting the Family

2
Rome at Last

Longman

Ecce Romani Combined 1 & 2

ISBN 0 8013 0439 3 (Combined 1 & 2) (78249)
ISBN 0 582 36664 X (1: Meeting the Family) (72458)
ISBN 0 582 36665 8 (2: Rome at Last) (72459)

Illustrated by Peter Dennis, Trevor Parkin, Hamish Gordon. *Cover illustration by Peter Dennis.*

This edition of *Ecce Romani* is based on *Ecce Romani: A Latin Reading Course*,
originally prepared by The Scottish Classics Group © copyright The Scottish Classics
Group 1971, 1982, and published in the United Kingdom by Oliver and Boyd, a
Division of Longman Group. This edition has been prepared by a team of American
and Canadian educators:
    Authors: Professor Gilbert Lawall, University of Massachusetts, Amherst,
          Massachusetts
          David Tafe, Rye Country Day School, Rye, New York
    Consultants: Dr. Rudolph Masciantonio, Philadelphia Public Schools, Pennsylvania
          Ronald Palma, Holland Hall School, Tulsa, Oklahoma
          Dr. Edward Barnes, C.W. Jefferys Secondary School, Downsview,
          Ontario
          Shirley Lowe, Wayland Public Schools, Wayland, Massachusetts

Longman, 10 Bank Street, White Plains, N.Y. 10606

Associated companies:
Longman Group Ltd., London
Longman Cheshire Pty., Melbourne
Longman Paul Pty., Auckland
Copp Clark Pitman, Toronto
Pitman Publishing Inc., Boston

5 6 7 8 9 10-MU-95949392

CONTENTS

1
Two Roman Girls

Ecce! In pictūrā est puella, nōmine Cornēlia. Cornēlia est puella Rōmāna quae in Italiā habitat. Etiam in pictūrā est vīlla rūstica ubi Cornēlia aestāte habitat. Cornēlia est laeta quod iam in vīllā habitat. Cornēlia iam sub arbore sedet. Etiam in pictūrā est altera puella, nōmine Flāvia. Flāvia est puella Rōmāna quae in vīllā vīcīnā habitat. Dum Cornēlia sedet, Flāvia cantat. 5 Laeta est Flāvia quod Cornēlia iam in vīllā habitat.

<table>
<tr><td>

Ecce! Look!
puella, (a, the) girl
nōmine, by name, called
quae, who
habitat, (he, she) is living, lives
etiam, also
ubi, where
aestāte, in summer
laeta, happy

</td><td>

quod, because
iam, now
sub arbore, under the tree
sedet, (he, she) is sitting, sits
altera, a second
vīcīna, neighboring
dum, while
cantat, (he, she) is singing, sings

</td></tr>
</table>

Exercise 1a

Respondē Latīnē:
1. Quis est Cornēlia?
2. Ubi habitat Cornēlia?
3. Cūr est Cornēlia laeta?
4. Quid facit Cornēlia?

5. Ubi habitat Flāvia?
6. Quid facit Flāvia?
7. Cūr est Flāvia laeta?

Quis . . . ? Who . . . ?

Cūr . . . ? Why . . . ?
Quid facit . . . ? What does . . . do?
What is . . . doing?

Exercise 1b

From the passage give the Latin for:
1. Cornelia is happy.
2. Cornelia is sitting under the tree.
3. Flavia is a Roman girl.
4. Cornelia now lives in the farmhouse.

2
A Happy Outing

Cornēlia est puella Rōmāna. Flāvia quoque est puella Rōmāna. Cornēlia et Flāvia sunt puellae Rōmānae quae in Italiā habitant. Cornēlia et Flāvia sunt amīcae. Hodiē puellae nōn sedent sed in agrīs ambulant. Puellae cantant quod laetae sunt. Brevī tempore Cornēlia dēfessa est. Nōn iam ambulat sed sub arbore sedet. Flāvia, quae est puella strēnua, in agrīs currit. Brevī tempore 5 Flāvia quoque est dēfessa. Iam Flāvia et Cornēlia sub arbore sedent quod dēfessae sunt. Tandem puellae dēfessae ex agrīs ad vīllam rūsticam lentē ambulant.

quoque, also	**dēfessa,** tired
et, and	**strēnua,** active, energetic
sunt, (they) are	**currit,** (he, she) is running, runs
amīcae, friends	**tandem,** at last
hodiē, today	**ex agrīs,** from the fields
sed, but	**ad vīllam rūsticam,** to or toward the
in agrīs, in the fields	farmhouse
ambulant, (they) are walking, walk	**lentē,** slowly
brevī tempore, in a short time, soon	

VERBS: The Endings -t and -nt

Look at these sentences:

Flāvia in Italiā habita**t**.	*Flavia lives in Italy.*
Puella in agrīs curri**t**.	*The girl is running in the fields.*
Flāvia et Cornēlia in Italiā habita**nt**.	*Flavia and Cornelia live in Italy.*
Puellae sub arbore sede**nt**.	*The girls are sitting under the tree.*

When the verb ends in **-t,** the subject of the sentence is singular, e.g., **Flāvia, puella.**

When the verb ends in **-nt,** the subject of the sentence is plural, e.g., **Flāvia et Cornēlia, puellae.**

6

Exercise 2a

Respondē Latīnē:
1. Ubi habitant Cornēlia et Flāvia?
2. Quid faciunt puellae hodiē?

   Quid faciunt . . . ?
   What are . . . doing?

3. Cūr puellae cantant?
4. Quid facit Cornēlia quod dēfessa est?
5. Quid faciunt puellae quod dēfessae sunt?

Exercise 2b

From the passage give the Latin for:
1. Cornelia and Flavia are Roman girls.
2. In a short time Cornelia is tired.
3. Flavia is running in the fields.
4. At last the girls walk slowly to the farmhouse.

Exercise 2c

Select the correct word, read the sentence aloud, and translate it into English:

1. Flāvia in vīllā vīcīnā _____.   habitat / habitant
2. Cornēlia et Flāvia sub arbore _____.   sedet / sedent
3. Cornēlia et Flāvia dēfessae _____.   est / sunt
4. Flāvia strēnua _____.   est / sunt
5. Cornēlia et Flāvia sunt _____.   puella Rōmāna / puellae Rōmānae

Exercise 2d

Read aloud and translate:

Cornēlia est puella Rōmāna quae in vīllā rūsticā aestāte habitat. In vīllā vīcīnā habitat altera puella, nōmine Flāvia, quae est amīca eius. Dum puellae in vīllā habitant, in agrīs saepe ambulant. Hodiē Cornēlia ad vīllam Flāviānam ambulat ubi in agrīs sub arbore sedet Flāvia. Iam puellae laetae currunt. Brevī tempore, quod dēfessae sunt, 5 nōn iam currunt sed sub arbore sedent.

eius, her   **saepe,** often

7

A Roman Family

The stories and pictures in this book are about a Roman family. When we first meet them, they are living not in Rome but on a farm (**fundus**) in the country near Baiae in Campania.

While spending their summers on the farm, the family occupies part of a large farmhouse called a **vīlla** or **vīlla rūstica** which has a central farmyard, court, or garden (**hortus**) surrounded by living quarters for the owner's family in one corner, a second farmyard with wine vats sunk in the ground, and various farm buildings including rooms for the slave laborers.

The date is A.D. 80.

In our family, there is a daughter, Cornelia, who is thirteen, and a son, Marcus, fifteen. Both wear the same dress as their respective parents, Cornelius and Aurelia, because the Romans did not have special clothes for children. Neither goes to school when at the **vīlla**, their education being in the hands of a Greek tutor, Eucleides. Although the father is called Gaius Cornelius Calvus and the son Marcus Cornelius Calvus, the daughter has to be content with the feminine form of her father's name, Cornelia. (What must Aurelia's father have been called?) Although Marcus has lessons from Eucleides, he gets a good deal of his education directly from his father, for Gaius is an old-fashioned Roman who thinks a father should superintend his son's education personally.

Gaius is responsible for the estate. As father, he is not only master of his own house, but legally has the power of life and death over his entire household, though he never exercises this power. Aurelia runs the household. She does some wool-spinning—a traditional practice which recalls the old Roman ideal of self-sufficiency—but, unlike the modern housewife, she has a miniature army of slaves to help with the chores.

They have living with them a younger boy, Sextus. He is not related to the family, but Cornelius is acting as his guardian while his father is on service overseas. Also with the family, from time to time, is Cornelia's friend, Flavia, who lives in a neighboring farmhouse referred to as the **vīlla Flāviāna** because it is owned by her father, Flavius.

Most Roman families had slaves who did the everyday work of the household and the farms. The tutor, Eucleides, is a slave, as is Davus, the overseer of the slaves and the farm.

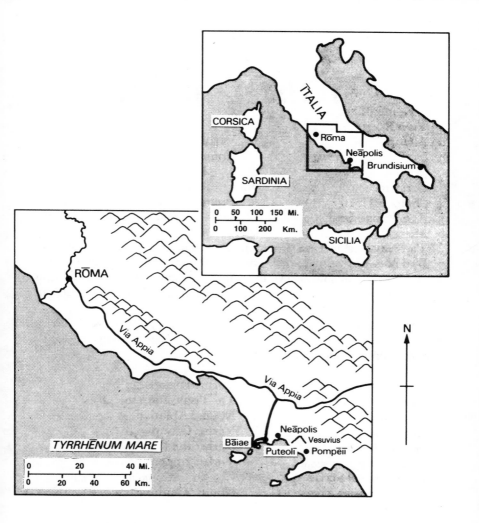

Baiae, on the Bay of Naples, was a fashionable resort for wealthy Romans, many of whom built splendid villas there. Puteoli, further around the Bay, was a thriving seaport where corn-ships from Egypt and Sicily would unload their cargo, to be taken to Rome by road. Nearby Naples (**Neāpolis**), a center of culture and learning for the Romans, was far enough from Vesuvius to survive when the eruption of A.D. 79 overwhelmed the prosperous town of Pompeii.

This whole area, part of the fertile province of Campania, in summer attracted Romans who were seeking relief from the heat and noise of Rome in this "Garden of Italy."

3
In the Garden

In pictūrā est puer Rōmānus, nōmine Marcus, quī in Italiā habitat. Etiam in pictūrā est alter puer, nōmine Sextus, quī in eādem vīllā rūsticā habitat. Marcus et Sextus sunt amīcī. Hodiē puerī in hortō clāmant et rīdent quod laetī sunt.

Vir quoque est in pictūrā, nōmine Dāvus, quī est servus. In Italiā sunt 5 multī servī quī in agrīs et in vīllīs rūsticīs labōrant. Puerī sunt Rōmānī, sed Dāvus nōn est Rōmānus. Est vir Britannicus quī iam in Italiā labōrat. Sextus et Marcus, quod sunt puerī Rōmānī, nōn labōrant. Dāvus sōlus labōrat, īrātus quod puerī clāmant.

Subitō Sextus in piscīnam cadit. Marcus rīdet, sed Dāvus, "Abīte, 10 molestī!" clāmat et ad piscīnam īrātus currit. Sextus madidus ex piscīnā exit, et puerī ex hortō currunt. Dāvus gemit.

puer, (a, the) boy	**in vīllīs rūsticīs,** in farmhouses
quī, who	**labōrant,** (they) are working, work
eādem, the same	**sōlus,** alone
in hortō, in the garden	**īrātus,** angry
clāmant, (they) are shouting, shout	**subitō,** suddenly
rīdent, (they) are laughing, laugh, smile	**in piscīnam,** into the fishpond
vir, (a, the) man	**cadit,** (he, she) falls
servus, (a, the) slave	**Abīte, molestī!** Go away, you pests!
multī, many	**madidus,** dripping, soaked
	gemit, (he, she) groans

10

Exercise 3a

Respondē Latīnē:
1. Quis est Dāvus?
2. Estne Marcus servus?
3. Quis est Marcus?
4. Suntne Marcus et Sextus amīcī?
5. Quid faciunt puerī hodiē?
6. Cūr Dāvus īrātus est?
7. Estne Dāvus vir Rōmānus?
8. Quid subitō facit Sextus?

Estne . . . ? Is . . . ?

Minimē! No!
Ita vērō! Yes!

Exercise 3b

From the passage give the Latin for:
1. Today the boys laugh because they are happy.
2. In Italy there are many slaves who work in farmhouses.
3. Davus now works in Italy.
4. Davus runs to the fishpond, and the boys run out of the garden.

NOUNS: Singular and Plural

Note how these words change in the plural:

Singular	Plural
puell**a**	puell**ae**
serv**us**	serv**ī**
puer	puer**ī**

Compare also: puell**a** Rōmān**a**   puell**ae** Rōmān**ae**
          puer Rōmān**us**   puer**ī** Rōmān**ī**

12

Exercise 3c

Select, read aloud, and translate:

1. Marcus et Sextus in eādem vīllā _____.   habitat / habitant
2. Dāvus vir Britannicus _____.   est / sunt
3. In agrīs labōrant _____.   servus / servī
4. Puerī et puellae saepe _____.   gemit / currit / currunt
5. In agrīs sunt multī _____.   puella / servus / servī
6. In Italiā habitat _____.   Marcus et Sextus/
   Marcus / puellae
7. Marcus et Sextus sunt puerī _____.   Rōmānus / Rōmānī /
   Rōmānae
8. Cornēlia et Flāvia sunt puellae _____.   Rōmānus / Rōmānī /
   Rōmānae

Exercise 3d

Read aloud and translate:

Hodiē Sextus in hortō ambulat sōlus quod Marcus in vīllā sedet. Sextus est puer strēnuus quī saepe in agrīs et in hortō currit. Brevī tempore Dāvus in hortum ambulat, sollicitus quod Sextus in hortō est. Dum Dāvus labōrat, Sextus eum spectat. Sextus Dāvum saepe vexat, sed hodiē nihil facit.   5

In hortum ad piscīnam currunt Flāvia et Cornēlia. Laetae rīdent et clāmant. Sextus fūrtim ad piscīnam ambulat. Subitō in piscīnam cadit statua rūstica. Madidae iam sunt puellae et īrātae. Dāvus est sollicitus quod statua est in piscīnā, sed Sextus, "Statua est salva," clāmat et ex hortō currit.   10

in hortum, into the garden	**vexat,** (he, she) annoys
sollicitus, anxious, worried	**nihil,** nothing
eum, him	**fūrtim,** stealthily
spectat, (he, she) watches	**salva,** undamaged, all right

Dress

Gaius' tunic is knee-length and, to show that he is a senator, it has a broad purple stripe running from the neck right down the front. On official occasions he wears over the tunic the **toga,** a very full garment requiring the services of two or three slaves before its folds can be successfully draped. Most Romans would wear the **toga virīlis,** a plain white toga, but Gaius has the privilege of wearing the **toga praetexta,** white with a purple edging, the distinctive dress of a senator who has held high office.

Aurelia wears a simple sleeveless white tunic and, over the tunic, a **stola**—a long, flounced dress, girdled at the waist and reaching to her ankles. For outdoor wear she adds the **palla,** a single piece of material draped around the body.

Cornelia, like her mother, is clad in the **stola.** Marcus, like his father, wears the tunic and, in public, a **toga** over it. A boy's **toga** was the same as a senior senator's—the **toga praetexta.** Both boys and girls wore around their necks a **bulla** or luck-charm which was given to them at their naming ceremony. Girls continued to wear the **bulla** until they were married. When boys came of age, at sixteen, they dedicated the **bulla** and the first scrapings of their beard to the household gods and thereafter wore the **toga virīlis.**

Romans generally went bare-headed. If protection from the wind or weather was needed, the **toga** or **palla** could be drawn over the head. Women used parasols to shield them from the sun, and men used the broad-brimmed hat (**petasus**) for this purpose.

BULLA, made of gold, bronze, lead, or leather

14

4
Show-off!

Sextus est puer molestus quī semper Cornēliam vexat. Cornēlia igitur
Sextum nōn amat. Hodiē sub arbore dormit Cornēlia. Sextus puellam cōn-
spicit et fūrtim appropinquat. Arborem ascendit et subitō magnā vōce clāmat.
Vōcem Cornēlia audit sed Sextum nōn videt. Magna vōx Cornēliam terret.
Sollicita est.   5

Tum Marcus ad arborem currit. Marcus puerum molestum cōnspicit et
clāmat, "Dēscende, Sexte!"

Sextus clāmat, "Marce, cūr tū nōn arborem ascendis? Nihil mē terret.
Quid tē terret?"

"Cavē, Sexte!" clāmat Marcus. "Rāmī sunt īnfirmī."   10

Subitō Marcus et Cornēlia magnum fragōrem audiunt; Sextus ex arbore
cadit. Rīdent Marcus et Cornēlia, sed nōn rīdet Sextus.

semper, always	**videt,** (he, she) sees
igitur, therefore	**terret,** (he, she, it) frightens
amat, (he, she) likes, loves	**tum,** at that moment, then
dormit, (he, she) sleeps	**Dēscende!** Come down!
cōnspicit, (he, she) catches sight of	**tū,** you (subject)
appropinquat, (he, she) approaches	**tē,** you (direct object)
ascendit, (he, she) climbs	**Cavē, Sexte!** Be careful, Sextus!
magnā vōce, in a loud voice	**rāmus,** (a, the) branch
vōx, (a, the) voice	**īnfirmus,** weak, shaky
audit, (he, she) hears, listens to	**fragor,** (a, the) crash, noise

In Latin, the form **Sexte** is used when Sextus is addressed by name. (Compare
Marce.) No such change is made in English.

16

Exercise 4a

Respondē Latīnē:
1. Quālis puer est Sextus?
2. Quid facit Cornēlia hodiē?
3. Quid facit Sextus?
4. Quid audit Cornēlia?
5. Quō Marcus currit?
6. Quid clāmat Sextus?
7. Quid audiunt Marcus et Cornēlia?

Quālis . . . ? What sort of . . . ?

Quō . . . ? Where . . . to?

Exercise 4b

Select, read aloud, and translate:

1. Marcus est puer _____.	Rōmānus / Rōmāna
2. Sextus est puer _____.	sollicitus / sollicita / molestus
3. Flāvia et Cornēlia in hortum _____.	currit / currunt
4. Marcus et Sextus sunt _____.	amīcus / amīcī
5. Marcus nōn est _____.	servus / servī
6. Puerī nōn sunt _____.	servus / servī
7. Marcus arborem nōn _____.	ascendit / ascendunt
8. Dāvus est vir _____.	Britannicus / Britannicī
9. Puerī _____ rīdent.	laetus / laetī
10. Cornēlia et Flāvia sunt _____.	dēfessa / dēfessae
11. _____ servī in Italiā _____.	Multī / Multae labōrat / labōrant
12. Servus Britannicus _____ est quod puerī nōn _____.	īrātus / īrātī labōrat / labōrant

NOUNS: The Ending -m

Look at these sentences taken from story 4:

Cornēlia Sextum nōn amat.	*Cornelia does not like Sextus.*
Sextus puellam cōnspicit.	*Sextus catches sight of the girl.*
Vōcem Cornēlia audit.	*Cornelia hears the voice.*
Marcus puerum molestum cōnspicit.	*Marcus catches sight of the annoying boy.*
Magnum fragōrem audiunt.	*They hear a great crash.*

In these sentences **Sextum, puellam, vōcem, puerum,** and **fragōrem** are the direct objects of the verbs.

The Latin nouns you have met so far end in **-m** when they are direct objects and are singular.

Versiculī: *"Serves Him Right," page 89.*

18

Word Study I

Latin and English

Over 60% of the words in the English language come from Latin. Look again at these words from Chapter 1:

pictūra **habitat**

It is not difficult to think of English words which come from them:

picture *inhabit*

The meanings and spellings of these English words show their relationship with Latin. Such words are called *derivatives*, since they are derived from (or come from) another language, in this case, Latin.

Of course, not all of English is derived from Latin. Most of the simple words of everyday English come from Anglo-Saxon, the Germanic ancestor of English. For this reason, many modern German words sound similar to English, such as "Buch" (*book*) and "Nacht" (*night*).

English words derived from Latin are usually the longer or more difficult words. For example, consider the two English words *water* and *aquatic*. The simpler word *water* is derived from the Anglo-Saxon "waeter" and is related to the German "Wasser." The more difficult word *aquatic* comes from the Latin word for water, **aqua**. Even if one did not know the meaning of *aquatic*, Latin would help to answer the following question:

Which of these is an aquatic sport?

(a) horseback riding   (b) tennis   (c) swimming   (d) soccer

Since *aquatic* means "related to water," the correct answer is "swimming." Knowledge of Latin will help with the meanings of over 60% of the words in the English language.

Exercise 1

Below are some Latin words from Chapters 1–4. Give the meaning of each word. Then, with the meaning in mind, think of at least one English word derived from each Latin word. Use each English word correctly in a sentence.

strēnua	sōlus	servus	agrīs	dēscende
multī	nōmine	spectat	terret	vōx (vōce)

19

Exercise 2

Match each English word in the column at the left with its meaning in the column at the right. Use the meaning of the Latin word in parentheses as a guide.

1. chant (**cantat**)
2. sedentary (**sedet**)
3. ridicule (**rīdet**)
4. virile (**vir**)
5. elaborate (**labōrat**)
6. audible (**audit**)
7. conspicuous (**cōnspicit**)
8. dormant (**dormit**)

a. manly
b. easy to catch sight of
c. to work out carefully
d. a type of singing
e. able to be heard
f. asleep, inactive
g. to make fun of, mock
h. seated, stationary

The Dictionary

An English dictionary is a useful source not only for finding the meanings of words but also for discovering the languages from which they are derived. Not all dictionaries provide information on derivation, but most larger ones do. In these more complete dictionaries, entries may include:

a. the word
b. a pronunciation guide
c. an abbreviation indicating the part of speech
d. derivation information
e. definition(s)

Locate these items of information in the following dictionary entry:

villain (vil′ ən), n. [O.Fr. *vilain* <L.L. *vīllānus* <L. *vīlla*, a farm, country house.] 1. a baseborn or clownish person. 2. a scoundrel.

This entry shows that the English word *villain* is a noun which comes from Old French "vilain," which is from the Late Latin **vīllānus**, which derives from Latin **vīlla**, meaning a farm or country house. This derivation is especially interesting since it reveals the negative feelings toward country people that must have been prevalent at the time when the word *villain* came into use in English.

The abbreviations used in notes on derivation will be different from dictionary to dictionary. All abbreviations are explained at the beginning of each dictionary.

Exercise 3

Using a dictionary large enough to contain information on derivation, look up the following English words and copy down the complete derivation for each. Be prepared to interpret these derivations as in the example above. All of these English words are derived from Latin words you have met.

nominal   cadence   virtue   alter   ramify   infirm

5
At a Loose End

Sextus, ubi in hortum māne exit, Dāvum cōnspicit et fūrtim appropinquat. Subitō, dum Dāvus est occupātus, clāmat, "Quid tū facis, Dāve?"
Dāvus, quī Sextum nōn amat, īrātus respondet, "Cūr tū mē vexās? Ego
clāmōrem tuum semper audiō. Tū semper clāmās, semper rīdēs, semper
curris. Ego semper sum occupātus. Ego in hortō labōrō. Ecce! Sunt multae   5
arborēs in agrīs. Sī tū puer strēnuus es, ascende arborem! Abī, moleste!"
Sextus, laetus quod Dāvus est īrātus, iam in agrōs abit. Arborem magnam
petit et statim ascendit. Ibi in rāmīs sedet et, "Ubi es, Marce?" clāmat.
"Ecce! Ego in arbore sedeō. Ego nōn sum timidus. Nihil mē terret. Cūr
tū quoque in agrōs nōn venīs? Arborēs nōn sunt magnae. Rāmī nōn sunt   10
īnfirmī."
Sed Marcus, quī adhūc dormit, Sextum nōn audit. Sextus igitur dēscendit
et lentē ad vīllam redit.

ubi, when	**magnus,** big, great
māne, early in the day	**petit,** (he, she) looks for, seeks
ego, I	**statim,** immediately
clāmor, shout, shouting	**ibi,** there
tuus, your	**venīs,** you come
sum, I am	**adhūc,** still
sī, if	**redit,** (he, she) returns

Exercise 5a

Using story 5 as a guide, give the Latin for:
1. Sextus catches sight of Davus.
2. What are you doing, Davus?
3. Why do you annoy me?
4. I am working in the garden.
5. Sextus immediately climbs a big tree.
6. Marcus does not hear Sextus.

21

Exercise 5b

Read aloud and translate:

1. Sextus Dāvum saepe vexat; Dāvus Sextum nōn amat.
2. Puellae Marcum et servum cōnspiciunt.
3. Magnam vōcem Cornēlia audit.
4. Magna vōx puellam terret.
5. Sextus arborem magnam ascendit.
6. Puerī clāmōrem audiunt et statim in hortum currunt.
7. Cūr nōn sollicita es, Cornēlia? Cornēlius, pater tuus, īrātus statuam petit.
8. Dāvus, ubi clāmōrem audit, est īrātus.
9. Aestāte dum Marcus in vīllā rūsticā habitat, amīcī eius saepe ad vīllam veniunt.

eius, his

6
Marcus to the Rescue

Cornēlia et Flāvia in hortō saepe ambulant. Sī diēs est calidus, ex hortō in silvam ambulant quod ibi est rīvus frīgidus. In eādem silvā puerī quoque saepe errant.

Hodiē, quod diēs est calidus, puellae sub arbore prope rīvum sedent. Dum ibi sedent, Flāvia, "Cūr Marcus arborēs ascendere nōn vult? Estne puer 5 ignāvus?"

"Minimē!" respondet Cornēlia. "Cūr tū Marcum nōn amās? Marcus neque ignāvus neque temerārius est."

Tum Flāvia, "Sed Marcus est semper sollicitus. Sextum nihil terret."

Subitō lupum cōnspiciunt quī ad rīvum fūrtim dēscendit. Perterritae sunt 10 puellae. Statim clāmant, "Marce! Sexte! Ferte auxilium! Ferte auxilium!"

Puerī, ubi clāmōrem audiunt, statim ad puellās currunt. Lupus eōs iam cōnspicit et statim petit. Tum Sextus, quod lupus eum terret, arborem petit et statim ascendit. Sed Marcus rāmum arripit et lupum repellit. Puellae ē silvā currunt et ad vīllam salvae adveniunt. Brevī tempore, ubi Marcus 15 advenit, eum laetae excipiunt. Sextus, puer ignāvus, adhūc sedet in arbore perterritus. Dēscendere timet.

diēs, (a, the) day	**lupus,** (a, the) wolf
calidus, warm	**perterritus,** frightened
in silvam, into the woods	**Ferte auxilium!** Bring help! Help!
rīvus, (a, the) stream	**ad puellās,** towards the girls
frīgidus, cool	**eōs,** them
errant, (they) wander	**arripit,** (he, she) grabs hold of,
prope, near	snatches
vult, (he, she) wishes, wants	**repellit,** (he, she) drives off
ignāvus, cowardly, lazy	**ē silvā,** out of the woods
neque . . . neque . . . ,	**adveniunt,** (they) reach, arrive at
neither . . . nor . . .	**excipiunt,** (they) welcome
temerārius, rash	**timet,** (he, she) fears, is afraid

Exercise 6a

Respondē Latīnē:
1. Ubi hodiē puellae sedent?
2. Estne Marcus ignāvus?
3. Estne Marcus sollicitus?
4. Cūr puellae perterritae sunt?
5. Quid puellae clāmant?
6. Ubi clāmōrem audiunt, quid faciunt puerī?
7. Cūr Sextus arborem ascendit?
8. Quem lupus terret?   **Quem** . . . ? Whom . . . ?
9. Quid facit Marcus?
10. Quid faciunt puellae?
11. Quid facit Sextus?
12. Quālis puer est Sextus?

Exercise 6b

Select, read aloud, and translate:
1. Hodiē Sextus _____ ascendit.
   arbor / arborem
2. Sextus _____ cōnspicit.
   Marcus / Marcum
3. Nihil _____ terret.
   Sextum / Sextus
4. _____ puellae cōnspiciunt.
   Lupus / Lupum
5. Puerī _____ audiunt.
   clāmōrem / clāmor
6. _____ lupus terret.
   Sextus / Sextum
7. Sextus arborem _____ ascendit.
   magnus / magnam
8. Puellae _____ laetae excipiunt.
   Marcus / Marcum

24

VERBS: *The Infinitive*

Look at these sentences:

Arborēs **ascendere** nōn vult.	*He does not wish to climb trees.*
Dēscendere timet.	*He is afraid to come down.*

The words **ascendere** and **dēscendere** are present infinitives. The present infinitive is a form of the verb that can be recognized by the ending *-re* and may be translated by "to . . . ," e.g., **errāre**, "to wander."

Exercise 6c

Read aloud and translate:

1. Ego ad hortum currō quod Dāvum vexāre volō.
2. Puellae saepe cantant, sed Sextus cantāre nōn potest.
3. Ego arborem nōn ascendō quod in rīvum cadere nōlō.
4. Quod diēs est calidus, tū prope rīvum errāre parās.
5. Lupus ad vīllam fūrtim appropinquat; servus eum repellere nōn potest.
6. Sextus ex arbore dēscendere nōn vult quod lupus eum terret.
7. Ego in silvā sōlus ambulāre timeō.
8. Prope piscīnam sedet puella. Advenit altera puella. Iam laetae cantant puellae.
9. Subitō statua rūstica in piscīnam cadit. Clāmant puellae.
10. Puer lupum cōnspicit, rāmum arripit, lupum repellere parat.
11. Sī diēs est calidus, Marcus ambulāre in silvam vult ubi prope rīvum frīgidum sedēre potest.
12. In hortum exīre nōlō quod in vīllā labōrāre volō.

volō, I wish, want	**potest**, (he, she) is able, can
nōlō, I do not wish	**parās**, you prepare, get ready

The Slave Market

Slaves, who were in the early days mainly prisoners of war, were plentiful, and even the poorest Roman household might own one or two. Davus had been captured in Britain and sent to Rome to be sold by auction in the Forum. When his feet were whitened with chalk by the slave-dealer, Davus was mystified, but he soon discovered that this had been done to all new arrivals from abroad. A placard was hung around his neck indicating that he was British and could read and write. He was then put on a revolving stand, and bidding for him began.

He felt pretty uncomfortable standing there like an exhibit at the cattle-market, but he put the best face on it, looking around challengingly at the bidders. Titus Cornelius, father of Gaius Cornelius, was in the Forum that day to purchase some new slaves. He did not pay much attention to the placard—**mangōnēs**, as slave-dealers were called, were notorious swindlers—but when he saw Davus' fine physique, fair hair, and blue eyes he made a bid of 5,000 sesterces, and Davus soon found himself beside the overseer and his new master.

By this time Titus was offering 10,000 sesterces for a Greek from Rhodes. This puzzled Davus because the fellow was a pale, half-starved individual who looked as if a hard day's work would kill him. The overseer, too, looked annoyed at this extravagant bid but said nothing. But when he heard Titus being forced up to 20,000, then 30,000, he could contain himself no longer and muttered angrily, "He's not worth half that, master!" But Titus ignored him and finally paid 35,000 for the Greek Eucleides. The odd qualifications on the placard, "skilled in geometry and rhetoric," must, Davus thought, have had something to do with the record price!

As Davus, along with the strange Greek, was packed on a cart with some tough-looking Thracians also bought that day, he was filled with fear and doubt as to what might happen to him. But he needn't have worried. Old Titus proved to be the kindest of masters, and now, thirty years later, Davus, himself a grizzled fifty-five, was overseer to Gaius. On some of the neighboring farms, he knew, things were not so good.

7
Bad News

In vīllā sedet vir Rōmānus, nōmine Gāius Cornēlius, quī est pater Marcī et Cornēliae. Cornēlius est senātor Rōmānus. Sōlus sedet quod multās epistulās scrībere vult. Dum pater occupātus est, Marcus et Sextus et Cornēlia in agrīs vīcīnīs errant. Ibi multōs servōs labōrantēs spectant. Subitō nūntium cōnspiciunt quī ad eōs venit. Nūntius, ubi advenit, 5 puerōs salūtat.

"Salvē!" respondet Marcus. "Quem tū petis?"

Nūntius, "Gāium Cornēlium petō," inquit.

Marcus, "Gāius Cornēlius est pater meus," inquit. "Est in vīllā." Nūntium in vīllam dūcit et patrem petit. 10

"Pater," inquit Marcus, "nūntius in vīllā est."

Cornēlius statim venit et nūntium salūtat. Epistulam nūntius trādit. Cornēlius, ubi epistulam legit, "Ēheu!" inquit. "Prīnceps senātōrēs Rōmānōs ad urbem revocat. Eōs cōnsulere vult. Necesse est ad urbem redīre."

"Eugepae!" clāmat Sextus, quī Rōmam redīre vult. Gemit Cornēlia quod 15 Flāvia ad urbem venīre nōn potest.

---

scrībere, to write
labōrantēs, working
nūntius, messenger
salūtat, (he, she) greets
Salvē! Greetings! Good morning!
  Hello!
inquit, (he, she) says
meus, my
dūcit, (he, she) leads, takes

trādit, (he, she) hands over
legit, (he, she) reads
Ēheu! Alas!
prīnceps, the emperor
ad urbem, to the city
revocat, (he, she) recalls
cōnsulere, to consult
necesse est, it is necessary
Eugepae! Hurray!

Exercise 7a

Respondē Latīnē:
1. Ubi sedet Cornēlius?
2. Cūr Cornēlius sōlus sedet?
3. Ubi Marcus et Sextus et Cornēlia errant?
4. Quōs spectant in agrīs?   **Quōs** . . . ? Whom . . . ? (plural)
5. Quis advenit?
6. Quem nūntius petit?
7. Quō Marcus nūntium dūcit?
8. Cūr prīnceps senātōrēs Rōmānōs ad urbem revocat?
9. Quis clāmat "eugepae"? Cūr?
10. Cūr gemit Cornēlia?

NOUNS: The Endings -ās, -ōs, -ēs

Look at these three sentences:

Multās epistulās scrībit.	He writes many letters.
Multōs servōs spectant.	They watch many slaves.
Senātōrēs Rōmānōs revocat.	He recalls the Roman senators.

The words **epistulās, servōs,** and **senātōrēs** introduce you to new endings. You already know that most singular Latin nouns end in **-m** when they are used as direct objects. Plural nouns used as direct objects usually end in **-s,** e.g., **epistulās, servōs,** and **senātōrēs.**

Exercise 7b

Using story 7 as a guide, give the Latin for:
1. Cornelius is the father of Marcus and Cornelia.
2. Cornelius wants to write many letters.
3. Marcus and Sextus watch many slaves working in the fields.
4. The messenger greets the boys.
5. The messenger is looking for Gaius Cornelius.
6. Marcus looks for (his) father.
7. The messenger hands over a letter.
8. It is necessary to return to the city immediately.
9. Sextus wishes to return to Rome, but Flavia cannot.

29

NOUNS: Cases and Declensions

Nominative and Accusative Cases

The form of the Latin noun when used as the *subject* of a verb is known as the *nominative case*.

The form of the Latin noun when used as the *direct object* of a verb is known as the *accusative case*.

For example:

Nominative	Accusative
Lup*us* eum terret.	Puellae lup*um* vident.
The wolf frightens him.	*The girls see the wolf.*
Lup*ī* puerōs terrent.	Servī lup*ōs* repellunt.
The wolves frighten the boys.	*The slaves drive back the wolves.*

The nouns you have met so far belong to three groups or declensions:

Number Case	*1st Declension*	*2nd Declension*		*3rd Declension*	
Singular					
Nominative	puell*a*	serv*us*	puer	pater	vōx
Accusative	puell*am*	serv*um*	puer*um*	patr*em*	vōc*em*
Plural					
Nominative	puell*ae*	serv*ī*	puer*ī*	patr*ēs*	vōc*ēs*
Accusative	puell*ās*	serv*ōs*	puer*ōs*	patr*ēs*	vōc*ēs*

Be sure to learn these forms thoroughly.

Notes

1. In the 2nd declension, most nouns end in -*us* in the nominative singular (e.g., **servus**), but there are a few like **puer, ager,** and **vir** which end in -*r.* In both types, however, the accusative singular ends in -*um* and the accusative plural in -*ōs.*
2. Although **arbor, pater,** and **māter** end in -*r,* their other endings put them in the 3rd declension.
3. In the 3rd declension, you will note that the nouns you have met can end in different ways in the nominative singular (e.g., **arbor, prīnceps, urbs, pater, vōx**). Nevertheless, their accusative singulars all end in -*em,* and both nominative and accusative plurals end in -*ēs.*

Building Up the Meaning I

When you are reading a Latin sentence, each word *as you meet it* gives you certain clues about its own meaning and about what is likely to come next. First you recognize the basic meaning of the word, and then you note the case of the word, since the case will help you decide what the function of the word is in the sentence.

Consider the following sentences:

1. **Servus currit.**

The first word we meet is **servus**. We know that it is the subject of the verb because we recognize that it is in the nominative case. We can expect a verb which will tell us what the slave is "doing."

2. **Servus Dāvum cōnspicit.**

We go from **servus** to **Dāvum** and recognize **Dāvum** as accusative case. It is likely that the slave is "doing" something to Davus and that a verb will follow to tell us what the slave is "doing" to Davus.

3. **Dāvum puerī vexant.**

The first word we meet is **Dāvum**. We know that it is the direct object of the verb because we recognize it as accusative case. It is likely that someone is doing something to Davus. The next word is **puerī**. We recognize that it is nominative, and therefore it is *the boys* who are doing something to Davus. The verb **vexant** tells us what they are doing.

4. **Rāmum arripit.**

We know immediately that someone is doing something to a branch, but, since there is no noun in the nominative case, the *ending* of the verb indicates the subject and the *meaning* of the verb completes the sense.

Exercise 7c

Read aloud and translate:

1. Lupus puellās terret.
2. Puellae silvam amant.
3. Aestāte arborēs Sextus ascendere vult.
4. Dāvum et servōs puerī vexāre timent.
5. Lupī puerōs et puellās semper terrent.
6. Clāmōrēs puerī audiunt; puellās petunt.
7. Servī lupōs ex agrīs repellunt.
8. Senātōrēs Rōmānī nūntiōs salūtant.
9. Senātōrēs Rōmānōs prīnceps cōnsulere vult.
10. Cornēlius, ubi nōn est occupātus, per agrōs errāre potest.

31

Building Up the Meaning II

In 3rd declension nouns the ending of both the nominative and accusative plural is -ēs. To decide which case is being used, you must look for further clues. Study these sentences, and, with the help of the clues, translate them:

1. Puerī clāmōrēs audiunt.
2. Puerōs clāmōrēs terrent.

3. Prīnceps senātōrēs ad urbem revocat.
4. Prīncipem senātōrēs excipiunt.

5. Clāmōrēs mātrēs audiunt.

In sentence 1, since **puerī** is in the nominative case and is therefore the subject of the verb, **clāmōrēs** must be in the accusative case and is therefore the direct object.

In sentence 2, since **puerōs** is accusative, **clāmōrēs** must be nominative.

In sentence 3, since **prīnceps** is nominative, **senātōrēs** must be accusative. An additional clue is the fact that the verb **revocat** is singular.

In sentence 4, since **prīncipem** is accusative, **senātōrēs** must be nominative. An additional clue is the fact that the verb **excipiunt** is plural.

In sentence 5, where both nouns end in -ēs and the verb is plural, it is the sense which indicates that **clāmōrēs** is accusative and **mātrēs** nominative.

Exercise 7d

Explain the clues in these sentences, read aloud, and translate:
1. Servus senātōrēs videt.
2. Arborēs puerī saepe ascendunt.
3. Clāmōrēs puellās terrent.
4. Patrem vōcēs vexant.
5. Vōcēs in hortō audit.
6. Mātrēs in viā cōnspiciunt.

Versiculī: *"Show-Off!"* page 89.

Review I

Exercise Ia

Change nominatives to accusatives and accusatives to nominatives, keeping the same number (singular or plural):

1. nūntius	5. lupus	9. puerōs
2. amīcam	6. virum	10. patrem
3. fragōrem	7. rīvī	11. rāmī
4. puellae	8. vōcem	12. clāmōrēs

Exercise Ib

Change singular subjects to plural and plural subjects to singular, and make the necessary changes in the endings of the verbs:

1. Servus clāmat.
2. Puellae cantant.
3. Virī sedent.
4. Puer ad vīllam advenit.
5. Lupus rīvum petit.
6. Nūntiī in agrīs currunt.
7. Vōx puerum terret.
8. Puella amīca est.
9. Servī fragōrem audiunt.
10. Nūntius puerum cōnspicit.

Exercise Ic

Select the appropriate adjective from the pool below to complete each of the following sentences. Be sure to use the right ending on the adjective. Translate each sentence.

1. Dāvus _____ est, quod puerī clāmant.
2. Sextus arborem ascendit, quod _____ est.
3. Flāvia in vīllā _____ habitat.
4. Marcus _____ rāmum arripit et lupum repellit.
5. Dāvus puerōs _____ in piscīnā cōnspicit.
6. Dāvus _____ est, quod Sextus in hortō ambulat.
7. Flāvia et Cornēlia puellae _____ sunt et saepe in agrīs currunt.
8. Sextus est puer _____ et puellās terret.
9. Ubi lupus venit, Sextus in arbore sedet, quod puer _____ est.
10. Cornēlius _____ sedet, quod epistulās scrībere vult.

sollicitus	madidus	temerārius	vīcīnus
strēnuus	ignāvus	sōlus	
īrātus	molestus	magnus	

Exercise Id

Read the following passage and answer the questions below in Latin:

Hodiē quod pater Marcum ad vīcīnam urbem dūcit, Sextus in agrōs
sōlus errat. Ibi arborēs ascendere potest. Ibi servōs in agrīs labōrantēs
spectāre potest. Subitō, dum per agrōs ambulat, clāmōrēs magnōs
audit quī eum terrent. Currit ad arborem quae prope rīvum est. Celeriter ascendere parat sed, quod perterritus est et rāmī sunt īnfirmī,   5
statim in rīvum cadit.
"Ferte auxilium!" clāmat. "Celeriter venīte! Ego natāre nōn possum."
Servī, ubi clāmōrēs audiunt, statim ad rīvum currunt, rāmōs arripiunt, ad Sextum extendunt. Sextus rāmum arripit. Tum servus quī   10
rāmum tenet ad rīpam Sextum trahere potest. Sextus madidus ex rīvō
exit lacrimāns. Servī miserum puerum spectant et rīdent.
"Cūr in rīvō natās?" inquiunt.
Sextus, quī servōs saepe vexat, respondēre nōn potest et miser ad
vīllam abit. Dum per agrōs currit, servōs rīdentēs audit.   15

in agrōs, into the fields	**tenet,** (he, she) holds
per agrōs, through the fields	**rīpa,** river bank
quī, which	**trahere,** to drag, pull
celeriter, quickly	**lacrimāns,** weeping
natāre, to swim	**miser,** wretched
extendunt, (they) stretch out	**rīdentēs,** laughing

1. Why is Sextus roaming in the fields by himself?
2. What two things is he able to do in the fields?
3. What frightens him?
4. What action does he take?
5. Why doesn't he succeed in climbing the tree?
6. Why is he upset when he falls into the stream?
7. How do the slaves help him?
8. What is Sextus doing as he gets out of the stream?
9. What do the slaves ask him?
10. Why doesn't Sextus reply?
11. How do the slaves show their feelings about Sextus?

Exercise Ie

*Locate the following in sequence as they occur in the Latin passage in
Exercise Id:*

1. All singular verbs; all plural verbs.
2. All nouns in the nominative singular, the accusative singular, the nominative plural, and the accusative plural.
3. All infinitives.

The Roman Villa

In cities, the majority of Romans lived in apartment buildings called insulae, which were several stories high; Cornelius, on the other hand, being a wealthy Roman, owned a self-contained house called a **domus**. We shall learn more of these town houses when Cornelius and his family reach Rome.

Like other rich Romans, Cornelius also had a house in the country. His farmhouse or **vīlla rūstica** near Baiae in Campania was similar to one actually discovered at Boscoreale near Pompeii. The ground plan of that **vīlla** is shown on the next page. The lower illustration on the next page includes the **piscīna** in Cornelius' **vīlla**.

The **vīlla** itself served two purposes: it housed the slaves who did the agricultural work, and it provided accommodation for the owner and his family when they went to the country from Rome, which they would usually do during the summer months to escape the noisy bustle and heat of the city. In addition to housing the owner's family and slaves, the **vīlla rūstica** had stables, two enclosed courts or farmyards, rooms for pressing grapes and olives, and an adjacent area for threshing.

Various features of the **vīlla rūstica** are described as follows by an ancient author who wrote a book on farming:

> The room of the overseer (**vīlicus**) should be near the entrance, and he should know who enters or leaves at night and what he is carrying, especially if there is no doorkeeper. Special care needs to be taken with the placement of the kitchen because many things are done there in the predawn hours, with food being prepared and eaten. You must see to it that the sheds in the farmyard are large enough for the wagons and all the other farming tools that might be harmed by the rain. . . . On a large farm (**fundus**) it is more convenient to have two farmyards, one with an exposed pool with running water, surrounded if you wish with columns—a sort of fishpond (**piscīna**). The cattle will drink and bathe here in the summer when brought back from plowing the fields, and also the geese, hogs, and pigs when they return from pasture. In the outer farmyard there should be a pool where lupines can be soaked along with other products that are made more fit for use by immersion in water.

Varro, *On Agriculture* I.13

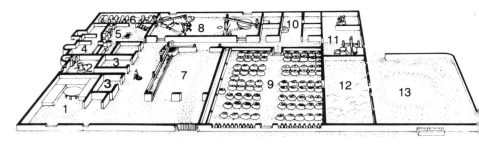

PLAN OF **VĪLLA RŪSTICA**

1. Dining Room
2. Bakery
3. Bedrooms (**cubicula**)
4. Baths
5. Kitchen
6. Stables
7. Farmyard, Court, or Garden (**hortus**)

8. Room for Pressing Grapes
9. Farmyard with Wine Vats
10. Slaves' Quarters
11. Olive-Pressing Room
12. Barn
13. Threshing Floor (**ārea**)

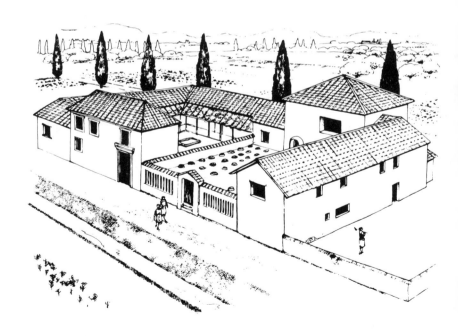

If Cornelius had been a very wealthy Roman, he might have had a country house separate from the farmhouse or even with no farm attached to it—just a large house standing in its own spacious grounds. This type of house was called a **vīlla urbāna**. Some Romans had more than one of these and often such houses were very luxurious indeed. The Roman author Pliny describes his Laurentine **vīlla urbāna** for us in a letter to a friend. Here is part of his description, and on the next page you will find a plan and a drawing of his country house:

> My **vīlla** is large enough for my use and cheap to keep up. It has a modest entrance-hall (**ātrium**) through which you enter D-shaped colonnades which enclose a small but pleasant courtyard. This provides protection in bad weather, as it is sheltered by windows and overhanging eaves. In the middle of this there is a very pleasant inner court, opening into a fairly handsome dining room which juts out over the shore. On each wall there is either a folding door or an equally large window. From the sides and front there are views of the sea. Look back and there is a view of the inner court, the colonnade, the outer court, and the hall, with the woods and mountains in the distance.
>
> Pliny, *Letters* II.17

Pliny had another **vīlla urbāna** in Tuscany with luxurious fountains, pools, and baths which he describes as follows:

> Opposite the dining-room at the corner of the colonnade is a large bedroom. From some of its windows you look onto the terrace, from others onto the meadow, while the windows in front overlook an ornamental pool which is a pleasure both to see and hear. For the water, falling from a height, foams white in the marble basin. The bedroom is very warm in winter, being so exposed to the sun, and on a cloudy day the hot air from the nearby furnace takes the place of the sun's heat. From here you pass through a spacious and pleasant changing-room into the "cold bath" room in which there is a large bath out of the full sunlight. But if you want more space to swim in and warmer water, there is a pool in the courtyard and near it a fountain in which you can cool yourself if you've had enough of the heat.

And later in the same letter he tells us why he liked this house so much:

> I can relax there with fuller and more carefree enjoyment. I need never wear a toga; nobody calls from next door. All is calm and quiet, which makes the place healthy, as do the clear sky and pure air. There I enjoy health of body and mind, for I keep my mind in training by study and my body by hunting.
>
> Pliny, *Letters* V.6

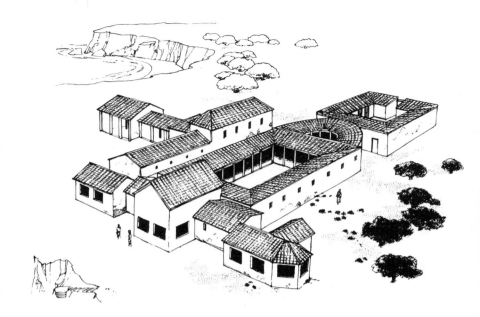

PLINY'S **VĪLLA URBĀNA**

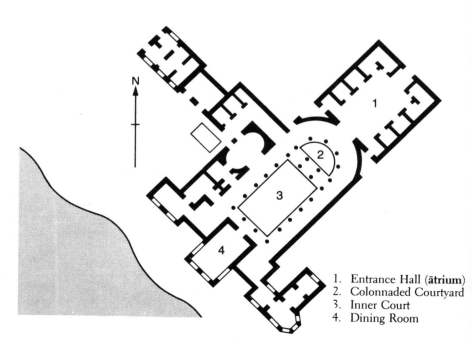

1. Entrance Hall (**ātrium**)
2. Colonnaded Courtyard
3. Inner Court
4. Dining Room

8
An Early Rise

Nōndum lūcet, sed Aurēlia, māter Marcī et Cornēliae, iam in vīllā
occupāta est. Īrāta est quod servōs sedentēs cōnspicit.
"Agite, molestī servī!" inquit. "Cūr nihil facitis? Cūr vōs ibi sedētis? Cūr
nōn strēnuē labōrātis? Omnia statim parāre necesse est quod nōs hodiē
Rōmam redīmus." Iam strēnuē labōrant servī. 5
    Tum puerōs excitāre parat. Intrat igitur cubiculum Marcī. Clāmat, "Age,
Marce! Tempus est surgere. Nōs ad urbem redīre parāmus."
    Marcus mātrem audit sed nihil respondet. Deinde Aurēlia cubiculum
Sextī intrat. Clāmat, "Age, Sexte! Tempus est surgere." Statim surgit Sextus.
Celeriter tunicam induit et brevī tempore ē cubiculō currit. 10
    Iterum Aurēlia cubiculum Marcī intrat. Iterum clāmat, "Age, Marce!
Nōs iam strēnuē labōrāmus. Cūr tū sōlus nōn surgis?"
    Gemit Marcus. "Ego nōn surgō," inquit, "quod Rōmam redīre nōlō.
Cūr mihi quoque necesse est ad urbem redīre? Patrem meum prīnceps ad
urbem revocat. Patrem cōnsulere vult. Nōn vult cōnsulere Marcum." 15
    Subitō intrat Gāius, pater Marcī, et clāmat, "Sed ego volō cōnsulere
Marcum! Cūr, Marce, hodiē mē vexās? Cūr nōn surgis? Cūr nōndum
tunicam induis, moleste puer?"
    Nihil respondet Marcus, sed statim surgit quod patrem timet.

nōndum, not yet	**intrat,** (he, she) enters
lūcet, it is light, it is day	**cubiculum,** room, bedroom
Age! Agite! Come on!	**tempus,** time
vōs, you (plural)	**surgere,** to get up
strēnuē, strenuously, hard	**deinde,** then, next
omnia, everything	**celeriter,** quickly
nōs, we, us	**induit,** (he, she) puts on
excitāre, to rouse, wake (someone) up	**iterum,** again, a second time
	mihi, for me

Exercise 8a

Respondē Latīnē:
1. Cūr est Aurēlia īrāta?
2. Cūr necesse est omnia statim parāre?
3. Quid Aurēlia in cubiculō Marcī clāmat?
4. Quid facit Marcus?
5. Surgitne Sextus?
6. Quid facit Sextus?
7. Cūr Marcus nōn surgit?
8. Quis subitō intrat?
9. Cūr Marcus surgit?

Exercise 8b

Using story 8 as a guide, give the Latin for:
1. It is necessary to work hard and prepare everything immediately because we are returning to Rome.
2. Aurelia enters Marcus' bedroom but does not wake him up.
3. "Come, Marcus! Why don't you get up?"
4. "Why do I have to return to the city?"
5. Gaius wishes to consult Marcus.

VERBS: Persons

Look at these sentences:

Rōmam redīre nōl*ō*.
Cūr nōn surgi*s*?
Aurēlia cubiculum Marcī intra*t*.
   Iterum clāma*t*.
Ad urbem redīre parā*mus*.

Cūr nōn strēnuē labōrā*tis*?
Līberī in agrīs erra*nt*. Servōs labōrantēs specta*nt*.

I *do not want to return to Rome.*
Why do you *not get up?*
Aurelia *goes into Marcus' bedroom.* **She** *calls again.*
We *are preparing to return to the city.*
Why do you *not work hard?*
The **children** *wander in the fields.*
They *watch the slaves working.*

The ending of the verb tells us who is doing something, i.e., whether the subject is 1st, 2nd, or 3rd *person*, singular or plural (I, you, he, she, it, we, you, they). In the 3rd person the subject may be a noun (e.g., **Aurēlia** and **līberī**). The personal pronouns **ego, tū, nōs,** and **vōs** are used only for emphasis.

40

Person	Singular		Plural	
1	-ō	I	-mus	we
2	-s	you	-tis	you
3	-t	he, she, it	-nt	they

These personal endings always have the same meaning wherever they occur.

Person	Singular		Plural	
1	parō	I prepare	parāmus	we prepare
2	parās	you prepare	parātis	you prepare
3	parat	he, she prepares	parant	they prepare

Note that the vowel that precedes the personal endings is short before final -t and -nt.

The following verb is irregular, but it uses the same endings as above (except for -m in place of -ō in the first person singular).

Person	Singular		Plural	
1	sum	I am	sumus	we are
2	es	you are	estis	you are
3	est	he, she, it is	sunt	they are

Be sure to learn all of the forms above thoroughly.

Exercise 8c

Take parts, read aloud, and translate:
1. NĀRRĀTOR: Sextus est laetus.
   MARCUS: Tū es laetus, Sexte. Cūr?
   SEXTUS: Ego sum laetus quod Rōmam redīre volō.
2. NĀRRĀTOR: Servī sunt dēfessī.
   MARCUS: Vōs estis dēfessī, servī. Cūr?
   SERVĪ: Dēfessī sumus quod strēnuē labōrāmus.
3. NĀRRĀTOR: Cornēlius epistulās legit.
   CORNĒLIA: Quid legis, Cornēlī?
   CORNĒLIUS: Epistulās legō.

41

4. NARRATOR: Marcus rāmum arripit.
   SEXTUS: Quid arripis, Marce?
   MARCUS: Rāmum arripiō.
5. NĀRRĀTOR: Cornēlia rīdet.
   FLĀVIA: Cūr rīdēs, Cornēlia?
   CORNĒLIA: Rīdeō quod laeta sum.
6. NĀRRĀTOR: Senātōrēs ad urbem redeunt.
   AURĒLIA: Cūr ad urbem redītis, senātōrēs?
   SENĀTŌRĒS: Redīmus quod prīnceps nōs cōnsulere vult.
7. NĀRRĀTOR: Puerī lupum nōn timent.
   PUELLAE: Cūr lupum nōn timētis, puerī?
   PUERĪ: Lupum nōn timēmus quod temerāriī sumus.
8. NĀRRĀTOR: Puellae cantant.
   PUERĪ: Cūr cantātis, puellae?
   PUELLAE: Cantāmus quod laetae sumus.

Exercise 8d

Read aloud and translate:
1. Cūr ē vīllā in silvam saepe ambulātis, puellae?
2. In eādem silvā puerī quoque ambulant.
3. Īrāta sum quod servōs sedentēs cōnspiciō.
4. Cūr sedēs adhūc in arbore, Sexte?
5. Arborēs ascendimus quod lupī nōs terrent.
6. "Sexte! Marce!" clāmat Cornēlia. "Cūr nōn surgitis?"
7. "Ēheu!" inquit Dāvus. "Semper ego labōrō; semper mē vexant puerī; ad Britanniam redīre volō."
8. Omnia parāmus quod Rōmam hodiē redīmus.
9. Puerōs excitō quod ad urbem redīre hodiē parāmus.
10. Servī in vīllā sedent; neque Aurēliam audiunt neque respondent, nam dēfessī sunt.

nam, for

Versiculī: *"Time to Go Home,"* page 90.

Word Study II

Latin Verbs into English Verbs

Often Latin verbs come into English with only minor changes. Some verbs drop the letters -āre, -ēre, -ere, or -īre from the infinitive and replace them with silent -e. For example, excitāre (to rouse) becomes *excite* in English. Other verbs simply drop these letters from the infinitive. For example, dēscendere (to go down) produces the English *descend*.

Sometimes additional minor spelling changes occur. For example, exclāmāre (to shout out) becomes *exclaim* in English, adding an *i* in the process.

Exercise 1

Identify the English verbs derived from these Latin verbs. Be sure that you know the meaning of the English verb; in many cases it has the same meaning as the Latin verb.

extendere	salūtāre	revocāre	respondēre	surgere
repellere	vexāre	trādere	errāre	ascendere

Latin Verbs into English Nouns and Adjectives

A Latin verb may be the source of an English noun or adjective. For example, errāre (to wander) provides English with the noun *error* and the adjective *erratic*.

Exercise 2

The English words in italics below are derived from the Latin verbs in parentheses. Determine the meaning of the English word from the meaning of the Latin verb. Is the English word a noun or an adjective?

1. Cornelius was not moved by the runaway slave's *petition*. (petere)
2. Sextus' rude behavior was *repellent* to Cornelia and Flavia. (repellere)
3. With the *advent* of summer, Cornelius moves his family to their farmhouse at Baiae. (advenīre)
4. Cornelius was dictating a letter to his *scribe*. (scrībere)
5. "Sextus," scolded Eucleides, "your writing is not *legible*." (legere)
6. The *insurgent* senators were severely punished by the emperor. (surgere)
7. The Roman army found the *descent* from the mountain more difficult than the *ascent*. (dēscendere, ascendere)

One Latin Word into Many English Words

Some Latin words are the source of several English words, representing different parts of speech. For example, **urbs** (city) is the source of:

1. *urban* — adjective, meaning "pertaining to a city"
2. *urbane* — adjective, meaning "elegant and polished in manner" (How does this idea relate to **urbs**?)
3. *urbanity* — noun, meaning "politeness, courtesy, the quality of being urbane"
4. *urbanize* — verb, meaning "to change from country to city"
5. *suburb* — noun, meaning "a residential area at the edge of a city"

Exercise 3

The words in each group below are derived from one Latin word. Identify the Latin word. With its meaning in mind, determine the meaning of each English word. Finally, give the part of speech of each English word.

1. *magnate, magnificent, magnify*
2. *contemporary, tempo, temporal*
3. *prince, principal, principally*
4. *inscribe, scribble, subscribe*
5. *paternal, paternity, patron*

Exercise 4

In the preamble to the Constitution of the United States, there are 22 different words derived from Latin, printed in italics below. Choose five of these words and look up their derivation in an English dictionary. Report on your findings to the class.

We the *people* of the *United States*, in *order* to *form* a more *perfect union, establish justice, insure domestic tranquillity, provide* for the *common defense, promote* the *general* welfare, and *secure* the blessings of *liberty* to ourselves and our *posterity*, do *ordain* and *establish* this *Constitution* for the *United States* of America.

Try this exercise on other famous passages, such as The Declaration of Independence, Lincoln's Gettysburg Address, and Martin Luther King's speech, "I Have a Dream."

9
Goodbye

Cornēlia, ubi surgit, ē vīllā suā fūrtim ambulat et per agrōs ad vīllam amīcae currit. Nōndum lūcet, sed nihil Cornēliam terret. Nēmō eam cōnspicit. Nūllī servī in agrīs labōrant. Etiam iānitor ad iānuam vīllae dormit. Cornēlia, quod tacitē intrat, iānitōrem nōn excitat.

Cornēlia cubiculum Flāviae tacitē intrat et eam excitāre temptat. Adhūc 5 dormit Flāvia. Iterum temptat Cornēlia. Flāvia sēmisomna, "Quis es? Cūr mē vexās?"

Cornēlia respondet, "Sum Cornēlia! Surge!"

Flāvia surgit. Laeta Cornēliam excipit et clāmat, "Quid tū hīc?"

Cornēlia, "Tacē, Flāvia! Nōlī servōs excitāre! Venī tacitē mēcum in agrōs. 10 Ibi nēmō nōs audīre potest."

Cornēlia Flāviam fūrtim ē vīllā in agrōs dūcit. Ubi puellae ad arborēs adveniunt, Cornēlia, "Misera sum," inquit, "quod ego et Marcus et Sextus et pater et māter Rōmam hodiē redīre parāmus. Prīnceps patrem meum cōnsulere vult. Nōbīs igitur necesse est statim discēdere." 15

Flāvia clāmat, "Cūr statim, Cornēlia? Cūr nōn pater tuus discēdit sōlus? Cūr vōs omnēs simul discēditis?"

Respondet Cornēlia, "Nesciō, Flāvia. Sed nōbīs secundā hōrā discēdere necesse est."

Flāvia lacrimat, "Ō mē miseram! Vōs omnēs Rōmam redītis. Mihi ne- 20 cesse est hīc manēre. Valē, Cornēlia! Multās epistulās ad mē mitte! Prōmittisne?"

Cornēlia, "Ego prōmittō. Et iam valē!" Cornēlia Flāviam complexū tenet et lacrimāns abit.

suā, her own	**discēdere,** to go away
per agrōs, through the fields	**vōs omnēs,** all of you
nēmō, no one	**simul,** together
nūllī, no	**nesciō,** I do not know
iānitor, doorkeeper	**secundā hōrā,** at the second hour (of
ad iānuam, at the door	daylight)
tacitē, silently	**lacrimāre,** to weep, cry
temptāre, to try	**Ō mē miseram!** Poor me! Oh dear
sēmisomna, half-asleep	me!
hīc, here	**manēre,** to remain
Tacē! Be quiet!	**Valē!** Goodbye!
Nōlī . . . excitāre! Don't wake	**mittere,** to send
(someone) up!	**prōmittere,** to promise
mēcum, with me	**complexū,** in an embrace
misera, unhappy, miserable	**tenet,** (he, she) holds
nōbīs, for us	**lacrimāns,** weeping

Exercise 9a

Respondē Latīnē:
1. Quō Cornēlia currit?
2. Cūr nēmō Cornēliam cōnspicit?
3. Quid facit iānitor?
4. Quid facit Cornēlia ubi cubiculum Flāviae intrat?
5. Quō Cornēlia Flāviam dūcit?
6. Quis lacrimāns abit?

Prepositions

Look at the examples in the columns below:

In vīll**am** currit.	In vīll**ā** sedet.
He runs into the house.	*He sits in the house.*
In rīv**um** cadit.	*In rīv**ō** natat.*
He falls into the river.	*He swims in the river.*
	In rām**ō** sedet.
	He sits on the branch.
In urb**em** venit.	Prīnceps in urb**e** est.
He comes into the city.	*The emperor is in the city.*

In the left-hand column, **in** is used with the *accusative case* and the meaning is "into."

In the right-hand column, **in** is used with the *ablative case* and the meaning is "in" or "on."

Other prepositions that you have seen with the accusative case are **ad**, **per**, and **prope**.

Ad vīllam redit.
He returns to the house.

Ad iānuam dormit.
He sleeps at the door.

Per agrōs currit.
He runs through the fields.

Puellae prope rīvum sedent.
The girls sit near the stream.

46

Other prepositions that you have seen with the ablative case are **sub** and **ex**:

Sub arbore dormit.
He sleeps under the tree.

Ex arbore cadit.
He falls out of the tree.

Note that **ex** may be written simply as **ē** when the next word begins with a consonant: **ē rāmīs**, "out of the branches."

From now on, Latin prepositions in the word lists will indicate in parentheses whether they are followed by the accusative or the ablative case, e.g., **ad** (+ *acc.*) and **sub** (+ *abl.*).

NOUNS: Cases and Declensions

Ablative Case

Here is a table showing the groups of nouns and cases you have met so far:

Number *Case*	*1st* *Declension*	*2nd* *Declension*		*3rd* *Declension*	
Singular					
Nominative	puell**a**	serv**us**	puer	pater	vōx
Accusative	puell**am**	serv**um**	puer**um**	patr**em**	vōc**em**
Ablative	puell**ā**	serv**ō**	puer**ō**	patr**e**	vōc**e**
Plural					
Nominative	puell**ae**	serv**ī**	puer**ī**	patr**ēs**	vōc**ēs**
Accusative	puell**ās**	serv**ōs**	puer**ōs**	patr**ēs**	vōc**ēs**
Ablative	puell**īs**	serv**īs**	puer**īs**	patr**ibus**	vōc**ibus**

Be sure to learn these forms thoroughly.

Note that the only difference between the nominative and ablative singular endings of 1st declension nouns is that the ablative has a long vowel: **-ā.**

Exercise 9b

Select, read aloud, and translate:

1. Marcus ad _____ sedet.   arborem / arbore
2. Puellae ē _____ ad _____ ambulant.   silvam / silvā   vīllam / vīllā
3. Multī servī in _____ labōrant.   agrōs / agrīs
4. Cornēlia amīcam ē _____ in _____ dūcit.   vīllam / vīllā   agrōs / agrīs
5. Servus sub _____ dormit.   statuam / statuā
6. Puerī per _____ natant.   rīvum / rīvō
7. Cornēlius ad _____ redīre parat.   urbem / urbe
8. Flāvia prope _____ sedet.   arbore / arborem
9. Sextus madidus ē _____ exit.   rīvō / rīvum
10. Geta per _____ festīnat.   agrīs / agrōs

natāre, to swim   festīnāre, to hurry

Exercise 9c

Read aloud and translate:

1. Marcus in vīllam currit. Nūntius in vīllā est.
2. Dāvus in hortō labōrat. Marcus in hortum festīnat.
3. Nūntius in Italiam redīre vult. Cornēlius in Italiā habitat.
4. Puer in arbore sedet. Puella in vīllam intrat.
5. In agrīs puerī ambulāre parant. Puellae in agrōs lentē ambulant.
6. In Italiā sunt multī servī. Aliī in agrīs labōrant, aliī in urbibus.
7. Servī sub arboribus sedēre volunt.
8. Servus ex arbore cadit; ad vīllam currit; in vīllā dormit.
9. Aliī nūntiī ex urbe celeriter veniunt; aliī ad urbem redeunt.
10. Puellae sub rāmīs sedent. Lupus ad puellās currit.
11. Puer ex arbore dēscendere nōn potest.
12. Cornēlia per iānuam in vīllam Flāviānam fūrtim intrat.

aliī . . . aliī . . . , some . . . others . . .

48

Exercise 9d

Select, read aloud, and translate:

1. Flāvia clāmat, "Ubi _____, Cornēlia?"   estis / es
2. Cornēlia iānitōrem nōn _____.   excitāre / excitat / excitās
3. Nōs omnēs hodiē Rōmam _____.   redīre / redīmus / redītis
4. Cūr vōs omnēs simul _____?   discēdere / discēdimus / discēdere parātis
5. Cūr patrem _____, Marce?   vexō / timēs / amātis
6. Necesse est epistulās statim _____.   trādit / legere / legimus
7. Prīnceps senātōrēs _____.   cōnsulere vult / cōnsulere volunt
8. Tacē, Flāvia! Nōlī servōs _____.   excitāmus / excitāre / surgere
9. Cornēlia amīcam in agrōs _____.   adveniunt / dūcit / amat
10. Cūr per agrōs _____, puellae?   curritis / excitātis / curris
11. Iānitor Cornēliam nōn _____.   audiō / audiunt / audit
12. Ego nōn _____ quod Rōmam redīre _____.   dormīmus / surgere / surgō nōlō / faciunt / vidētis
13. _____ Cornēlia in agrīs nōn cōnspicit.   Servōs / Servī / Servus
14. Nōlī _____ excitāre!   puellās / puellae / puella
15. Senātōrēs _____ omnēs in urbe sunt.   Rōmānōs / Rōmānī / Rōmānum

Exercise 9e

Using story 9 as a guide, give the Latin for:
1. Cornelia tries to wake Flavia up.
2. We are preparing to return to Rome today.
3. Why are you all leaving at the same time?
4. Send many letters to me! Do you promise?
5. Cornelia goes off in tears.

Versiculī: "Bad News," page 90.

10
Departure

Intereā in vīllā Cornēliānā omnēs strēnuē labōrant. Aurēlia multās ancillās habet. Eās iubet tunicās et stolās in cistīs pōnere. In cubiculō Marcī
servus togam praetextam in cistā pōnit quod in urbe omnēs puerī togam
praetextam gerere solent. In cubiculō Gāiī servus togam parat quod Gāius
in urbe togam gerere solet.   5

Dāvus, quī ipse omnia cūrat, ad iānuam stat. Servōs iubet cistās ē cubiculīs
in viam portāre. Baculum habet et clāmat, "Agite, servī scelestī! Dormītisne?
Hodiē, nōn crās, discēdimus."

Marcus quoque servōs incitat et iubet eōs cistās in raedā pōnere. Servus
quīdam, nōmine Geta, cistam Sextī arripit et in raedam iacit.   10

"Cavē, Geta!" exclāmat Sextus sollicitus. "Cūrā cistam meam! Nōlī eam
iacere!"

Tandem omnēs cistae in raedā sunt. Ascendunt Marcus et Sextus. Ascendit Eucleidēs. Ascendit Aurēlia. Gāius ipse ascendere est parātus. Syrus,
raedārius, quoque ascendit et equōs incitāre parat. Subitō exclāmat Aurēlia,   15
"Ubi est Cornēlia?"

Eō ipsō tempore in viam currit Cornēlia. Eam Gāius iubet in raedam
statim ascendere. Statim raedārius equōs incitat. Discēdunt Cornēliī.

inter**eā**, meanwhile
ancilla, slave-woman
habēre, to have, hold
iubēre, to order
cista, trunk, chest
pōnere, to place
gerere solent, (they) are accustomed
   to wear, usually wear
ipse, himself
cūrāre, to look after, attend to
stāre, to stand
via, road
portāre, to carry

baculum, a stick
scelestus, wicked
crās, tomorrow
incitāre, to spur on, urge on
raeda, carriage
servus quīdam, a certain slave
iacere, to throw
parātus, ready
raedārius, coachman
equus, horse
eō ipsō tempore, at that very
   moment

Exercise 10a

Respondē Latīnē:
1. Quid Aurēlia ancillās facere iubet?
2. Cūr togam praetextam in cistā pōnit servus?
3. Quid facit Dāvus?
4. Quid clāmat Sextus?
5. Quid raedārius facere parat?
6. Quō currit Cornēlia?
7. Quid tum facit raedārius?
8. Quid faciunt Cornēliī?

VERBS: Conjugations

Latin verbs, with very few exceptions, fall into four major groups or conjugations. You can distinguish the group or conjugation of a verb by looking at two parts—the 1st person singular of the present tense and the present infinitive. For example:

	1st Person Sing. Present Tense	Present Infinitive
1st Conjugation	par*ō*	par*āre*
2nd Conjugation	hab*eō*	hab*ēre*
3rd Conjugation	mitt*ō* iac*iō*	mitt*ere* iac*ere*
4th Conjugation	aud*iō*	aud*īre*

Note the differences between verbs of the 2nd and 3rd conjugations. Note also that some verbs of the 3rd conjugation end in **-iō** in the 1st person singular of the present tense.

Hereafter, verbs will be given in the word lists in the 1st person singular form (present tense), followed by the present infinitive and conjugation number, e.g., **habeō, habēre** (2), to have. The few exceptions that do not fit neatly into any of the four conjugations will be marked as irregular (*irreg.*).

VERBS: The Present Tense

			1st Conjugation	2nd Conjugation	3rd Conjugation		4th Conjugation
		Infinitive	par*āre*	hab*ēre*	mitt*ere*	iac*ere* (**-iō**)	aud*īre*
Number and Person	*Singular*	1	par*ō*	hab*eō*	mitt*ō*	iac*iō*	aud*iō*
		2	par*ās*	hab*ēs*	mitt*is*	iac*is*	aud*īs*
		3	par*at*	hab*et*	mitt*it*	iac*it*	aud*it*
	Plural	1	par*āmus*	hab*ēmus*	mitt*imus*	iac*imus*	aud*īmus*
		2	par*ātis*	hab*ētis*	mitt*itis*	iac*itis*	aud*ītis*
		3	par*ant*	hab*ent*	mitt*unt*	iac*iunt*	aud*iunt*

Be sure to learn these forms thoroughly.

52

Note that the vowel that precedes the personal endings is short before final -*t* and -*nt*.

In addition to **iaciō, iacere**, you have met the following -*iō* verbs of the 3rd conjugation:

arripiō, arripere	**excipiō, excipere**
cōnspiciō, cōnspicere	**faciō, facere**

Exercise 10b

Read the following verbs aloud and give the conjugation number and meaning of each:

ascendō, ascendere	repellō, repellere	cūrō, cūrāre
terreō, terrēre	ambulō, ambulāre	excipiō, excipere
arripiō, arripere	excitō, excitāre	timeō, timēre
discēdō, discēdere	iaciō, iacere	nesciō, nescīre
audiō, audīre	currō, currere	rīdeō, rīdēre

Exercise 10c

Using the verbs in Exercise 10b, give the Latin for the following:
1. We are running.
2. You (singular) are afraid.
3. They drive the wolf back.
4. We hear the noise.
5. You (plural) throw the chest.
6. I snatch the branch.
7. They go away.
8. They welcome the girls.
9. You (singular) frighten Cornelia.
10. We climb the tree.
11. We wake the boys up.
12. I throw the stick.
13. I run to the farmhouse.
14. They hear the voice.
15. They snatch the letter.
16. You (singular) go away.
17. You (singular) hear the noise.
18. We hear the voice.
19. We throw the stick.
20. We drive the wolf back.

VERBS: Imperative

The imperative is the part of the verb used in issuing orders, e.g.:

Cūrā cistam meam, Geta!
Take care of my trunk, Geta!

Nōlī eam iacere, Geta!
Don't throw it, Geta! (literally, *refuse, be unwilling to throw it, Geta!*)

Cūrāte cistam meam, servī!
Take care of my trunk, slaves!

Nōlīte eam iacere, servī!
Don't throw it, slaves! (literally, *refuse, be unwilling to throw it, slaves!*)

	1st Conjugation	*2nd Conjugation*	*3rd Conjugation*	*4th Conjugation*
Infinitive	par*āre*	hab*ēre*	mitt*ere* iac*ere* (*-iō*)	aud*īre*
Imperative Singular Plural	par*ā* par*āte*	hab*ē* hab*ēte*	mitt*e* iac*e* mitt*ite* iac*ite*	aud*ī* aud*īte*

Be sure to learn these forms thoroughly.

Exercise 10d

Read aloud and translate:

1. Dāvus omnēs strēnuē labōrāre iubet.
2. "Tunicam, nōn togam, gerere volō," clāmat Marcus.
3. In urbe Gāius togam gerere solet.
4. Eō ipsō tempore Aurēlia, "Cavē!" inquit. "Nōlī cistam iacere!"
5. Eucleidēs, "Nōlīte dormīre!" clāmat. "Strēnuē labōrāte, servī!"
6. "Cūr nōn in raedam ascenditis, puerī?" "Nōn ascendimus quod nōndum parātī sumus."
7. "Audīsne vōcem Cornēliī, Sexte?" "Ita vērō! Eius vōcem audiō."
8. Flāvia, "Scrībe ad mē saepe!" inquit. Cornēlia, "Ego prōmittō," respondet.
9. Gāius, "Ascendite, omnēs!" inquit. "Eucleidēs, cūrā puerōs! Cornēlia, sedē prope mātrem! Aurēlia, nōlī lacrimāre! Syre, incitā equōs!"
10. "Quid tū aestāte facere potes, Marce?" "Possum in agrīs currere, arborēs ascendere, in rīvō natāre, prope piscīnam sedēre."

Versiculī: *"To Rome Tomorrow," page 91.*

Treatment of Slaves

Some masters treated their slaves well and were rewarded by loyalty and good service, but, even when conditions were good, slaves were keenly aware of their inferior position and by way of protest sometimes rebelled or tried to run away. If they were recaptured, the letters FUG (for **fugitīvus**, "runaway") were branded on their foreheads.

Some owners treated their slaves very badly. Even if the owner were not as bad as the despised Vedius Pollio, who fed his slaves to lampreys, slaves were liable to be severely punished, often at the whim of their master:

> Does Rutilus believe that the body and soul of slaves are made the same as their masters? Not likely! Nothing pleases him more than a noisy flogging. His idea of music is the crack of the whip. To his trembling slaves he's a monster, happiest when some poor wretch is being branded with red-hot irons for stealing a pair of towels. He loves chains, dungeons, branding, and chain-gang labor camps. He's a sadist.
>
> Juvenal, *Satires* XIV. 16

There were also large numbers of female slaves, and even they were often subjected to ill-treatment. Juvenal tells how a slave-woman was at the mercy of her mistress:

> If the mistress is in a bad mood, the wool-maid is in trouble, the dressers are stripped and beaten, the litter-bearers accused of coming late. The rods are broken over one poor wretch's back, another has bloody weals from the whip, and a third is flogged with the cat-o'-nine-tails. The slave-girl arranging her mistress's hair will have her own hair torn and the tunic ripped from her shoulders, because a curl is out of place.
>
> Juvenal, *Satires* VI.475

Pliny tells a story about some slaves who tried to murder their master:

> Larcius Macedo was a cruel, arrogant master, and he suffered a terrible fate at the hands of his slaves. He was taking a bath at his house at Formiae when his slaves suddenly surrounded him. One grabbed his throat while others punched him in the face, chest, and stomach. When they thought he was dead, they threw him on the hot paving-stones to see if they were right. Either because he was really unconscious or only pretending, he lay there motionless, so that they believed he was quite dead. Then he was

55

carried out as though he had fainted with the heat. The more loyal slaves took over; the maids came running with shrieks and screams. Roused by their cries and revived by the cool air, he opened his eyes and moved, showing that he was alive, now that it was safe to do so. The guilty slaves ran away. Most have been arrested; the rest are still being hunted. Macedo was nursed back to life, but a few days later he died. At least he had the satisfaction of knowing he was avenged. Before their victim died, the culprits suffered the penalty for murder.

Pliny, Letters III.14

On the other hand, Tacitus speaks of "slaves whose loyalty did not waver under torture." There were owners who treated their slaves fairly and sympathetically. In a letter to a friend Pliny writes:

> I have noticed how kindly you treat your slaves; so I shall openly admit my own easy treatment of my own slaves. I always keep in mind the Roman phrase, "father of the household." But even supposing I were naturally cruel and unsympathetic, my heart would be touched by the illness of my freedman Zosimus. He needs and deserves my sympathy; he is honest, obliging, and well educated. He is a very successful actor with a clear delivery. He plays the lyre well and is an accomplished reader of speeches, history, and poetry. A few years ago he began to spit blood and I sent him to Egypt. He has just come back with his health restored. However, he has developed a slight cough. I think it would be best to send him to your place at Forum Julii where the air is healthy and the milk excellent for illness of this kind.

Pliny, Letters V.19

It was possible for a slave to buy his freedom if he could save enough from the small personal allowance he earned; some masters gave their slaves their freedom as a reward for long service. A slave who had been set free was called a **lībertus.** Many who were freed and became rich used to hide with "patches" the marks which had been made on their bodies and faces when they were slaves.

> I am very upset by illness among my slaves. Some of them have actually died, including even younger men. In cases like this I find comfort in two thoughts. I am always ready to give my slaves their freedom, so I don't think their deaths so untimely if they die free men. I also permit my slaves to make a "will," which I consider legally binding.

Pliny, Letters VIII.16

Gaius, a jurist of the second century A.D., mentions certain legal measures which were introduced to check the ill-treatment of slaves:

> But at this time neither Roman citizens nor subjects of the Empire may maltreat their slaves excessively or without good reason; for, under a regulation of the emperor Antoninus, to kill one's own slave without reason is just as serious an offense as killing another man's slave. Excessively harsh treatment by owners is also controlled by a regulation of the same emperor. He ruled that in the case of slaves who had fled for refuge to the shrines of the gods or to the statues of the emperors, the owners should be compelled to sell their slaves if their treatment was intolerably harsh.
>
> Gaius, *Institutes* 1.53

Columella, a Roman writer on agriculture, recommends securing a reliable slave as overseer (**vīlicus**) of a farm:

> I advise you not to choose an overseer from slaves who are physically attractive nor from those that have practiced the refinements of the city. These slaves are lazy and sleepy and accustomed to leisure, the Campus, the Circus, the theater, gambling, food-shops, and other such attractions and constantly day-dream of such nonsense. You should rather choose a slave hardened with farm work from infancy and tested by experience.

Friendliness and respect on the part of the master toward his slaves pay off:

> I would speak on quite familiar terms with my country slaves (if they have behaved themselves) more frequently than I would with my city slaves. And, since I have noticed that their constant toil is lightened by this friendliness of their master, I sometimes even joke with them and allow them to joke even more. Nowadays, I often consult with them about some new task as if they knew more about it than I, and this way I find out what sort of ability and intelligence each one has. Then, too, I notice that they undertake a task more willingly if they think they have been consulted about it and are undertaking it according to their own advice.
>
> Columella, *On Agriculture* I.8

11
A Slave Runs Away

Omnēs Cornēliī iam sunt in raedā. Rōmam per Viam Appiam petunt.
Intereā in vīllā Dāvus est sollicitus. Dāvus est vīlicus Cornēliī et, sī
dominus abest, vīlicus ipse vīllam dominī cūrat. Dāvus igitur omnēs servōs
in āream quae est prope vīllam venīre iubet. Brevī tempore ārea est plēna
servōrum et ancillārum quī magnum clāmōrem faciunt.   5
Tum venit Dāvus ipse et, "Tacēte, omnēs!" magnā vōce clāmat. "Audīte
mē! Quamquam dominus abest, necesse est nōbīs strēnuē labōrāre."
Tum servī mussant, "Dāvus dominus esse vult. Ecce! Baculum habet.
Nōs verberāre potest. Necesse est igitur facere id quod iubet." Redeunt igitur
ad agrōs servī quod baculum vīlicī timent.   10
Sed nōn redit Geta. Neque vīlicum amat neque īram vīlicī timet. Illā
nocte igitur, quod in agrīs nōn iam labōrāre vult, cibum parat et ē vīllā
effugit. Nēmō eum videt, nēmō eum impedit. Nunc per agrōs, nunc per
viam festīnat. Ubi diēs est, in rāmīs arboris sē cēlat. Ibi dormit.
Intereā, quamquam nōndum lūcet, Dāvus omnēs servōs excitat. In agrōs   15
exīre et ibi labōrāre eōs iubet. Sed Getam nōn videt. Ubi est Geta? Dāvus
igitur est īrātus, deinde sollicitus. Ad portam vīllae stat et viam spectat; sed
Getam nōn videt.

Via Appia, the Appian Way	**id quod,** that which, what
vīlicus, overseer, farm manager	**īra,** anger
dominus, master	**illā nocte,** that night
absum, abesse (*irreg.*), to be away,	**cibus,** food
absent	**effugiō, effugere** (3), to run away,
ārea, open space, threshing-floor	escape
plēnus, full	**impediō, impedīre** (4), to hinder
quamquam, although	**nunc,** now
mussō, mussāre (1), to mutter	**sē cēlāre,** to hide (himself)
verberō, verberāre (1), to beat	**porta,** gate

NOUNS: Cases and Declensions

Genitive Case

Compare the following sentences:

Dāvus ad portam stat.
Davus stands near the door.

Dāvus ad portam **vīllae** stat.
Davus stands near the door of the farmhouse.

Servī baculum timent.
The slaves fear the stick.

Servī baculum **vīlicī** timent.
The slaves fear the overseer's stick.

In rāmīs sē cēlat.
He hides in the branches.

In rāmīs **arboris** sē cēlat.
He hides in the branches of the tree.

In the right-hand column other nouns have been added to the sentences of the left-hand column. These additional nouns are in the *genitive case*. This case is used to connect two nouns in a single phrase, e.g., **portam vīllae.** It often indicates possession, e.g., **baculum vīlicī.**

This table shows the declensions and cases you have met so far:

Number Case	*1st* *Declension*	*2nd* *Declension*		*3rd* *Declension*	
Singular					
Nominative	puell*a*	serv*us*	puer	pater	vōx
Genitive	puell*ae*	serv*ī*	puer*ī*	patr*is*	vōc*is*
Accusative	puell*am*	serv*um*	puer*um*	patr*em*	vōc*em*
Ablative	puell*ā*	serv*ō*	puer*ō*	patr*e*	vōc*e*
Plural					
Nominative	puell*ae*	serv*ī*	puer*ī*	patr*ēs*	vōc*ēs*
Genitive	puell*ārum*	serv*ōrum*	puer*ōrum*	patr*um*	vōc*um*
Accusative	puell*ās*	serv*ōs*	puer*ōs*	patr*ēs*	vōc*ēs*
Ablative	puell*īs*	serv*īs*	puer*īs*	patr*ibus*	vōc*ibus*

Be sure to learn these forms thoroughly.

Hereafter, nouns will be given in the word lists as follows: **puella, -ae** (*f*); **servus, -ī** (*m*); **vōx, vōcis** (*f*); i.e., the nominative singular (**puella**), the genitive singular (**puellae**), and the gender (*feminine*).

N.B. It is the genitive singular ending that indicates the declension to which a noun belongs.

59

Exercise 11a

Translate the following sentences, completing them where necessary with reference to the family tree:

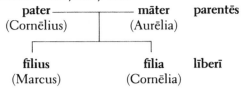

pater ———┬——— māter   parentēs
(Cornēlius)   (Aurēlia)

┌——————————————┐
filius   fīlia   līberī
(Marcus)   (Cornēlia)

1. Marcus est frāter Cornēliae.
2. Cornēlia est soror Marcī.
3. Aurēlia est uxor Cornēliī.
4. Marcus est fīlius Aurēliae.
5. Cornēlia est _____ Cornēliī.
6. Cornēlius et Aurēlia sunt _____ Marcī et Cornēliae.
7. Marcus et Cornēlia sunt _____ Cornēliī et Aurēliae.
8. Aurēlia est _____ Marcī et Cornēliae.
9. Cornēlius est _____ Marcī et Cornēliae.

Exercise 11b

Supply the ending, read the sentence aloud, and translate:
1. Līberī in raedā senātor___ sunt.
2. Marcus est frāter Cornēli___.
3. Nūntius fīlium Cornēli___ salūtat.
4. Servī īram vīlic___ timent.
5. Effugit Geta et in rāmīs arbor___ sē cēlat.
6. Magna vōx Dāv___ eum terret.
7. Dāvus, vīlicus Cornēli___, Getam vidēre nōn potest.
8. Sī Cornēlius abest, Dāvus vīllam domin___ cūrat.
9. Magnus numerus līber___ est in āreā.

       numerus, -ī (*m*), number

Exercise 11c

Using story 11 as a guide, give the Latin for:
1. The overseer looks after the master's farmhouse.
2. In a short time the threshing-floor is full of slaves.
3. The slaves fear the overseer's stick.
4. Geta is afraid of Davus' anger.
5. Geta is sleeping in the branches of a tree.

Building Up the Meaning III

In the 1st and 2nd declensions, the endings of the genitive singular are the same as the endings of the nominative plural. To decide which case is used, you must look for further clues.

Look at these sentences:

1. **Celeriter redeunt servī.**

The genitive usually forms a phrase with another noun. Since **servī** is the only noun in the sentence, it must be nominative plural.

2. **Puerī pater est senātor Rōmānus.**

The word **puerī** could be genitive singular or nominative plural. It is only when we reach **pater** (which can only be nominative singular) and **est** (which is a singular verb) that we know that **puerī** must be genitive singular, forming a phrase with **pater**, i.e., "the boy's father."

3a. **In agrīs dominī servī strēnuē labōrant.**
3b. **In agrīs dominī servōs habent.**

In 3a **dominī** and **servī** cannot both be nominative plural since they are not linked by **et**. One of them, therefore, must be genitive singular. There is a second clue: the order of the words suggests that **dominī** forms a phrase with **in agrīs** and that **servī** is the subject of **labōrant**.

In 3b **dominī** could be genitive singular or nominative plural, but it makes more sense to take **dominī** as the subject of **habent** than to assume some unknown subject.

4. **In vīllā puerī sedent.**

Again, **puerī** could be genitive singular or nominative plural. Only the context will help you to decide whether the sentence means *The boys sit in the house*, or *They sit in the boy's house*.

12
Capture

Dāvus est sollicitus, nam necesse est Getam invenīre. Ubi servī effugiunt, dominī saepe vīlicōs reprehendunt. Saepe etiam eōs verberant. Cornēlius est dominus bonus, sed ubi Cornēlius īrātus est —
Servōs igitur Dāvus in āream statim convocat et rogat, "Ubi est Geta?" Nēmō respondēre potest. Dāvus igitur aliōs servōs in hortum, aliōs in agrōs, 5 aliōs in vīneās mittit. In hortō et agrīs et vīneīs Getam petunt. Neque in hortō neque in fossīs agrōrum neque in arboribus vīneārum Getam inveniunt.
Dāvus igitur servōs iubet canēs in āream dūcere. Aliī servī tunicam Getae in āream ferunt. Canēs veniunt et tunicam olfaciunt. Mox Dāvus servōs 10 cum canibus in agrōs dūcit. Lātrant canēs. Per agrōs Cornēliī, deinde per agrōs vīcīnārum vīllārum currunt. Neque rīvī neque fossae eōs impediunt. Vestīgia Getae inveniunt, sed Getam invenīre nōn possunt. Tandem Dāvus eōs in silvam incitat.
Geta in arbore adhūc manet et ibi dormit. Canēs lātrantēs eum excitant. 15 Nunc tamen Geta effugere nōn potest et in rāmīs sedet, immōbilis et perterritus. Canēs, ubi ad arborem appropinquant, Getam ipsum nōn cōnspiciunt, sed olfaciunt. Lātrant canēs; appropinquant servī. Miserum servum vident quī in rāmīs arboris sē cēlat.
"Dēscende, Geta!" clāmat Dāvus. Geta dēscendit. Dāvus eum tunicā 20 arripit et baculō verberat. Deinde servōs iubet Getam ad vīllam trahere et in fronte litterās FUG inūrere.

nam, for	**olfaciō, olfacere** (3), to catch the scent
inveniō, invenīre (4), to find	of, smell
reprehendō, reprehendere (3), to	**mox,** soon
blame, scold	**cum** (+ *abl.*), with
bonus, good	**lātrō, lātrāre** (1), to bark
convocō, convocāre (1), to call to-	**vestīgia,** tracks, footprints, traces
gether	**tamen,** however
rogō, rogāre (1), to ask	**immōbilis,** motionless
vīnea, -ae (*f*), vineyard	**tunicā,** by the tunic
fossa, -ae (*f*), ditch	**trahō, trahere,** to drag
canis, canis (*m/f*), dog	**in fronte litterās inūrere,** to brand
ferō, ferre (*irreg.*), to bring, carry	the letters on his forehead

Exercise 12a

Respondē Latīnē:

1. Cūr est Davus sollicitus?
2. Quō Dāvus servōs mittit?
3. Inveniuntne Getam?
4. Quid canēs faciunt?
5. Cūr Geta effugere nōn potest?
6. Ubi servī litterās FUG inūrunt?

NOUNS: *Ablative Case*

The ablative case is used both with and without prepositions.

1. With a preposition, e.g.:

ē rīvō	*out of the stream*
in hortō	*in the garden*
cum patre	*with his father*
sub arboribus	*under the trees*

2. Without a preposition:

   a. Expressions referring to time, e.g.:

septimā hōrā	*at the seventh hour*
illā nocte	*on that night*
nocte	*at night*
tribus diēbus	*in three days*
aestāte	*in summer*
brevī tempore	*in a short time*

   b. Other uses of the ablative without a preposition can often be translated "by" or "with," e.g.:

Getam tunicā arripit.	*He seizes Geta by the tunic.*
Servum baculō verberat.	*He beats the slave with a stick.*

   c. Sometimes English requires a different form of expression, e.g.:

Magnā vōce clāmat.	*He shouts loudly* (literally, *in a loud voice).*
Servus, nōmine Geta, . . .	*a slave called Geta* (literally, *Geta by name),* . . .

Exercise 12b

Supply the ending, read aloud, and translate:

1. Ē vīll___ currit Gāius ipse.
2. Vīlicus ancillam tunic___ arripit.
3. Servus, nōmin___ Geta, effugit.
4. Quis togās in cist___ pōnit?
5. Per viās urbis cum patr___ ambulāre volō.
6. Dāvus servōs iubet canēs ex agr___ in āream dūcere.

Exercise 12c

Select, read aloud, and translate:

1. Geta in _____ sē cēlat.
2. Prope _____ vīllae servī stant.
3. Aliī in _____, aliī in
   _____ sedent.
4. Servī in fossīs _____ Getam nōn
   vident.
5. Dāvus servōs cum _____ in agrōs
   dūcit.
6. Est magnus numerus _____ et
   _____ in vīllā vīcīnā.
7. Ubi est vīlicus _____ _____?
8. Dāvus Getam _____ verberat.

arborem / arbore / arboris
portae / portam / porta
cubiculum / cubiculō
āreā / āreae / āream
agrīs / agrī / agrōs

canēs / canem / canibus

puerī / puerōs / puerōrum
puellārum / puella / puellam
dominus / dominō / dominī
bonō / bonī / bonum
baculum / baculī / baculō

Exercise 12d

Read aloud and translate:

1. Vōcēs servōrum in agrīs audīmus.
2. Puerōrum clāmōrēs puellae timent.
3. In vīllā senātōris Rōmānī sedent amīcae Aurēliae.
4. Sub rāmīs arboris Cornēlia sedet.
5. Omnēs Cornēliī servī vestīgia Getae petunt; brevī tempore eum inveniunt.
6. Ē cubiculō Marcī servī cistās ferunt.
7. Līberī cum patre et mātre in raedam ascendunt.
8. Magnus fragor rāmōrum puellās terret; ē rāmīs arboris cadit subitō Sextus.

Versiculī: "Spoken by Geta," page 91.

65

Review II

Exercise IIa

Change singulars to plurals and plurals to singulars, keeping the same case:

1. vīlicō	9. vōx	17. portārum
2. cistae (gen.)	10. fossae (nom.)	18. virōrum
3. noctem	11. cibī (gen.)	19. fragōrēs (acc.)
4. dominī (nom.)	12. patribus	20. fīlia
5. ancillā	13. puerum	21. raedāriīs
6. canēs (nom.)	14. raedīs	22. canis (gen.)
7. equōs	15. frontem	23. equum
8. āream	16. fīlius	24. arbore

Exercise IIb

Read and translate each sentence below with the appropriate form of each of the following verbs:

portō, portāre   iaciō, iacere   habeō, habēre
inveniō, invenīre   pōnō, pōnere

1. Ego cistam _____.
2. Tū cistam _____.
3. Puer cistam _____.
4. Nōs cistam _____.
5. Vōs cistam _____.
6. Puerī cistām _____.
7. _____ cistam, puer!
8. _____ cistam, puerī!

Exercise IIc

Give the first person singular, infinitive, conjugation number, and meaning of each of the following verbs:

For example: surgimus   Answer: surgō, surgere (3), to rise

1. intrātis	8. manē
2. iubēs	9. mussātis
3. habent	10. cūrō
4. impedīte	11. prōmittis
5. reprehendimus	12. festīnāte
6. convocā	13. verberāmus
7. rogat	14. olfaciunt

Exercise IId

Read the following passage and answer the questions in Latin:

Hodiē servus novus ad vīllam Cornēliī venit. Dāvus eum ex urbe vīcīnā dūcit.

DĀVUS:	Ego sum Dāvus, vīlicus Gāiī Cornēliī. Gāius Cornēlius est senātor Rōmānus. Quod est senātor, in urbem saepe redit. Nunc Cornēlius, dominus meus, abest sed aestāte in vīllā habitat cum Aurēliā et Marcō et Cornēliā et Sextō. Aurēlia est uxor Cornēliī.
SERVUS:	Sed quis est Marcus?
DĀVUS:	Marcus est fīlius Cornēliī et frāter Cornēliae. Cornēlia igitur est fīlia Cornēliī et soror Marcī.
SERVUS:	Sed quis est Sextus? Estne frāter Marcī?
DĀVUS:	Minimē vērō! Nōn est frāter sed amīcus Marcī. Pater Sextī est amīcus Cornēliī. Pater Sextī nōn in Italiā sed in Asiā habitat. Sextus cum Marcō in Italiā habitat.
SERVUS:	Suntne multī servī in vīllā Cornēliī?
DĀVUS:	Est magnus numerus servōrum et ancillārum. Aliī servī in vīllā labōrant, aliī in agrīs et in vīneīs et in olīvētīs.
SERVUS:	Quid faciunt ancillae?
DĀVUS:	Togās et tunicās līberōrum et parentum cūrant. Cibum quoque parant.
SERVUS:	Laetī sunt servī Gāiī Cornēliī. Amantne dominum?
DĀVUS:	Ita vērō! Sum vīlicus virī bonī.

Line markers: 5, 10, 15, 20, 25

novus, new
olīvētīs, olive groves

1. Who comes to Cornelius' farmhouse?
2. Who brings him there?
3. Why does Cornelius often return to Rome?
4. Where is Cornelius now?
5. Who is Marcus?
6. Who is Cornelia?
7. Is Sextus Marcus' brother?
8. Who is Marcus' friend?
9. Where does Sextus' father live?
10. In what four places do the slaves work?
11. What do the slave-women do?
12. What is the slaves' attitude toward their master?

Exercise IIe

Select the appropriate adjective from the list below to complete each of the following sentences. Be sure to use the right ending on the adjective. Translate each sentence.

1. Dāvus ad āream _____ servōrum et ancillārum advenit.
2. Gāius in raedam ascendere est _____.
3. Cornēlia Flāviam _____ excitāre temptat.
4. Servī _____ ē vīllā effugiunt.
5. Cornēlia ē vīllā _____ ambulat et ad vīllam amīcae currit.

parātus	suus	plēnus	sēmisomnus	scelestus

Exercise IIf

Complete the following sentences to match the English:

1. Cornēlia et Marcus et Sextus _____ in vīllā habitant. (in summer)
2. Marcus et Sextus _____ sedent. (under the tree)
3. Nūntius sollicitus _____ currit. (to the farmhouse)
4. Puer temerārius _____ cadit. (out of the tree)
5. Cornēlia _____ ad vīllam vīcīnam fūrtim ambulat. (that night)
6. Servus _____ dormit. (at the door)
7. Cornēlius sōlus _____ epistulam scrībit. (in the farmhouse)
8. Servī _____ per agrōs currunt. (with the dogs)
9. Puer molestus _____ cadit. (into the fishpond)
10. Dāvus _____ Getam verberat. (with a stick)

Exercise IIg

In the passage in Exercise IId above, find the Latin for:

1. the house of Cornelius
2. from the neighboring city
3. the overseer of Gaius Cornelius
4. in summer
5. the wife of Cornelius
6. the sister of Marcus
7. the friend of Marcus
8. with Marcus
9. large number of slaves and slave-women
10. in the olive groves

68

13
Disaster

Intereā Cornēliī per Viam Appiam iter faciēbant. Cornēlius, quod ad urbem tribus diēbus advenīre volēbat, Syrum identidem iubēbat equōs incitāre. Syrus igitur equōs virgā verberābat. Dum per viam ībant, Aurēlia et Cornēlia spectābant rūsticōs quī in agrīs labōrābant. Marcus et Sextus spectābant omnēs raedās quae per Viam Appiam ībant.   5
Septima hōra erat. Diēs erat calidus. In agrīs rūsticī nōn iam labōrābant, sed sub arboribus quiēscēbant. In raedā Cornēlius et Aurēlia iam dormiēbant. Marcus pede vexābat Cornēliam quae dormīre volēbat. Sextus cum raedāriō Syrō sedēbat; viam et vehicula spectābat.
Subitō, "Ecce, Marce!" exclāmat Sextus. "Est aurīga!"   10
Marcus magnō rīsū respondet, "Nōn est aurīga, fatue! Est tabellārius quī epistulās cīvium praeclārōrum ab urbe fert. Tabellāriī semper celeriter iter faciunt quod epistulās ab urbe ad omnēs partēs Italiae ferunt."
"Quam celeriter iter facit!" clāmat Sextus. "Equōs ferōciter virgā incitat. Cavē tabellārium, Syre! Tenē equōs! Cavē fossam! Cavē fossam!"   15
Syrus equōs tenet et tabellārium vītat, sed raeda in fossam magnō fragōre dēscendit.

iter faciēbant, (they) were traveling
tribus diēbus, in three days
volēbat, (he, she) wanted
identidem, again and again
iubēbat, he ordered, kept ordering
virga, -ae (f), stick
verberābat, he kept beating, whipping
rūsticus, -ī (m), peasant
ībant, (they) were going
septimus, seventh
erat, it was
quiēscēbant, (they) were resting

pēs, pedis (m), foot
vehicula, vehicles
aurīga, -ae (m), charioteer
magnō rīsū, with a loud laugh
fatuus, stupid
tabellārius, -ī (m), courier
cīvis, cīvis (m), citizen
praeclārus, distinguished
ab or **ā** (+ abl.), from
pars, partis (f), part
Quam . . . ! How . . . !
ferōciter, fiercely
vītō, vītāre (1), to avoid

69

Exercise 13a

Respondē Latīnē:
1. Quid Cornēliī faciēbant?
2. Cūr Cornēlius Syrum identidem iubēbat equōs incitāre?
3. Quid faciēbat Syrus?
4. Quid faciēbant Aurēlia et Cornēlia dum per viam ībant?
5. Cūr rūsticī nōn iam labōrābant?
6. Cūr Cornēlia nōn dormiēbat?
7. Ubi sedēbat Sextus?
8. Quis celeriter appropinquat?
9. Cūr tabellāriī celeriter iter faciunt?
10. Quō īnstrumentō tabellārius equōs incitat?
11. Vītatne Syrus tabellārium?
12. Quō dēscendit raeda?

> **Quō īnstrumentō . . . ?** With what instrument . . . ?
> How . . . ?

Exercise 13b

Using story 13 as a guide, give the Latin for:
1. Again and again Cornelius kept ordering Syrus to spur on the horses.
2. While they were going along the road, Marcus and Sextus were looking at all the carriages.
3. The day was warm and it was the seventh hour.
4. The peasants were resting under the trees, and Cornelius and Aurelia were asleep in the carriage.
5. Marcus kept annoying Cornelia again and again.
6. Sextus was looking at a courier who was going along the road.
7. Couriers quickly carry letters to all parts of Italy.
8. How fiercely he spurs on the horses with (his) stick!
9. Syrus avoids the courier but not the ditch.

VERBS: The Imperfect Tense

Look at these examples from the story:

Per Viam Appiam iter **faciēbant.**	*They* **were traveling** *along the Via Appia.*
Ad urbem tribus diēbus advenīre **volēbat.**	*He* **wanted** *to reach the city in three days.*
Syrus equōs **verberābat.**	*Syrus* **kept whipping** *the horses.*

The Latin verbs in dark type are examples of the *imperfect tense.* This tense is easily recognized because the letters *-ba-* appear before the personal ending.

N.B. The imperfect forms of **sum, esse** (to be) and **possum, posse** (to be able) are irregular:

erat, (he, she, it) was	**poterat,** (he, she, it) was able
erant, (they) were	**poterant,** (they) were able

Exercise 13c

Read aloud, say whether the verb is present or imperfect, and translate:
1. Cornēlia sub arbore sedet.
2. Flāvia in agrīs ambulābat.
3. Rōmānī in Italiā habitant.
4. Servī Getam invenīre nōn poterant.
5. Lātrant canēs; appropinquant servī.
6. Marcus et Sextus raedās spectābant.
7. Rūsticī erant in agrīs.
8. Puerī saepe currunt in agrīs.
9. Geta labōrāre nōlēbat.
10. Tabellāriī epistulās ab urbe in omnēs partēs Italiae ferēbant.

Versiculī: *"Disaster," page 92.*

71

Word Study III

Latin Suffix -or

The suffix *-or,* when added to the base of a Latin verb, creates a 3rd declension noun which means "the act of" or "the result of" that particular verb. The base of a verb is found by subtracting the *-āre, -ēre, -ere,* or *-īre* ending from its infinitive. For example, **clāmāre** (base: **clām-**) becomes **clāmor, clāmōris** (*m*), a shout. The Latin noun formed in this way often comes into English unchanged. The derivative *clamor* means "a loud outcry."

Exercise 1

Create a 3rd declension noun from each verb below. Give the nominative and genitive singular of the noun. Give an English derivative, if there is one.

terrēre	**tenēre**	**stupēre** (to be amazed)
errāre	**timēre**	**valēre** (to be strong)

English Suffix -(i)fy

The Latin verb **facere** (to do, make) is the source of the English verb suffix *-(i)fy,* meaning "to make." The English word *beautify* means "to make beautiful." Often the base to which the suffix is added is also of Latin origin. The Latin word **magnus** provides the base for the English word *magnify,* "to make large."

Exercise 2

Identify the English verbs made by adding the suffix *-(i)fy* to the bases of these Latin words.

terrēre	**satis** (enough)
quālis	**ūnus** (one)
nūllus	**signum** (sign)

72

Exercise 3

Match each English word in the column at the left with its meaning in the column at the right. Use the meaning of the Latin word in parentheses as a guide.

1. fraternity (**frāter**)
2. novelty (**novus**)
3. pedestrian (**pēs, pedis**)
4. procrastinate (**crās**)
5. ancillary (**ancilla**)
6. tacit (**tacitē**)
7. simultaneous (**simul**)
8. dominate (**dominus**)

a. unspoken
b. put off until tomorrow
c. brotherhood
d. be master over
e. traveler on foot
f. something new
g. at the same time
h. serving as helper

Latin Mottoes

Although Latin is an ancient language, its words and phrases are still part of our life today. Look at the inscriptions on a penny, nickel, dime, or quarter. Find the Latin words E PLURIBUS UNUM. This is the motto of the United States, meaning "out of many, one." It refers to the many colonies which were united to make one nation.

Many states, universities, and other organizations have Latin mottoes which serve as symbols of their purpose, for example:

SEMPER FIDELIS "always faithful" (U.S. Marine Corps)
LABOR OMNIA VINCIT "Work conquers everything." (Oklahoma)
VOX CLAMANTIS IN DESERTO "the voice of one crying in the wilderness" (Dartmouth College)
A MARI USQUE AD MARE "from sea to sea" (national motto of Canada)
GRANDESCUNT AUCTA LABORE "By work, all things increase and grow." (McGill University)

Exercise 4

Find further examples of mottoes in English, Latin, or other languages used by any of the following:

a. your home state or city
b. military units, such as the army, navy, or air force
c. local colleges, universities, or academies
d. local organizations: community service groups, political groups, unions, or clubs.

73

14
Who Is to Blame?

Ubi dēscendit raeda in fossam, concidunt omnēs. Nēmō tamen ē raedā cadit. Mox cūnctī in viam ē raedā dēscendunt, sollicitī sed incolumēs. Cornēlius, quamquam gaudet quod omnēs sunt incolumēs, raedārium miserum reprehendit.

"Age, Syre! Nōlī cessāre! Extrahe statim raedam ē fossā!" 5
Syrus igitur equōs incitat. Equī raedam strēnuē trahunt, sed frūstrā. Raeda in fossā haeret immōbilis. Syrus eam movēre nōn potest.
"Ō sceleste!" inquit Cornēlius. "Tuā culpā raeda est in fossā. Quid tū faciēbās ubi cisium appropinquābat? Dormiēbāsne?"
Interpellat Sextus, "Syrus nōn dormiēbat, sed per viam placidē ībat dum 10
appropinquābat cisium. Ego et Marcus spectābāmus cisium quod celerrimē appropinquābat. Deinde tabellārius equōs ad raedam nostram dēvertēbat. Perīculum erat magnum. Syrus cisium vītāre poterat et iam nōs omnēs sumus incolumēs quod Syrus raedam magnā arte agēbat."
Tum Cornēlius rogat, "Tūne cisium spectābās, Marce, ubi appropin- 15
quābat?"
"Ita vērō, pater!" respondet Marcus. "Omnia observābam. Erat culpa tabellāriī, nōn Syrī. Syrus raedam magnā arte agēbat."
Sed Cornēlius, magnā īrā commōtus, virgam arripit et raedārium miserum verberat. 20

concidō, concidere (3), to fall down	interpellō, interpellāre (1), to interrupt
cūnctī, all	
incolumis, unhurt, safe and sound	placidē, gently, peacefully
gaudeō, gaudēre (2), to be glad	quod, which
cessō, cessāre (1), to be idle, do nothing	celerrimē, very fast
extrahō, extrahere (3), to drag out	noster, our
frūstrā, in vain	dēvertēbat, he began to turn aside
haereō, haerēre (2), to stick	perīculum, danger
moveō, movēre (2), to move	ars, artis (f), skill
culpa, -ae (f), fault, blame	agō, agere (3), to drive
cisium, light two-wheeled carriage	commōtus, moved

Exercise 14a

Respondē Latīnē:

1. Quid accidit ubi dēscendit raeda in fossam?   **accidit,** happens
2. Quō cūnctī dēscendunt?
3. Cūr Cornēlius gaudet?
4. Potestne Syrus raedam ē fossā extrahere?
5. Dormiēbatne Syrus ubi cisium appropinquābat?
6. Cuius culpa erat?   **Cuius . . . ?** Whose . . . ?
7. Quōmodo Syrus raedam agēbat?   **Quōmodo . . . ?** In what way . . . ?
    How . . . ?
8. Quōmodo commōtus est Cornēlius?
9. Quid facit Cornēlius īrātus?

75

VERBS: The Imperfect Tense

You have now met all the endings of the imperfect tense:

	1	-bam		1	-bāmus
Singular	2	-bās	Plural	2	-bātis
	3	-bat		3	-bant

Note that the vowel is short before final -m, -t, and -nt.

These are the endings of the imperfect tense of *all* Latin verbs (except **esse** and its compounds, of which **posse** is one; see page 101).

The Imperfect Tense

Number and Person			1st Conjugation	2nd Conjugation	3rd Conjugation		4th Conjugation
	Infinitive		par*āre*	hab*ēre*	mitt*ere*	iac*ere* (*-iō*)	aud*īre*
	Singular	1	parā*bam*	habē*bam*	mittē*bam*	iaciē*bam*	audiē*bam*
		2	parā*bās*	habē*bās*	mittē*bās*	iaciē*bās*	audiē*bās*
		3	parā*bat*	habē*bat*	mittē*bat*	iaciē*bat*	audiē*bat*
	Plural	1	parā*bāmus*	habē*bāmus*	mittē*bāmus*	iaciē*bāmus*	audiē*bāmus*
		2	parā*bātis*	habē*bātis*	mittē*bātis*	iaciē*bātis*	audiē*bātis*
		3	parā*bant*	habē*bant*	mittē*bant*	iaciē*bant*	audiē*bant*

Be sure to learn these forms thoroughly.

Note that the personal endings are the same as those given for the present tense on page 41, except that in this tense the first person singular ends in -m (compare **sum**).

The following is a summary of the meanings of the imperfect tense:

Syrus nōn **dormiēbat.**	*Syrus was not sleeping.*
Cornēlia dormīre **volēbat.**	*Cornelia wanted to sleep.*
Marcus Cornēliam **vexābat.**	*Marcus kept annoying Cornelia.*
Dāvus in Britanniā **habitābat.**	*Davus used to live in Britain.*
Equōs ad raedam nostram **dēvertēbat.**	*He began to turn the horses in the direction of our coach.*

76

Exercise 14b

Read aloud and translate:
1. Tabellārium līberī spectābant.
2. Cornēlius, ubi epistulās scrībēbat, uxōrem et līberōs vidēre nōlēbat.
3. Gaudēbat Cornēlius quod omnēs ē raedā incolumēs dēscendēbant.
4. Prīnceps tabellāriōs ex urbe saepe mittēbat.
5. Syrus tabellārium vītāre poterat quod equōs tenēbat.
6. Dormiēbāsne, Syre? Minimē vērō, domine! Ego placidē per viam ībam.
7. Quid vōs faciēbātis, puerī? Nōs omnēs raedās spectābāmus, pater.
8. Appropinquābatne cisium placidē? Minimē! Celerrimē per viam ībat.
9. Cūr mē semper vexābās, Marce? Dormīre volēbam.

Exercise 14c

Select, read aloud, and translate:
1. Tabellārius equōs ferōciter _____.
   incitābam / incitābat / incitābant
2. Pater et māter ē raedā _____.
   dēscendēbās / dēscendēbat / dēscendēbant
3. Cūr tū celeriter iter _____ ?
   faciēbās / faciēbant / faciēbāmus
4. Nōs omnēs in raedā _____.
   dormiēbam / dormiēbātis / dormiēbāmus
5. Ego et Marcus saepe in agrīs _____.
   currēbāmus / currēbant / currēbat

Exercise 14d

Supply the imperfect tense endings, read aloud, and translate:
1. Tabellārius multās epistulās ab urbe portā___.
2. Cornēlia, quae dēfessa era___, in cubiculō dormiē___.
3. Nōs omnēs raedam magnā arte agē___.
4. Sub arboribus vīneārum et in olīvētīs vōs Getam petē___.
5. Latrā___ canēs; per agrōs curre___; Getam invenīre nōn
   potera___.
6. "Dāve, servumne baculō verberā___?"
7. Aliī servī in vīllā, aliī in vīneīs labōrā___.
8. Sextus identidem clāmā___, "Ecce! aurīga!"

olīvētīs, olive groves

15
Vehicle Spotting

Dum raeda in fossā manēbat, Marcus et Sextus vehicula exspectābant.
Longum erat silentium.

Diū nūllum vehiculum appāret. Tandem Marcus murmur rotārum audit
et procul vim pulveris cōnspicit.

Sextus, "Quid est, Marce? Estne plaustrum?" 5

Marcus, "Minimē, fatue! Plaustra onera magna ferunt. Tarda igitur sunt.
Sed illud vehiculum celeriter appropinquat."

Sextus, "Ita vērō! Praetereā equī illud vehiculum trahunt. Bovēs plaustra
trahunt. Fortasse est raeda."

"Nōn est raeda," inquit Marcus, "Nam quattuor rotās habet raeda. Illud 10
vehiculum duās tantum rotās habet."

"Est cisium!" clāmat Sextus. "Ecce, Marce! quam celeriter appropinquat!
Fortasse est alius tabellārius."

"Minimē, Sexte!" respondet Marcus. "Nōn est tabellārius. Tabellāriī
tunicās gerere solent. Ille togam gerit. Fortasse est vir praeclārus quī ab urbe 15
Neāpolim iter facit."

Praeterit cisium. Tum vim pulveris tantum vident et murmur rotārum
audiunt. Tandem silentium.

---

exspectō, exspectāre (1), to look out
  for
longus, -a, -um, long
diū, for a long time
appāreō, appārēre (2), to appear
rota, -ae (*f*), wheel
procul, in the distance, far off
vim pulveris, a cloud of dust
plaustrum, -ī (*n*), wagon, cart
onus, oneris (*n*), load, burden

tardus, -a, -um, slow
ille, illa, illud, that, he, she, it
praetereā, besides
bōs, bovis (*m/f*), ox
tantum, only
fortasse, perhaps
alius, alia, aliud, another
Neāpolim, to Naples
praetereō, praeterīre (*irreg.*), to go
  past

RAEDA

PLAUSTRUM

CISIUM

Numerals and Numbers

I	**ūnus, -a, -um**, one	VIII	**octō**, eight
II	**duo, -ae, -o**, two	IX	**novem**, nine
III	**trēs, trēs, tria**, three	X	**decem**, ten
IV	**quattuor**, four	L	**quīnquāgintā**, fifty
V	**quīnque**, five	C	**centum**, a hundred
VI	**sex**, six	D	**quīngentī, -ae, -a**, five hundred
VII	**septem**, seven	M	**mīlle**, a thousand

Full sets of the forms of **ūnus, duo,** and **trēs** are given on page 99.

Exercise 15a

Complete these sentences with the Latin words for the appropriate numbers, read aloud, and translate:

1. Quot rotās habet raeda? _____ rotās habet raeda.
2. Quot rotās habet cisium? _____ rotās habet cisium.
3. Quot līberī in raedā erant? _____ līberī in raedā erant.
4. Duo et _____ sunt decem.
5. Duo et trēs sunt _____.
6. Sex et _____ sunt novem.
7. Quīnque et trēs sunt _____.
8. Quattuor et sex sunt _____.
9. Quattuor et quīnque sunt _____.
10. Quattuor et _____ sunt septem.

   Quot . . . ? How many . . . ?

Neuter Nouns

Some nouns in Latin have the same ending in the accusative as in the nominative. They have -a as the ending in the nominative and accusative plural. These are neuter nouns.

You have met sentences like:

Davus **baculum** habet.	*Davus has a stick.*
Vestīgia Getae inveniunt.	*They find Geta's tracks.*

The words **baculum** and **vestīgia** are neuter nouns. The 2nd and 3rd declensions have neuter nouns.

Number Case	2nd Declension	3rd Declension
Singular		
Nominative	bacul**um**	nōmen
Genitive	bacul**ī**	nōmin**is**
Accusative	bacul**um**	nōmen
Ablative	bacul**ō**	nōmin**e**
Plural		
Nominative	bacul**a**	nōmin**a**
Genitive	bacul**ōrum**	nōmin**um**
Accusative	bacul**a**	nōmin**a**
Ablative	bacul**īs**	nōmin**ibus**

There are three genders of Latin nouns: masculine, feminine, and neuter. Most nouns of the 1st declension are feminine (e.g., **puella**). The 2nd declension contains both masculine nouns (such as those in the chart on page 59) and neuter nouns as in the chart on page 80. The 3rd declension contains nouns of all three genders (e.g., **pater** and **vōx** in the chart on page 59, which are masculine and feminine respectively, and **nōmen** in the chart on page 80, which is neuter).

All of this is brought together in the chart on page 97 at the end of this book, which shows the forms of nouns of all three genders in the three declensions.

Other examples of neuter nouns are:

2nd Declension	3rd Declension
auxilium, -ī (*n*), help	**iter, itineris** (*n*), journey
cisium, -ī (*n*), light two-wheeled carriage	**murmur, murmuris** (*n*), murmur, rumble
cubiculum, -ī (*n*), room, bedroom	**onus, oneris** (*n*), load
olīvētum, -ī (n), olive grove	**tempus, temporis** (*n*), time
perīculum, -ī (*n*), danger	
plaustrum, -ī (*n*), wagon, cart	
silentium, -ī (*n*), silence	
vehiculum, -ī (*n*), vehicle	
vestīgium, -ī (*n*), track, footprint, trace	

Exercise 15b

Read aloud and translate:

1. Nūllum vehiculum puerī cōnspicere poterant.
2. Nox erat; raeda in fossā immōbilis manēbat; nēmō auxilium ferēbat.
3. Marcus et Sextus spectābant vehiculum quod celerrimē appropinquābat.
4. Canis lātrābat quod murmur rotārum audiēbat.
5. Marcus baculum iaciēbat; canis baculum petēbat.
6. Plaustra onera magna ferēbant.
7. Erant multa vehicula in viā; cisium tarda vehicula praeterībat.
8. "Quot vehicula vidēre potes, Marce?" rogat Sextus. "Ūnum cisium et tria plaustra procul videō."
9. Vestīgia vehiculōrum vidēre poterāmus, nam via erat madida.
10. Quot līberōs in raedā vidēs? In raedā ūnam puellam et duōs puerōs videō.
11. Quot līberī Rōmam raedā iter faciēbant? Ūna puella et duo puerī cum parentibus Rōmam ībant.
12. Raedārius baculō equōs incitat; equī celerrimē currunt.
13. Nescīmus nōmina omnium servōrum; sed Dāvus cūnctōs servōs nōmine saepe convocābat.
14. Quamquam tabellāriī multa itinera faciēbant, perīcula magna in viīs identidem vītābant.

81

Word Study IV

Numbers

The Latin words for numbers provide English with a great many words. For example, the English word *unite* (to bring together as *one*) comes from the Latin number **ūnus**. The English word *duet* (music for *two* performers) is derived from **duo** in Latin, and *triple* (*three* fold) traces its ancestry to the Latin **trēs**.

Exercise 1

Match these English words with their meanings.

1.	sextet	a.	five babies born together
2.	unique	b.	an eight-sided figure
3.	decimate	c.	one-of-a-kind, without equal
4.	quadrant	d.	people in their seventies
5.	duplex	e.	to destroy one tenth of
6.	septuagenarians	f.	a set of three
7.	octagon	g.	one fourth of a circle
8.	triad	h.	a period of 100 years
9.	quintuplets	i.	a group of six
10.	century	j.	a two-family house or an apartment on two levels

The Roman Number System

The origin of Roman numerals from one to ten is in the human hand. The Roman numeral **I** is one finger held up; the numeral **II** is two fingers, and so on. The numeral **V** comes from the v-shape between the thumb and the other four fingers pressed together, and it therefore represents five. When two **V**'s are placed with their points touching, the numeral **X** is formed, representing ten.

The number system of the Romans was awkward compared to the Arabic system we use today. As Roman numerals grew larger, they became increasingly hard to read. Since the Romans had no zero, arithmetic calculation was difficult. Although no longer used in mathematics, Roman numerals are still part of our everyday experience: on the face of a clock, in the chapter headings of our books, and in writing the year of an important date.

Here are some rules to remember about Roman numerals:

1. A numeral followed by a smaller numeral represents addition: **VI** = 5 + 1 = 6.
2. A numeral followed by a larger numeral represents subtraction: **IV** = 5 − 1 = 4.
3. A smaller numeral between two larger numerals is subtracted from the second of the larger numerals: **MCM** = 1000 + (1000 − 100) = 1900.

Exercise 2

Give the following in Arabic numerals:

1. **XXI**		6. **XXXIV**	
2. **DC**		7. **LXXXVIII**	
3. **XL**		8. **MDLXXIII**	
4. **LVII**		9. **MCMXLVI**	
5. **XIX**		10. **MDCCCLXIV**	

Exercise 3

Give the following in Roman numerals:

1. your age
2. the year of our story, A.D. 80
3. the current year
4. the year Rome was founded, 753 B.C.
5. your age in 25 years time

Exercise 4

Find ten examples of Roman numerals in use in your environment.

16
Do We Stay at an Inn?

Erat decima hōra. Raeda adhūc in fossā manēbat quod raedārius eam movēre nōn poterat. Aurēlia sollicita erat; Cornēlia lacrimābat; etiam puerī perīcula iam timēbant; Cornēlius in viā stābat sollicitus et caelum spectābat quod iam advesperāscēbat.

Tandem Eucleidēs, "Vidēsne illud aedificium, domine?" inquit. 5
"Videō," Cornēlius respondet. "Quid est?"
"Caupōna est. Vīsne igitur ibi pernoctāre, domine?"
Clāmat Aurēlia, "Ō mē miseram! Caupōnās nōn amō. Saepe ibi perīcula sunt magna. Fortasse caupō aliōs equōs habet. Fortasse equī caupōnis raedam ē fossā extrahere possunt. In caupōnā pernoctāre timeō." 10
"Cūr timēs, mea domina?" Eucleidēs rogat. "Nūllum est perīculum. Omnēs caupōnae nōn sunt perīculōsae. Omnēs caupōnēs nōn sunt scelestī. Ille caupō est amīcus meus. Graecus est et vir bonus."
Tum Aurēlia, "Cornēlius est senātor Rōmānus. Senātōrēs Rōmānī in caupōnā nōn pernoctant." 15
Cornēlius tamen, "Quid facere possumus?" inquit. "Hīc in Viā Appiā pernoctāre nōn possumus. Nūlla vehicula iam appārent quod advesperāscit. Est nūllum auxilium. Illa caupōna nōn procul abest. Necesse est igitur ad caupōnam īre. Agite, puerī!"
Itaque, dum Eucleidēs Cornēliōs ad caupōnam dūcēbat, raedārius sōlus 20
in viā manēbat; raedam et equōs custōdiēbat.

---

decimus, -a, -um, tenth
caelum, -ī (n), sky
advesperāscere (3), to get dark
aedificium, -ī (n), building
caupōna, -ae (f), inn
Vīsne . . . ? Do you want . . . ?
pernoctō, pernoctāre (1), to spend the night

caupō, caupōnis (m), innkeeper
perīculōsus, -a, -um, dangerous
Graecus, -a, -um, Greek
eō, īre (irreg.), to go
itaque, and so, therefore
custōdiō, custōdīre (4), to guard

Exercise 16a

Respondē Latīnē:
1. Cūr raeda in fossā manēbat?
2. Cūr Cornēlius sollicitus erat?
3. Quid videt Eucleidēs?
4. Ubi pernoctāre possunt?
5. Cūr Aurēlia in caupōnā pernoctāre nōn vult?
6. Quālis vir est caupō?
7. Ubi Cornēliī pernoctāre nōn possunt?
8. Quō īre necesse est?
9. Quis ad raedam et equōs manēbat?

Exercise 16b

Read aloud and translate:
1. Caupōnēs cīvēs Rōmānī nōn amant, nam saepe scelestī caupōnēs cīvēs in caupōnā verberant.
2. Puellārum nōmina ancilla nova vocat; sed strēnuae puellae vōcem ancillae nōn audiunt.
3. Perīculōsum erat iter per Viam Appiam facere, nam servī fugitīvī sub arboribus sē cēlābant et, ubi advesperāscēbat, viātōrēs baculō verberābant.
4. Aliī servī equōs dominī in viam dūcēbant, aliī ē vīllā currēbant et cistās in raedā pōnēbant.
5. Ubi Cornēlius epistulās scrībit, nēmō eum impedit. Sī magnae līberōrum vōcēs patrem vexant, Aurēlia puerōs in hortum mittit.
6. Plaustrum duās habet rotās; in plaustrīs onera magna rūsticī pōnunt; plaustra bovēs per viās in urbem nocte trahunt.
7. Aurēlia in caupōnā pernoctāre nōlēbat; caupōnēs timēbat. "Caupōnēs," inquit, "scelestī sunt omnēs et caupōnae perīculōsae."
8. Nōn omnēs caupōnēs scelestī sunt. Eucleidis amīcus est caupō bonus, et viātōrēs in caupōnā eius salvī sunt.
9. Bacula canis petere parat. Marcus baculum longum iacit, sed baculum canis petere nōn potest quod in arboris rāmīs haeret.
10. Magnum numerum servōrum Cornēlius in vīneā spectābat. Servī spectābant Getam, quī in rāmō arboris dormiēbat.

Versiculī: "Proserpina," pages 92-93
"Phaëthon," pages 94-95.

Review III

Exercise IIIa

Read and translate each sentence below with the appropriate form of each of the following verbs in the imperfect tense:

exspectō, exspectāre   cōnspiciō, cōnspicere   extrahō, extrahere
moveō, movēre   custōdiō, custōdīre

1. Ego raedam _____.
2. Tū raedam _____.
3. Servus raedam _____.
4. Nōs raedam _____.
5. Vōs raedam _____.
6. Servī raedam _____.

Exercise IIIb

Change the words in italics to plural, make any other necessary changes, read aloud, and translate:

1. Puerī in *cubiculō* dormiēbant.
2. Servus *onus magnum* portat.
3. Sextus *murmur* rōtārum in viā audiēbat.
4. Cornēliī in *cisiō* iter faciēbant.
5. *Perīculum* in viīs est magnum.
6. Cornēlius servōs *baculō* verberābat.
7. Senātor ad urbem *iter* facit.
8. Raeda est *vehiculum Rōmānum.*
9. *Rūsticus* in *plaustrō* dormit.
10. *Rōta cisiī* īnfirma erat.

Exercise IIIc

Complete the sentences with Latin words for the appropriate numbers, read aloud, and translate:

1. Quot fīliōs habet Cornēlius? Cornēlius _____ fīlium habet.
2. Quot fīliās habet Cornēlius? Cornēlius _____ fīliam habet.
3. Numerus līberōrum Cornēliī est _____.
4. Quot pedēs habet lupus? Lupus _____ pedēs habet.
5. Quot līberī ad urbem iter faciunt? _____ līberī ad urbem iter faciunt.
6. Quot rotās habent raeda et cisium? Raeda et cisium _____ rotās habent.
7. Quot pedēs habent duo lupī? Duo lupī habent _____ pedēs.
8. Quot nōmina habet Cornēlius? Cornēlius _____ nōmina habet.
9. Quot nōmina habet Cornēlia? Cornēlia _____ nōmen habet.
10. Quot pedēs habent trēs puerī? Trēs puerī _____ pedēs habent.

Exercise IIId

Select the correct word, read the sentence aloud, and translate it into English:

1. In agrīs errābant _____.
   puerōs / puerī / puerōrum

2. Aurēlia _____ cibum parāre iubēbat.
   ancillae / ancillās / servī / Dāvus

3. Cornēlius multōs _____ habēbat.
   canēs / servum / ancillās / amīcī

4. Quid facit _____ ?
   Aurēliam / Aurēlia / Aurēliae

5. Sextus neque puellās neque _____ timet.
   fossae / vīlicus / Dāvum / ancilla

6. Rūsticī _____ baculīs excitant.
   canis / bovēs / equus

7. Quam molesta est _____ !
   Sextus / puellae / Flāvia / Cornēliam

8. Sub arborum rāmīs dormit _____.
   cīvēs / servus / rūsticōs

9. Procul arborēs, _____, vīneās vident.
   agrī / vīllae / vīllās

10. Canēs lātrantēs timēbant _____.
    puerōs / puerī / puella

11. In agrīs _____ sunt multae arborēs.
    Cornēliī / vīllā / vīneam

12. In āreā Marcus videt magnum numerum _____.
    ancillae / servōrum / virum / puellās

13. Ancillae līberōrum _____ cūrābant.
    tunica / tunicae / canis / cistās

14. Servī cum _____ per vīneās festīnābant.
    canēs / amīcōs / canibus / agrīs

15. _____ novās _____ induere vult.
    puella / puellae / stola / stolās

16. Marcus multōs servōs in agrīs _____ videt.
    omnis / patris / Cornēliō / patribus

17. Puerī in _____ effugiēbant.
    hortō / hortum / hortīs / hortōrum

18. Pater puerōs in hortum _____.
    mittunt / est / mittit / reprehendit

19. Rūsticī sub rāmīs arborum _____.
    dormiēbat / labōrābat / sedēbat / labōrābant

20. Cornēlius arborēs _____ nōn iam potest.
    ascendit / ascendēbat / ascendere

21. Tabellārius multās epistulās _____.
    ferēbant / ferēbat / scrībēbant / habēbant

22. Servī Getam in arbore _____.
    invenit / mittit / inveniunt / reprehendit

Exercise IIIe

Read the following passage and answer the questions in Latin:

Raeda in fossā haerēbat immōbilis. Raedārius sōlus manēbat quod
necesse erat raedam et equōs custōdīre. "Ō mē miserum!" inquit.
"Dominus meus est īrātus quod raedam ē fossā movēre nōn possum.
Hīc pernoctāre nōlō. Ēsuriō etiam, sed cibum nōn habeō."
Iam advesperāscēbat. Nūlla vehicula praeterībant. Nēmō per viam 5
ad urbem ībat. Equī sub arboribus quiēscēbant. Dormiēbat in raedā
raedārius. Longum erat silentium.
Subitō appropinquant trēs latrōnēs quī ab urbe per Viam Appiam
iter faciunt. Cistās in viā cōnspiciunt et statim petunt. Vestēs extrahunt.
Ad urbem redīre parant. Subitō stertit raedārius. Latrōnēs, quī rae- 10
dārium nōn vident, aufugiunt perterritī. Vestēs in viā relinquunt.
Iam diēs est. Raedārius surgit. Tunicās et stolās et togās spectat.
"Cūr vestēs ̄in viā sunt? Quis hoc faciēbat ubi ego dormiēbam?"
Hoc mussābat et vestēs in cistīs pōnēbat. Tum cistās in raedam
iacit, raedam ipse ascendit, auxilium exspectat. 15

> ēsuriō, ēsurīre (4), to be hungry
> latrō, latrōnis (m), robber
> vestēs, vestium (f pl), clothes
> stertō, stertere (3), to snore
> aufugiō, aufugere (3), to run away
> relinquō, relinquere (3), to leave

1. Why did the coachman remain alone?
2. Why is he unhappy?
3. Why is he hungry?
4. Why were there no more vehicles passing by?
5. What were the horses doing under the trees?
6. In what direction are the thieves going?
7. What do they do after they take the clothes out of the trunks?
8. Why are the thieves startled when they hear the coachman snore?
9. What does the coachman see the next morning?
10. What does he do?
11. What does he wait for?

Exercise IIIf

*In the first five lines above identify the subjects and the direct objects,
and identify the tense of each verb.*

VERSICULĪ

1 Serves Him Right
(after Chapter 4)

Arbor habet fēlem. Sextus petit (ecce!) superbus.
    Ad terram fēlēs dēsilit, ille manet.

habet, (he, she, it) has
fēlēs, (a, the) cat
petit, (he, she) seeks, goes after
superbus, boastful
ad terram, to the ground
dēsilit, (he, she) jumps down
ille, he
manet, (he, she) stays

2 Show-off!
(after Chapter 7)

Ambulat in mūrō Sextus spectantque puellae.
    "Nōn timeō mūrōs!" clāmat, humīque cadit.

in mūrō, on the wall
-que, and
humī, to or on the ground

3 Time to Go Home
(after Chapter 8)

Nōn laetīs, puer, ambulāre in agrīs
aut ascendere in arborēs licēbit,
Lātrācemve tuum vidēre amīcum.
Crās urbem petere et forum necesse est.

nōn . . . licēbit, it will not be permitted (to you), you will not be able
aut, or
Lātrāx, name of a dog (cf. **lātrat,** barks)
-ve, or
crās, tomorrow
forum, market place

4 Bad News
(after Chapter 9)

Nōn iam errāre in agrīs, nōn iam lātrante licēbit
    cum cane per tōtum lūdere, Sexte, diem;
aut in frondōsōs, ignāve, ascendere rāmōs
    arboris, et lentōs inde vidēre bovēs;
aut tua dum clāmant mīrantēs facta puellae,   5
    saltāre in mūrō, "Vae tibi, caute parum!"

nōn . . . licēbit, it will not be permitted (to you), you will not be able
lātrante . . . cum cane, with a barking dog
per tōtum . . . diem, the whole day through
lūdere, to play
aut . . . aut, either . . . or (with **nōn,** 1 = nor . . . nor)
in frondōsōs . . . rāmōs arboris, up into leafy branches of a tree
lentus, slow-moving
inde, from there
bovēs, oxen, cows
tua . . . mīrantēs facta, marveling at your exploits
saltāre, to jump
in mūrō, on the wall
Vae tibi, caute parum! Serves you right, you reckless boy!

5 To Rome Tomorrow
(after Chapter 10)

Ad Rōmāna iterum fora festīnāre necesse est,
    crās iterum plēnās plēbe vidēre viās.
Iam domina īrāta est; iam ancilla hūc currit et illūc;
    dūcit iam invītōs ad iuga servus equōs.

fora, market places
plēnās plēbe, full of people
domina, mistress
hūc . . . et illūc, hither and thither
invītus, unwilling
ad iuga, to their harness

6 Spoken by Geta
(after Chapter 12)

Ō servī, spectāte Getam mē nōmine servum,
    cui grave vōx dominī continuusque labor.
Iam tergō baculī vestīgia, iamque figūra
    (heu mōnstrum!) mediā stat mihi fronte triplex!

cui grave, to whom . . . were annoying
tergō, on my back
figūra . . . triplex, the threefold mark
heu mōnstrum, alas the terrible warning
mediā . . . mihi fronte, on the middle of my forehead

7 Disaster
(after Chapter 13)

Nōn dēfessī urbem petimus laetīque vidēmus
    multa; sed occurrit vix bene sānus homō.
Tum dēvertit equōs servus. Cornēlia clāmat.
    In fossā raeda est, in tabulīsque sumus.

multa, many things (acc. pl.)
occurrō, occurrere (3), to meet
vix bene sānus, scarcely in his right mind
homō, hominis (*m*), man
dēvertō, dēvertere (3), to turn aside
tabula, -ae (*f*), plank, floorboard

8 Proserpina
(after Chapter 16)

Proserpina was the daughter of Ceres, the goddess of the earth and crops. One day she was picking flowers in the fields of Enna in Sicily, when the ground suddenly opened beneath a very beautiful flower and she was snatched away by Dis, the god of the underworld, who desired her for his wife. Her mother, in terrible distress, searched for her the whole world over, and out of sympathy with the great goddess, the earth bore no fruit or grain. When Ceres at last learned what had happened to her daughter, she begged her back from the king of the dead and was told that Proserpina might return, provided she had eaten nothing during her stay below. Alas, she had eaten four pomegranate seeds and so was destined every year thereafter to spend four months with her husband while her mother mourned and all the face of the earth mourned with her. The poem tells part of this story.

Dum petit in terrā Siculā Proserpina flōrēs,
  errat ab ancillīs saepe puella suīs;
nam, "Prope nōn flōs est pulcherrimus," inquit, "amīcae.
  Saepe in dēsertōs īre necesse locōs."
Sōla ōlim sōlīs in agrīs dēfessa puella   5
  (heu!) sedet, et flōrem multum habet atque bonum,
cum prope sub parvā magnum videt arbore flōrem
  et petit. At flōrem nōn superāre potest.
Tum magis atque magis Proserpina parva labōrat
  strēnua—sed frūstrā! Flōs magis haeret ibi.   10
Ecce! Puella, cavē! Mōnstrum est! Temerāria, mōnstrum
  (esque sine ancillīs sōla), puella, cavē!
At subitō parvā est discissa sub arbore terra,
  appārent ātrī quattuor intus equī.
"Ancillae, ferte auxilium!" Proserpina clāmat,   15
  "Māter," et "auxilium fer, dea magna, mihi!
Dīs mē habet!" At cēlat lacrimantem terra puellam.
  Invenit et dominam servula nūlla suam.

9 Phaëthon
(after Chapter 16)

Phaëthon was really the Sun-god's son, but none of his friends would believe him when he boasted about it. In fact, he began to doubt it himself. So one day he journeyed far to the east to the palace of the Sun-god, the stately golden fortress from which every morning he begins his journey through the skies. The god laughed when he heard of his son's doubts and distress and said, "To prove to you beyond doubt that I am your father, ask anything at all of me and I promise you on my unbreakable word that I will grant it." Phaëthon asked to be allowed for one day to drive the great sun-chariot with its four huge horses.

There was nothing the Sun-god was less willing to grant. He looked at Phaëthon and at the great horses and knew that the boy would not be able to control them. But he had given his word, and the youth set off to his certain death. The horses got the bit between their teeth and came so near the earth with their blazing chariot that Jupiter, king of gods and men, had no choice but to destroy them with his thunderbolts to save the earth and everyone on it from being destroyed by fire.

> Sūmit ab invītō genitōre ēlātus habēnās
>   et puer immēnsōs incitat ācer equōs.
> Mox procul ā summō timidus videt aethere terrās,
>   tum dextrā sociīs (ēn!) equus hinnit equīs.
> Et, "Sociī, nōn est onus hoc solitum," inquit. "Habēnās   5
>   quae tenet hās hodiē, nōnne remissa manus?
> Est aurīga puer! Puer hōrum at nūllus equōrum
>   est dominus. Retinet nōn mea colla puer!
> Noster abest dominus. Nunc lūdere tempus, amīcī,
>   nunc dēvertere iter. Quō placet īre licet."   10
> Currus deinde patris vestīgia certa relinquit.
>   Dēscendit, Phaëthon nec retinēre potest.
> Incipit et iam vīcīnōs nimis ūrere montēs;
>   vīcīnōs currus iam nimis ūrit agrōs.
> Mox urbēs nūllae incolumēs; mox oppida nūlla,   15
>   nūlla propinquantēs nōn timet aula rotās.
> Iuppiter illa videt; quī, "Nōn placet," inquit, "equōrum
>   sī terrās omnēs ūrere turba potest.
> Ō Cyclōpes, ubī sunt fulmina?" Fulmina mittit.
>   Servat sīc terrās. Heu! Phaëthonta necat.   20

sūmō, sūmere (3), to take
invītus, -a, -um, unwilling
genitor, genitōris (m), father
ēlātus, -a, -um, delighted
habēnae, -ārum (f pl), reins
ācer, ācris, ācre, eager
ā summō . . . aethere, from the
heights of heaven
terra, -ae (f), land
dextrā, on the right
sociīs . . . equīs, to the horses
accompanying (him)
ēn, look, behold
hinniō, hinnīre (4), to whinny
socius, -ī (m), companion
hoc, this
solitus, -a, -um, usual
hās, these
nōnne remissa manus? is it not a
feeble hand?
hōrum, of these
at, but
retineō, retinēre (2), to hold
back, restrain
colla, -ōrum (n pl), neck
lūdō, lūdere (3), to play

quō placet īre licet, we may go
where we please
currus, chariot
certus, -a, -um, fixed, usual
relinquō, relinquere (3), to leave
nec, and not
incipiō, incipere (3), to begin
nimis, too, too much
ūrō, ūrere (3), to burn
mōns, montis (m), mountain
oppidum, -ī (n), town
propinquantēs, approaching
aula, -ae (f), hall, palace
Iuppiter, Iovis (m), Jupiter
illa, those things, that
nōn placet, I don't like it
turba, -ae (f), crowd
Cyclōpes, Cyclōpum (m pl), Cyclopes
(giants who manufactured
thunderbolts for Jupiter)
fulmen, fulminis (n), thunderbolt
servō, servāre (1), to save
sīc, in this way
Heu! Alas!
Phaëthonta, Phaëthon (acc. case)
necō, necāre (1), to kill

PRONUNCIATION

The pronunciation of Latin is best learned by imitation of the teacher. Most consonants are pronounced as in English, but the following should be noted:

b before **s** or **t** is pronounced as English *p*: **urbs.**
c is always hard and pronounced as English *k*: **cibus.**
g is hard, as in English "get": **gemit.**
gn in the middle of a word may be pronounced as the *ngn* in English "hangnail": **magnus.**
i before a vowel is a consonant and pronounced as English *y*: **iānua.**
r should be rolled: **rāmus.**
s is pronounced as in English "sing," never as in "roses": **cīvis.**
v is pronounced as English *w*: **vīlla.**

The following approximations are offered for the pronunciation of short and long vowels. In addition, long vowels should be held for a longer time than short ones.

SHORT	LONG
a = English "alike" (**pater**)	**ā** = English "father" (**māter**)
e = English "pet" (**ego**)	**ē** = English "date" (**dēscendō**)
i = English "sip" (**iterum**)	**ī** = English "sleep" (**īrātus**)
o = English "for" (**omnēs**)	**ō** = English "holy" (**in hortō**)
u = English "foot" (**ubi**)	**ū** = English "boot" (**ūnus**)

The diphthong **ae** is pronounced as the *y* in English "sky" (**amīcae**). The diphthong **au** is pronounced as the *ow* in English "how" (**audit**). The diphthong **ei** is pronounced as the "ay" in English "say" (**deinde**).

Latin words are accented according to simple rules. If the next to the last syllable has a long vowel or a diphthong, it will receive the accent:

discḗdō

If the next to the last syllable has a short vowel followed by two consonants, it will usually receive the accent:

exténdō

Otherwise, the accent falls on the third syllable from the end:

Británnicus

Careful observation of the long marks (macrons) over the vowels will thus help with both pronunciation and accenting of Latin words.

FORMS

The following charts show the forms of typical Latin nouns, adjectives, and verbs in the cases and tenses presented in this book. As an aid in pronunciation, markings of long vowels and of accents are included.

I. Nouns

Number / Case	1st Declension Fem.	2nd Declension Masc.	2nd Declension Neut.	3rd Declension Masc.	3rd Declension Fem.	3rd Declension Neut.
Singular						
Nominative	puélla	sérvus	púer	báculum	páter	vōx	nṓmen
Genitive	puéllae	sérvī	púerī	báculī	pátris	vṓcis	nṓminis
Accusative	puéllam	sérvum	púerum	báculum	pátrem	vṓcem	nṓmen
Ablative	puéllā	sérvō	púerō	báculō	pátre	vṓce	nṓmine
Plural						
Nominative	puéllae	sérvī	púerī	bácula	pátrēs	vṓcēs	nṓmina
Genitive	puellárum	servōrum	puerṓrum	baculṓrum	pátrum	vṓcum	nṓminum
Accusative	puéllās	sérvōs	púerōs	bácula	pátrēs	vṓcēs	nṓmina
Ablative	puéllīs	sérvīs	púerīs	báculīs	pátribus	vṓcibus	nōmínibus

II. Adjectives

Number	1st and 2nd Declension			3rd Declension		
Case	Masc.	Fem.	Neut.	Masc.	Fem.	Neut.
Singular						
Nominative	mágnus	mágna	mágnum	ómnis	ómnis	ómne
Genitive	mágnī	mágnae	mágnī	ómnis	ómnis	ómnis
Accusative	mágnum	mágnam	mágnum	ómnem	ómnem	ómne
Ablative	mágnō	mágnā	mágnō	ómnī	ómnī	ómnī
Plural						
Nominative	mágnī	mágnae	mágna	ómnēs	ómnēs	ómnia
Genitive	magnórum	magnárum	magnórum	ómnium	ómnium	ómnium
Accusative	mágnōs	mágnās	mágna	ómnēs	ómnēs	ómnia
Ablative	mágnīs	mágnīs	mágnīs	ómnibus	ómnibus	ómnibus

98

III. Numbers

Case	Masc.	Fem.	Neut.	Masc.	Fem.	Neut.	Masc.	Fem.	Neut.
Nominative	únus	úna	únum	dúo	dúae	dúo	trēs	trēs	tría
Genitive	ūníus	ūníus	ūníus	duốrum	duắrum	duốrum	tríum	tríum	tríum
Accusative	únum	únam	únum	dúōs	dúās	dúo	trēs	trēs	tría
Ablative	únō	únā	únō	duóbus	duábus	duóbus	tríbus	tríbus	tríbus

IV. Regular Verbs

The Present Tense

Number and Person		1st Conjugation	2nd Conjugation	3rd Conjugation		4th Conjugation
Infinitive		paráre	habére	míttere	iácere (-iō)	audíre
Imperative		párā	hábē	mítte	iáce	aúdī
		paráte	habéte	míttite	iácite	audíte
Singular	1	párō	hábeō	míttō	iáciō	aúdiō
	2	párās	hábēs	míttis	iácis	aúdīs
	3	párat	hábet	míttit	iácit	aúdit
Plural	1	parámus	habémus	míttimus	iácimus	audímus
	2	parátis	habétis	míttitis	iácitis	audítis
	3	párant	hábent	míttunt	iáciunt	aúdiunt

The Imperfect Tense

Number and Person		1st Conjugation	2nd Conjugation	3rd Conjugation		4th Conjugation
Singular	1	parábam	habébam	mittébam	iaciébam	audiébam
	2	parábās	habébās	mittébās	iaciébās	audiébās
	3	parábat	habébat	mittébat	iaciébat	audiébat
Plural	1	parābámus	habēbámus	mittēbámus	iaciēbámus	audiēbámus
	2	parābátis	habēbátis	mittēbátis	iaciēbátis	audiēbátis
	3	parábant	habébant	mittébant	iaciébant	audiébant

V. Irregular Verbs

The Present Tense

Number and Person		Infinitive	ésse	pósse	vélle	nólle	íre	férre
Singular	1		sum	póssum	vólō	nólō	éō	férō
	2		es	pótes	vīs	nōn vīs	īs	fers
	3		est	pótest	vult	nōn vult	it	fert
Plural	1		súmus	póssumus	vólumus	nólumus	ímus	férimus
	2		éstis	potéstis	vúltis	nōn vúltis	ítis	fértis
	3		sunt	póssunt	vólunt	nólunt	éunt	férunt

The Imperfect Tense

Number and Person		éram	póteram	volébam	nōlébam	íbam	ferébam
Singular	1	éram	póteram	volébam	nōlébam	íbam	ferébam
	2	érās	póterās	volébās	nōlébās	íbās	ferébās
	3	érat	póterat	volébat	nōlébat	íbat	ferébat
Plural	1	erámus	poterámus	volēbámus	nōlēbámus	ībámus	ferēbámus
	2	erátis	poterátis	volēbátis	nōlēbátis	ībátis	ferēbátis
	3	érant	póterant	volébant	nōlébant	íbant	ferébant

Note: The imperatives of **nólle** are **nōli** (*sing.*) and **nōlite** (*pl.*).

*Vocabulary**

A

13	ā or ab (+ *abl.*)	from
3	ábeō, abíre (*irreg.*)	to go away
11	ábsum, abésse (*irreg.*)	to be away, absent
14	áccidit, accídere (3)	to happen
2	ad (+ *acc.*)	to, towards, at, near
5	adhúc	still
6	advéniō, adveníre (4)	to reach, arrive at
16	advesperáscit, advesperáscere (3)	to get dark
16	aedifícium, -ī (*n*)	building
1	aestáte	in summer
8	Áge! Ágite!	Come on!
2	áger, ágrī (*m*)	field
14	ágō, ágere (3)	to do, drive
15	álius, ália, áliud	another, other
9	áliī . . . áliī . . .	some . . . others . . .
1	álter, áltera, álterum	the other, a second
2	ámbulō, ambuláre (1)	to walk
2	amíca, -ae (*f*)	friend
3	amícus, -ī (*m*)	friend
4	ámō, amáre (1)	to like, love
10	ancílla, -ae (*f*)	slave-woman
15	appáreō, appārére (2)	to appear
4	appropínquō, appropinquáre (1)	to approach
1	árbor, árboris (*f*)	tree
11	área, -ae (*f*)	open space, threshing-floor
6	arrípiō, arrípere (3)	to grab hold of, snatch
14	ars, ártis (*f*)	skill
4	ascéndō, ascéndere (3)	to climb, go up, climb into (a carriage
4	aúdiō, audíre (4)	to hear, listen to
13	auríga, -ae (*m*)	charioteer
6	auxílium, -ī (*n*)	help

B

10	báculum, -ī (*n*)	stick
12	bónus, -a, -um	good
15	bōs, bóvis (*m/f*)	ox, cow
2	brévī témpore	in a short time, soon
8	Británnia, -ae (*f*)	Britain
3	Británnicus, -a, -um	British

*Numbers at the left refer to the chapter in which the word first appears.

C

3	cádō, cádere (3)	to fall
16	caélum, -ī (n)	sky
6	cálidus, -a, -um	warm
12	cánis, cánis (m/f)	dog
1	cántō, cantáre (1)	to sing
16	caúpō, caupónis (m)	innkeeper
16	caupóna, -ae (f)	inn
4	Cávē! Cavéte!	Be careful!
8	celériter	quickly
14	celérrimē	very fast, quickly
11	célō, cēláre (1)	to hide
15	céntum	a hundred
14	céssō, cessáre (1)	to be idle, do nothing
11	cíbus, -ī (m)	food
14	císium, -ī (n)	light two-wheeled carriage
10	císta, -ae (f)	trunk, chest, box
13	cívis, cívis (m)	citizen
3	clámō, clāmáre (1)	to shout
5	clámor, clāmóris (m)	shout, shouting
14	commótus, -a, -um	moved
9	compléxū	in an embrace
14	cóncidō, concídere (3)	to fall down
4	cōnspíciō, cōnspícere (3)	to catch sight of
7	cónsulō, cōnsúlere (3)	to consult
12	cónvocō, convocáre (1)	to call together
10	crās	tomorrow
8	cubículum, -ī (n)	room, bedroom
14	Cúius . . . ?	Whose . . . ?
14	cúlpa, -ae (f)	fault, blame
12	cum (+ abl.)	with
14	cúnctī, -ae, -a	all
1	Cūr . . . ?	Why . . . ?
10	cúrō, cūráre (1)	to look after, attend to
2	cúrrō, cúrrere (3)	to run
16	custódiō, custōdíre (4)	to guard

D

15	décem	ten
16	décimus, -a, -um	tenth
2	dēféssus, -a, -um	tired
8	deínde	then, next
4	dēscéndō, dēscéndere (3)	to come or go down, climb down
14	dēvértō, dēvértere (3)	to turn aside
6	díēs, diéī (m)	day

9	discédō, discédere (3)	to go away, depart
15	díū	for a long time
16	dómina, -ae (f)	mistress, lady of the house
11	dóminus, -ī (m)	master
4	dórmiō, dormíre (4)	to sleep
7	dúcō, dúcere (3)	to lead, take, bring
1	dum	while, as long as
15	dúo, dúae, dúo	two

E

2	ē or ex (+ abl.)	from, out of
9	éam	her, it
10	éās	them
1	Écce!	Look! Look at . . . !
11	effúgiō, effúgere (3)	to run away, escape
5	égo	I
7	Éheu!	Alas!
2	éius	his, her, its
13	éō, íre (irreg.)	to go
10	éō ípsō témpore	at that very moment
6	éōs	them
7	epístula, -ae (f)	letter
10	équus, -ī (m)	horse
13	érat	(he, she, it) was
6	érrō, erráre (1)	to wander
	ésse (see sum)	
2	et	and
1	étiam	also
7	Eúgepae!	Hurray!
3	éum	him, it
2	ex or ē (+ abl.)	from, out of
6	excípiō, excípere (3)	to welcome
8	éxcitō, excitáre (1)	to rouse, wake (someone) up
10	exclámō, exclāmáre (1)	to exclaim, shout out
3	éxeō, exíre (irreg.)	to go out
15	exspéctō, exspectáre (1)	to look out for, wait for
14	éxtrahō, extráhere (3)	to drag out

F

1	fáciō, fácere (3)	to make, do
13	fátuus, -a, -um	stupid
6	férō, férre (irreg.)	to bring, carry
13	feróciter	fiercely
6	Férte auxílium!	Bring help! Help!
9	festínō, festināré (1)	to hurry
11	fília, -ae (f)	daughter

11	fílius, -ī (*m*)		son
15	fortásse		perhaps
12	fóssa, -ae (*f*)		ditch
4	frágor, fragóris (*m*)		crash, noise, din
11	fráter, frátris (*m*)		brother
6	frígidus, -a, -um		cool, cold
12	frōns, fróntis (*f*)		forehead
14	frústrā		in vain
3	fúrtim		stealthily

G

14	gaúdeō, gaudére (2)	to be glad, rejoice
3	gémō, gémere (3)	to groan
10	gérō, gérere (3)	to wear
16	Graécus, -a, -um	Greek

H

10	hábeō, habére (2)	to have, hold
1	hábitō, habitáre (1)	to live, dwell
14	haéreō, haerére (2)	to stick
9	hīc (*adverb*)	here
2	hódiē	today
9	hóra, -ae (*f*)	hour
3	hórtus, -ī (*m*)	garden

I

10	iáciō, iácere (3)	to throw
1	iam	now, already
9	iánitor, iānitóris (m)	doorkeeper
9	iánua, -ae (*f*)	door
5	íbi	there
11	id quod	that which, what
3	ídem, éadem, ídem	the same
13	idéntidem	again and again
4	ígitur	therefore
6	ignávus, -a, -um	cowardly, lazy
11	ílle, ílla, íllud	that, he, she, it
12	immóbilis, -is, -e	motionless
11	impédiō, impedíre (4)	to hinder, prevent
1	in (+ *abl.*)	in, on
3	in (+ *acc.*)	into
10	íncitō, incitáre (1)	to spur on, urge on
14	incólumis, -is, -e	unhurt, safe and sound
8	índuō, indúere (3)	to put on
4	īnfírmus, -a, -um	weak, shaky
7	ínquit	(he, she) says, said
10	intéreā	meanwhile

14	interpéllō, interpelláre (1)	to interrupt
8	íntrō, intráre (1)	to enter, go in
12	inúrō, inúrere (3)	to brand
12	invéniō, invenīre (4)	to come upon, find
10	ípse, ípsa, ípsum	-self, very
11	íra, -ae (f)	anger
14	īrā commótus	made angry, in a rage
3	īrátus, -a, -um	angry
	íre (see éō)	
3	Íta vérō!	Yes!
1	Itália, -ae (f)	Italy
16	ítaque	and so, therefore
13	íter, itíneris (n)	journey
13	íter fácere	to travel
8	íterum	again, a second time
10	iúbeō, iubére (2)	to order

L

3	labórō, labōráre (1)	to work
9	lácrimō, lacrimáre (1)	to weep, cry
1	laétus, -a, -um	happy, glad
12	látrō, lātráre (1)	to bark
7	légō, légere (3)	to read
2	léntē	slowly
11	líberī, -órum (m pl)	children
12	líttera, -ae (f)	letter (of the alphabet)
15	lóngus, -a, -um	long
8	lúcet, lūcére (2)	to be light, to be day
6	lúpus, -ī (m)	wolf

M

3	mádidus, -a, -um	dripping, soaked, wet
4	mágnus, -a, -um	big, great, large, loud (voice, laugh)
5	máne	early in the day, in the morning
9	máneō, manére (2)	to remain, stay
8	máter, mátris (f)	mother
4	mē	me
9	mécum	with me
7	méus, -a, -um	my
8	míhi	for me, to me
15	mílle	a thousand
3	Mínimē!	No!
9	míser, mísera, míserum	unhappy, miserable
9	míttō, míttere (3)	to send
4	moléstus, -a, -um	troublesome, annoying
3	moléstus, -ī (m)	pest

14	móveō, movḗre (2)	to move
12	mox	soon, presently
3	múltī, -ae, -a	many
15	múrmur, múrmuris (n)	murmur, rumble
11	mússō, mussā́re (1)	to mutter

N

8	nam	for
8	nārrā́tor, nārrātṓris (m)	narrator
9	nátō, natā́re (1)	to swim
3	-ne	(indicates a question)
15	Neā́polis	Naples
7	necésse	necessary
9	nḗmō	no one
6	néque . . . néque . . .	neither . . . nor . . .
9	nésciō, nescī́re (4)	to be ignorant, not know
3	níhil	nothing
9	nṓbīs	for us
12	nócte	at night
6	nṓlō, nṓlle (irreg.)	to be unwilling, not wish
1	nṓmen, nṓminis (n)	name
1	nṓmine	by name, called
2	nōn	not
8	nṓndum	not yet
8	nōs	we, us
14	nóster, nóstra, nóstrum	our
15	nóvem	nine
11	nox, nóctis (f)	night
9	núllus, -a, -um	no
11	númerus, -ī (m)	number
11	nunc	now
7	núntius, -ī (m)	messenger

O

14	obsérvō, observā́re (1)	to watch
5	occupā́tus, -a, -um	busy
15	óctō	eight
12	olfáciō, olfácere (3)	to catch the scent of, smell
14	olīvḗtum, -ī (n)	olive grove
8	ómnēs, ómnia	all, everyone, everything
15	ónus, óneris (n)	load, burden

P

10	parā́tus, -a, -um	ready, prepared
11	párēns, paréntis (m/f)	parent
6	párō, parā́re (1)	to prepare, get ready
13	párs, pártis (f)	part

5	páter, pátris (m)	father
9	per (+ acc.)	through, along
16	perīculósus, -a, -um	dangerous
14	perículum, -ī (n)	danger
16	pernóctō, pernoctáre (1)	to spend the night
6	pertérritus, -a, -um	frightened, terrified
13	pēs, pédis (m)	foot
5	pétō, pétere (3)	to look for, seek, aim at, attack
1	pictúra, -ae (f)	picture
3	piscína, -ae (f)	fishpond
14	plácidē	gently, peacefully
15	plaústrum, -ī (n)	wagon, cart
11	plénus, -a, -um	full
10	pốnō, pốnere (3)	to put, place
11	pórta, -ae (f)	gate
10	pórtō, portáre (1)	to carry
6	póssum, pósse (irreg.)	to be able
13	póterat	(he, she) was able
13	praeclárus, -a, -um	distinguished, famous
15	praetéreā	besides, too, moreover
15	praetéreō, praeterfre (irreg.)	to go past
10	praetéxta (tóga)	with purple edge
7	prínceps, príncipis (m)	emperor
15	prócul	in the distance, far off
9	prōmíttō, prōmíttere (3)	to promise
6	própe (+ acc.)	near
1	puélla, -ae (f)	girl
3	púer, púerī (m)	boy

Q

1	quae	who
4	Quális . . . ?	What sort of . . . ?
13	Quam . . . !	How . . . !
11	quámquam	although
15	quáttuor	four
6	Quem . . . ?	Whom . . . ?
1	quī, quae, quod	who, which
10	quídam, quaédam, quóddam	a certain
1	Quid fácit . . . ?	What does . . . do?
13	quiéscō, quiéscere (3)	to rest, keep quiet
15	quīngéntī, -ae, -a	five hundred
15	quīnquāgíntā	fifty
15	quínque	five
1	Quis . . . ? Quid . . . ?	Who . . . ? What . . . ?
4	Quō . . . ?	Where . . . to?

108

1	quod	because, which
13	Quō īnstruméntō . . . ?	With what implement . . . ?
		How . . . ?
14	Quómodo . . . ?	In what way . . . ? How . . . ?
2	quóque	also
7	Quōs . . . ?	Whom . . . ?
15	Quot . . . ?	How many . . . ?

R

10	ráeda, -ae (f)	traveling carriage, coach
10	raedárius, -ī (m)	coachman
4	rámus, -ī (m)	branch
5	rédeō, redíre (irreg.)	to return
6	repéllō, repéllere (3)	to drive off, drive back
12	reprehéndō, reprehéndere (3)	to blame, scold
5	respóndeō, respondére (2)	to reply
7	révocō, revocáre (1)	to recall, call back
3	rídeō, rīdére (2)	to laugh, smile
13	(mágnō) rísū	with a loud laugh
6	rívus, -ī (m)	stream
12	rógō, rogáre (1)	to ask
7	Róma, -ae (f)	Rome
1	Rōmánus, -a, -um	Roman
15	róta, -ae (f)	wheel
1	rústicus, -a, -um	rustic, country-style
13	rústicus, -ī (m)	peasant

S

2	saépe	often
7	salútō, salūtáre (1)	to greet, welcome
7	Sálvē! Salvéte!	Greetings! Good morning! Hello!
3	sálvus, -a, -um	undamaged, all right, safe
10	sceléstus, -a, -um	wicked
7	scríbō, scríbere (3)	to write
11	sē	himself, herself, itself, themselves
9	secúndus, -a, -um	second
2	sed	but
1	sédeō, sedére (2)	to sit
9	sēmisómnus, -a, -um	half-asleep
4	sémper	always
7	senátor, senātóris (m)	senator
15	séptem	seven
13	séptimus, -a, -um	seventh
3	sérvus, -ī (m)	slave
15	sex	six

5	sī	if
15	siléntium, -ī (*n*)	silence
6	sílva, -ae (*f*)	woods, forest
9	símul	together, at the same time
10	sóleō, solére (2)	to be accustomed, in the habit of
3	sollícitus, -a, -um	anxious, worried
3	sólus, -a, -um	alone
11	sóror, soróris (*f*)	sister
3	spéctō, spectáre (1)	to watch, look at
5	státim	immediately
3	státua, -ae (*f*)	statue
10	stō, stáre (1)	to stand
10	stóla, -ae (*f*)	stola, a woman's outer-garment
8	strénuē	strenuously, hard
2	strénuus, -a, -um	active, energetic
1	sub (+ *abl.*)	under, beneath
3	súbitō	suddenly
1	sum, ésse (*irreg.*)	to be
8	súrgō, súrgere (3)	to get up, rise
9	súus, -a, -um	his, her, its, their (own)

T

13	tabellárius, -ī (*m*)	courier
9	táceō, tacére (2)	to be quiet
9	tácitē	silently
12	támen	however
2	tándem	at last
15	tántum	only
15	tárdus, -a, -um	slow
	tē (*see* tū)	
6	temerárius, -a, -um	rash, reckless, bold
9	témptō, temptáre (1)	to try
2	témpus, témporis (*n*)	time
9	téneō, tenére (2)	to hold
4	térreō, terrére (2)	to frighten, terrify
6	tímeō, timére (2)	to fear, be afraid of
5	tímidus, -a, -um	afraid
10	tóga, -ae (*f*)	toga
7	trádo, trádere (3)	to hand over
12	tráhō, tráhere (3)	to drag, pull
12	trēs, trēs, tría	three
4	tū (*acc.* tē)	you (*sing.*)
4	tum	at that moment, then
8	túnica, -ae (*f*)	tunic
5	túus, -a, -um	your

U	5	**Úbi . . . ?**	Where . . . ?
	1	**úbi**	where, when
	15	**ū́nus, -a, -um**	one
	7	**urbs, úrbis** (*f*)	city
	11	**úxor, uxṓris** (*f*)	wife
V	9	**Válē! Valḗte!**	Goodbye!
	13	**vehículum, -ī** (*n*)	vehicle
		vélle (*see* **vólō**)	
	5	**véniō, venī́re** (4)	to come
	11	**vérberō, verberā́re** (1)	to beat
	12	**vestī́gium, -ī** (*n*)	track, footprint, trace
	3	**véxō, vexā́re** (1)	to annoy
	10	**vía, -ae** (*f*)	road, street
	16	**viā́tor, viātṓris** (*m*)	traveler
	1	**vīcī́nus, -a, -um**	neighboring
	4	**vídeō, vidḗre** (2)	to see
	11	**vī́licus, -ī** (*m*)	overseer, farm manager
	1	**vī́lla, -ae** (*f*)	farmhouse
	1	**vī́lla rū́stica**	farmhouse
	12	**vī́nea, -ae** (*f*)	vineyard
	3	**vir, vírī** (*m*)	man
	13	**vírga, -ae** (*f*)	stick
	16	**vīs** (from **vólō**)	you want
	15	**vīs púlveris**	cloud of dust
	13	**vī́tō, vītā́re** (1)	to avoid
	6	**vólō, vélle** (*irreg.*)	to wish, want, be willing
	8	**vōs**	you (*pl.*)
	4	**vōx, vṓcis** (*f*)	voice
	6	**vult** (*from* **vólō**)	(he, she) wishes, wants

Ecce Romani

A Latin Reading Program
Revised Edition

2
Rome at Last

Longman

Ecce Romani Student's Book 2   Rome at Last

First Printing 1984

ISBN 0 582 36665 8
(72459)

Illustrated by Peter Dennis, Trevor Parkin, Hamish Gordon and Claudia Karabaic Sargent. Cover illustration by Peter Dennis.

This edition of *Ecce Romani* is based on *Ecce Romani: A Latin Reading Course*, originally prepared by The Scottish Classics Group © copyright The Scottish Classics Group 1971, 1982, and published in the United Kingdom by Oliver and Boyd, a Division of Longman Group. This edition has been prepared by a team of American and Canadian educators:
  Authors: Professor Gilbert Lawall, University of Massachusetts, Amherst,
        Massachusetts
        David Tafe, Rye Country Day School, Rye, New York
  Consultants: Dr. Rudolph Masciantonio, Philadelphia Public Schools, Pennsylvania
        Ronald Palma, Holland Hall School, Tulsa, Oklahoma
        Dr. Edward Barnes, C.W. Jefferys Secondary School, Downsview,
        Ontario
        Shirley Lowe, Wayland Public Schools, Wayland, Massachusetts

For providing us with photographs or permission to publish extracts from their publications, we would like to thank:
Page 62: The Montreal Museum of Fine Arts, photograph of Roman Magistrates and Lictors by Jean Lemaire, French 1598-1659, oil on canvas. A gift of Lord Strathcona and family.
Page 58: Harvard University Press, publisher of Loeb Classical Library, Pliny *Natural History*, Volume X Book XXXVI-XXXVII, copyright © 1962 by the President and Fellows of Harvard College.
Pages 21, 47, and 91: Carol Clemeau Esler, *Roman Voices: Everyday Latin in Ancient Rome* and *Teacher's Guide to Roman Voices: Everyday Latin in Ancient Rome*, published by Gilbert Lawall, 71 Sand Hill Road, Amherst, MA 01002.

Longman
95 Church Street
White Plains, New York 10601

Distributed in Canada by Academic Press Ltd., 55 Barber Greene Road, Don Mills, Ontario MC3 2A1, Canada.

9 10-MU-9594939291   .

CONTENTS

17
Arrival at the Inn

Raeda in fossā haerēbat. Cornēliī per viam ībant ad caupōnam quae nōn procul aberat. Cornēlia, quae nōn iam lacrimābat, cum Eucleide ambulābat. Puerōs, quod praecurrēbant, identidem revocābat Cornēlius. Aurēlia, quamquam in caupōnā pernoctāre adhūc nōlēbat, lentē cum Cornēliō ībat. Mox ad caupōnam appropinquābant. Nēminem vidēbant; vōcēs tamen 5 hominum audiēbant.

Subitō duo canēs ē iānuā caupōnae sē praecipitant et ferōciter lātrantēs Cornēliōs petunt. Statim fugit Sextus. Stat immōbilis Marcus. Aurēlia perterrita exclāmat. Cornēlius ipse nihil facit. Cornēlia tamen nōn fugit sed ad canēs manum extendit.   10

"Ecce, Marce!" inquit. "Hī canēs lātrant modo. Nūllum est perīculum. Ecce, Sexte! Caudās movent."

Eō ipsō tempore ad iānuam caupōnae appāruit homō obēsus quī canēs revocāvit.

"Salvēte, hospitēs!" inquit. "In caupōnā meā pernoctāre vultis? Hīc multī 15 cīvēs praeclārī pernoctāvērunt. Ōlim hīc pernoctāvit etiam lēgātus prīncipis."

"Salvē, mī Apollodōre!" interpellāvit Eucleidēs. "Quid agis?"

"Mehercule!" respondit caupō. "Nisi errō, meum amīcum Eucleidem agnōscō."

"Nōn errās," inquit Eucleidēs. "Laetus tē videō. Quod raeda dominī meī 20 in fossā haeret immōbilis, necesse est hīc in caupōnā pernoctāre."

"Doleō," inquit caupō, "quod raeda est in fossā, sed gaudeō quod ad meam caupōnam nunc venītis. Intrāte, intrāte, omnēs!"

praecurrō, praecurrere (3), to run ahead
homō, hominis (m), man
sē praecipitant, (they) hurl themselves, rush
fugiō, fugere (3), to flee
manum, hand
hī canēs, these dogs
modo, only
cauda, -ae (f), tail
appāruit, (he) appeared
obēsus, -a, -um, fat

revocāvit, (he) called back
hospes, hospitis (m), friend, host, guest
pernoctāvērunt, (they) have spent the night
ōlim, once (upon a time)
lēgātus, -ī (m), envoy
Quid agis? How are you?
Mehercule! By Hercules! Goodness me!
nisi errō, unless I am mistaken
agnōscō, agnōscere (3), to recognize
doleō, dolēre (2), to be sad

Exercise 17a

Respondē Latīnē:

1. Quō ībant Cornēliī?
2. Cūr Cornēlius puerōs identidem revocābat?
3. Volēbatne Aurēlia in caupōnā pernoctāre?
4. Quid canēs faciunt?
5. Quālis homō ad iānuam caupōnae appāruit?
6. Quālēs cīvēs in caupōnā pernoctāvērunt?
7. Quis ōlim in caupōnā pernoctāvit?
8. Cūr necesse est in caupōnā pernoctāre?
9. Gaudetne caupō quod raeda est in fossā?

Exercise 17b

Using story 17 as a guide, give the Latin for:

1. The inn was not far away.
2. Cornelius kept calling the boys back.
3. Aurelia was unwilling to spend the night in the inn.
4. Two dogs head for the boys.
5. The two dogs are wagging their tails.
6. I am glad to see you.
7. The innkeeper is sorry that the coach is in the ditch.

Cavē canem! *Beware of the dog!* (Pompeian inscription)

Errāre est hūmānum. *To err is human.* (Seneca)

Manus manum lavat. *One hand washes the other.*
(Petronius, *Satyricon* 45)

6

Regular Verbs

Most Latin verbs belong to one of four conjugations:

		THE PRESENT TENSE			
		1st _Conjugation_	2nd _Conjugation_	3rd _Conjugation_	4th _Conjugation_
Infinitive		par*āre*	hab*ēre*	mitt*ere*	iac*ere* (**-iō**)	aud*īre*
Imperative		par*ā*	hab*ē*	mitt*e*	iac*e*	aud*ī*
		par*āte*	hab*ēte*	mitt*ite*	iac*ite*	aud*īte*
Singular	1	par*ō*	habe*ō*	mitt*ō*	iaci*ō*	audi*ō*
	2	par*ās*	hab*ēs*	mitt*is*	iac*is*	aud*īs*
	3	para*t*	habe*t*	mitt*it*	iac*it*	audi*t*
Plural	1	par*āmus*	hab*ēmus*	mitt*imus*	iac*imus*	aud*īmus*
	2	par*ātis*	hab*ētis*	mitt*itis*	iac*itis*	aud*ītis*
	3	para*nt*	habe*nt*	mittu*nt*	iaciu*nt*	audiu*nt*

Number and Person (left label for present tense table rows: Singular / Plural)

		THE IMPERFECT TENSE			
		1st _Conjugation_	2nd _Conjugation_	3rd _Conjugation_	4th _Conjugation_
Singular	1	par*ābam*	hab*ēbam*	mitt*ēbam*	iaci*ēbam*	audi*ēbam*
	2	par*ābās*	hab*ēbās*	mitt*ēbās*	iaci*ēbās*	audi*ēbās*
	3	par*ābat*	hab*ēbat*	mitt*ēbat*	iaci*ēbat*	audi*ēbat*
Plural	1	par*ābāmus*	hab*ēbāmus*	mitt*ēbāmus*	iaci*ēbāmus*	audi*ēbāmus*
	2	par*ābātis*	hab*ēbātis*	mitt*ēbātis*	iaci*ēbātis*	audi*ēbātis*
	3	par*ābant*	hab*ēbant*	mitt*ēbant*	iaci*ēbant*	audi*ēbant*

Number and Person (left label for imperfect tense table rows: Singular / Plural)

Be sure you know all of these forms thoroughly.

Irregular Verbs

A few verbs do not belong to any of the four conjugations shown on the previous page, but you will notice that, except for the forms **sum** and **possum,** they have the same personal endings as the regular verbs.

THE PRESENT TENSE						
Infinitive	esse	posse	velle	nōlle	īre	ferre
Imperative	es	—	—	nōlī	ī	fer
	es*te*	—	—	nōlī*te*	ī*te*	fer*te*
Number and Person *Singular* 1	su*m*	possu*m*	volō	nōlō	eō	ferō
2	e*s*	pote*s*	vīs	nōn vīs	ī*s*	fer*s*
3	es*t*	potes*t*	vul*t*	nōn vul*t*	i*t*	fer*t*
Plural 1	su*mus*	possu*mus*	volu*mus*	nōlu*mus*	ī*mus*	feri*mus*
2	es*tis*	potes*tis*	vul*tis*	nōn vul*tis*	ī*tis*	fer*tis*
3	su*nt*	possu*nt*	volu*nt*	nōlu*nt*	eu*nt*	feru*nt*

THE IMPERFECT TENSE						
Number and Person *Singular* 1	era*m*	potera*m*	volē*bam*	nōlē*bam*	ī*bam*	ferē*bam*
2	erā*s*	poterā*s*	volē*bās*	nōlē*bās*	ī*bās*	ferē*bās*
3	era*t*	potera*t*	volē*bat*	nōlē*bat*	ī*bat*	ferē*bat*
Plural 1	erā*mus*	poterā*mus*	volē*bāmus*	nōlē*bāmus*	ī*bāmus*	ferē*bāmus*
2	erā*tis*	poterā*tis*	volē*bātis*	nōlē*bātis*	ī*bātis*	ferē*bātis*
3	era*nt*	potera*nt*	volē*bant*	nōlē*bant*	ī*bant*	ferē*bant*

Be sure to learn these forms thoroughly.

Exercise 17c

Read and translate the following short sentences, paying particular attention to the tenses of the verbs:

1. Ubi manēbat?
2. Unde veniunt?
3. Cūr īre nōn poterant?
4. Quid fers?
5. Quid faciēbātis?
6. Tum erāmus in fossā.
7. Quō īre volunt?
8. Quid respondēbant?
9. Cūr praecurrēbant?
10. Quid facere iubēbat?
11. Nōn poteram clāmāre.
12. Quō ītis?

8

13. Quid ferēbās?
14. Quid facitis?
15. Quid vidēs?
16. Ubi haeret raeda?
17. In viā pernoctāre nōlumus.
18. Quō ībant?
19. Ad urbem īre nōn vult.

20. Unde veniēbās?
21. Scelestī estis.
22. Quō equōs dūcit?
23. Quō fugiēbant?
24. Cūr īre nōlunt?
25. Caupōna nōn procul aberat.
26. Manēre nōlēbāmus.

Unde . . . ? Where . . . from?

Adjectives

Some adjectives have endings like those of 1st and 2nd declension nouns, and others have 3rd declension endings, as shown in the following chart:

Number Case	1st and 2nd Declension			3rd Declension		
	Masc.	*Fem.*	*Neut.*	*Masc.*	*Fem.*	*Neut.*
Singular						
Nom.	magn*us*	magn*a*	magn*um*	omn*is*	omn*is*	omn*e*
Gen.	magn*ī*	magn*ae*	magn*ī*	omn*is*	omn*is*	omn*is*
Acc.	magn*um*	magn*am*	magn*um*	omn*em*	omn*em*	omn*e*
Abl.	magn*ō*	magn*ā*	magn*ō*	omn*ī*	omn*ī*	omn*ī*
Plural						
Nom.	magn*ī*	magn*ae*	magn*a*	omn*ēs*	omn*ēs*	omn*ia*
Gen.	magn*ōrum*	magn*ārum*	magn*ōrum*	omn*ium*	omn*ium*	omn*ium*
Acc.	magn*ōs*	magn*ās*	magn*a*	omn*ēs*	omn*ēs*	omn*ia*
Abl.	magn*īs*	magn*īs*	magn*īs*	omn*ibus*	omn*ibus*	omn*ibus*

Be sure to learn these forms thoroughly.

Notes

1. Some adjectives that have endings of the 1st and 2nd declensions end in -er in the masculine nominative singular, e.g., **miser.** The feminine and neuter of this adjective are **misera** and **miserum.** In some words, the -e- is dropped from all forms except the masculine nominative singular, e.g., **noster, nostra, nostrum; nostrī, nostrae, nostrī.** Compare with the noun **ager, agrī** (*m*).

2. Many adjectives of the 3rd declension have identical forms in the masculine and feminine, as does **omnis** above.

3. The ablative singular of 3rd declension adjectives ends in -ī (not -e), and the genitive plural ends in **-ium.** The neuter nominative and accusative plurals end in -ia. Compare these endings with those of 3rd declension nouns that you learned in Chapters 11 and 15.

9

Agreement of Adjectives

The gender, case, and number of an adjective are determined by the noun with which it *agrees*. Consider the following sentence:

Multōs agrōs, multās arborēs, multa plaustra vident.

Since **agrōs** is a masculine noun in the accusative plural, **multōs** has a masculine accusative plural ending. Similarly, **multās** is feminine accusative plural *agreeing* with **arborēs**, and **multa** is neuter accusative plural *agreeing* with **plaustra**. An adjective will *agree* with the noun it describes in *gender, case,* and *number.*

There are five clues which help you to decide with which noun an adjective agrees. These are *gender, case, number, sense,* and *position.*

1. Let us look at the first three clues (agreement of gender, case, and number):

    a. Sometimes any one of the three *agreement* clues will show which noun an adjective modifies:

        Māter bonōs puerōs laudat.
        The mother praises the good boys.

        Māter and **puerōs** are different in gender, case, and number, and therefore all the clues in **bonōs** are decisive.

    b. Sometimes only two of these clues are present:

        Māter bonās puellās laudat.
        The mother praises the good girls.

        In this sentence **māter** and **puellās** have the same gender, but either of the two other clues (case and number) will help.

    c. In the following sentences only one of the *agreement* clues is present:

        Māter bonam puellam laudat.
        The mother praises the good girl.

        Since **māter** and **puellam** have the same gender and number, only the case of **bonam** is decisive.

        Mātrem bonum puerum laudāre iubēmus.
        We order the mother to praise the good boy.

        Here, it is the gender alone which is decisive.

        Mātrem bonās puellās laudāre iubēmus.
        We order the mother to praise the good girls.

        Here, only the number is decisive.

10

2. You will find examples where none of the clues of agreement will help you. When this happens, you must rely on position or sense:

   Puellam ignāvam epistulam scrībere iubēmus.
   We order the lazy girl to write the letter.

3. Note that either adjectives that take 1st and 2nd declension endings or adjectives of the 3rd declension may be used with nouns of any declension, as is shown in the following phrases:

māter bona	omnium puellārum
patrem bonum	omnēs puerī
iter bonum	omnī puerō
itinerī bonō	omnī itinere
itinera bona	omnia itinera

   The important thing is that the adjective must *agree* with the noun it modifies in *gender, case,* and *number.*

Exercise 17d

In the following sentences, the most important clues to meaning are those of agreement of adjectives. Sometimes words appear in an unusual order with adjectives separated from the nouns they modify.

Read aloud and translate:

1. Canis magnus ossa habet.
2. Canis magna ossa habet.
3. Multī canēs ossa habent.
4. Canis magnum os habet.
5. Omnia ossa magnus canis habet.
6. Magna habent multī canēs ossa.
7. Magnum canis habet os.
8. Omnēs canēs dominōs nōn habent.
9. Magnum habet dominus canem.
10. Canem dominus magnum habet.
11. Habent multī puerī magnōs canēs.
12. Magnōs multī habent puerī canēs.

   os, ossis (*n*), bone

Nōn omnia possumus omnēs. *We cannot all do everything.*
(Vergil, *Eclogues* VIII.63)

Versiculī: *"Arrival at the Inn,"* page 99.

Word Study V

Latin Suffixes -(i)tūdō and -(i)tās

A Latin adjective may form a noun by adding the suffix -(i)tūdō or the suffix -(i)tās to its base. The base of a Latin adjective may be found by dropping the ending from the genitive singular, e.g., the base of **magnus** (genitive, **magnī**) is **magn-**. Nouns formed in this way are in the 3rd declension, they are feminine, and they convey the meaning of the adjective in noun form.

Adjective			Base	Noun
Nom.	*Gen.*			
magnus	**magnī**	big, great	**magn-**	**magnitūdō, magnitūdinis** (*f*) size, greatness
obēsus	**obēsī**	fat	**obēs-**	**obēsitās, obēsitātis** (*f*) fatness

In English words derived from these nouns, -(i)tūdō becomes -*(i)tude* and -(i)tās becomes -*(i)ty*. The meaning of the English derivative is usually the same as that of the Latin noun, e.g., *magnitude* (size), *obesity* (fatness).

Exercise 1

Give the Latin nouns which may be formed from the bases of the adjectives below. In numbers 1–4, use the suffix -(i)tūdō, and in numbers 5–10, use the suffix -(i)tās. Give the English word derived from each noun formed, and give the meaning of the English word.

1. sōlus, -a, -um
2. multus, -a, -um
3. longus, -a, -um
4. sollicitus, -a, -um
5. ūnus, -a, -um

6. brevis, -is, -e
7. īnfirmus, -a, -um
8. timidus, -a, -um
9. vīcīnus, -a, -um
10. hūmānus, -a, -um

Latin Suffixes -īlis, -ālis, -ārius

The suffixes -īlis, -ālis, and -ārius may be added to the bases of many Latin nouns to form adjectives. The base of a Latin noun may be found by dropping the ending from the genitive singular, e.g., the base of vōx (genitive, vōcis) is vōc-. Adjectives formed in this way mean "pertaining to" the meaning of the noun from which they are formed.

	Noun		Base		Adjective
Nom.	*Gen.*				
vir	virī	man	vir-		virīlis, -is, -e manly
vōx	vōcis	voice	vōc-		vōcālis, -is, -e pertaining to the voice
statua	statuae	statue	statu-		statuārius, -a, -um pertaining to statues

Some adjectives ending in -ārius are used as nouns, e.g., statuārius, -ī (m), *sculptor*. Can you think of similar words made from the nouns **raeda**, -ae (*f*), *coach*, and **tabella**, -ae (*f*), *tablet, document?*

English words derived from these adjectives make the following changes in the suffixes:

-īlis becomes -il or -ile, e.g., virīlis, virile
-ālis becomes -al, e.g., vōcālis, vocal
-ārius becomes -ary, e.g., statuārius, statuary

The meaning of the English derivative is similar to or the same as that of the Latin adjective, e.g., virīlis in Latin and *virile* in English both mean "manly." Sometimes the English word ending in -ary may be used as a noun, e.g., *statuary*, "a group or collection of statues," "sculptor," or "the art of sculpting."

Exercise 2

For each English word below, give the following:

a. the Latin adjective from which it is derived
b. the Latin noun from which the adjective is formed
c. the meaning of the English word.

You may need to consult a Latin and/or English dictionary for this exercise.

auxiliary	principal
civil	puerile
literary	servile
nominal	temporal

13

Combining Suffixes

Some English words end with a combination of suffixes derived from Latin. For example, the English word *principality* (domain of a prince) is derived from the Latin **prīnceps, prīncipis** (*m*) by the combination of the suffixes **-ālis** (*-al* in English) and **-itās** (*-ity* in English).

Exercise 3

For each word below, give the related English noun ending in the suffix *-ity*. Give the meaning of the English word thus formed and give the Latin word from which it is derived.

civil	immobile
dual	partial
facile	servile
hospital	virile

English Replaced by Latin Derivatives

In the following exercise, the italicized English words are not derived from Latin. Note that these words are usually simpler and more familiar than the Latin derivatives which replace them. Latin can help with the meanings of many of these more difficult English words.

Exercise 4

Replace the italicized words with words of equivalent meaning chosen from the pool on page 15. Use the Latin words in parentheses to determine the meanings of the English words in the pool.

1. Staying at an inn was much too *risky* for Aurelia.
2. While he was away, Cornelius left the children in the *guardianship* of Eucleides.
3. Although the driver *handled* the reins skillfully, he was unable to avoid disaster.
4. It was *easy to see* that Eucleides was a friend of the innkeeper.
5. The *runaway* slave was captured and returned to the farm.
6. The innkeeper offered his *friendly welcome* to the Cornelii.
7. The heat made the slaves' work more *burdensome*.
8. The Via Appia is full of *traveling* merchants, who sell their wares from town to town.
9. Cornelia cast a *sorrowful* glance as she waved goodbye to Flavia.
10. This *country* inn was host to all the local farmers.

14

custody (**custōs**)	hospitality (**hospes**)
itinerant (**iter**)	fugitive (**fugere**)
apparent (**appārēre**)	perilous (**perīculum**)
doleful (**dolēre**)	onerous (**onus**)
manipulated (**manus**)	rustic (**rūsticus**)

Latin Words in English

Some Latin words are used in English in their Latin form. Many of these words have become so familiar in English that they are pluralized using English rules, e.g.:

senator   plural: senators
area   plural: areas

Others retain their Latin plurals, e.g.:

alumnus   plural: alumni
alumna   plural: alumnae
medium   plural: media

Sometimes both an English and a Latin plural are used, e.g.:

index   plurals: indexes, indices
memorandum   plurals: memorandums, memoranda

Occasionally the use of two plurals may reflect more than one meaning of the word. For example, the word indexes usually refers to reference listings in a book, whereas indices are signs or indicators, e.g., "the indices of economic recovery."

Exercise 5

Look up these nouns in both an English and a Latin dictionary. For each noun, report to the class on similarities or differences between the current meaning in English and the original meaning in Latin. Be sure to note carefully the English plurals and their pronunciation.

antenna	consensus	formula
appendix	crux	stadium
campus	focus	stimulus

18
Settling In

Cūnctī in caupōnam intrāvērunt.

"Nōnne cēnāre vultis?" inquit caupō. "Servī meī bonam cēnam vōbīs statim parāre possunt."

"Ego et Cornēlia," inquit Aurēlia, "hīc cēnāre nōn possumus. Dūc nōs statim ad cubiculum nostrum." 5

Servōs caupō statim iussit cēnam Cornēliō et Marcō et Sextō parāre. Ipse Aurēliam et Cornēliam ad cubiculum dūxit. Aurēlia, ubi lectum vīdit, gemuit.

"Hic lectus est sordidus," inquit. "Mea Cornēlia in sordidō lectō dormīre nōn potest. Necesse est alium lectum in cubiculum movēre." 10

Caupō respondit, "Cūr mē reprehendis? Multī viātōrēs ad meam caupōnam venīre solent. Nēmō meam caupōnam reprehendit."

Iam advēnit Eucleidēs. Ubi Aurēlia rem explicāvit, Eucleidēs quoque caupōnem reprehendit.

Caupō mussāvit, "Prope viam Appiam caupōnam meliōrem invenīre nōn 15 potestis. In caupōnā meā nūllī lectī sunt sordidī."

Sed servōs iussit alium lectum petere. Brevī tempore servī alium lectum in cubiculum portāvērunt. Caupō iam cum rīsū clāmāvit, "Ecce, domina! Servī meī alium lectum tibi parāvērunt. Nōnne nunc cēnāre vultis?"

"Ego nōn iam ēsuriō," inquit Cornēlia. "Volō tantum cubitum īre." 20

"Ego quoque," inquit Aurēlia, "sum valdē dēfessa."

Nōn cēnāvērunt Aurēlia et Cornēlia, sed cubitum statim īvērunt. Mox dormiēbant.

---

intrāvērunt, (they) entered
cēnō, cēnāre (1), to dine, eat dinner
cēna, -ae (f), dinner
vōbīs, for you
Dūc! Take! Lead!
iussit, (he) ordered
Cornēliō, for Cornelius
dūxit, (he) led
lectus, -ī (m), bed
hic lectus, this bed
sordidus, -a, -um, dirty

viātor, viātōris (m), traveler
venīre solent, (they) are in the habit of coming
rem explicāre, to explain the situation
melior, better
tibi, for you
ēsuriō, ēsurīre (4), to be hungry
cubitum īre, to go to bed
valdē, very, exceedingly, very much
īvērunt, they went

16

Exercise 18a

Respondē Latīnē:

1. Quid servī caupōnis parāre possunt?
2. Vultne Aurēlia statim cēnāre?
3. Quid fēcit Aurēlia ubi lectum vīdit?
4. Quālis est lectus?
5. Quid fēcit Eucleidēs ubi Aurēlia rem explicāvit?
6. Quid servī in cubiculum portāvērunt?
7. Cūr Cornēlia cēnāre nōn vult?
8. Quid fēcērunt Aurēlia et Cornēlia?

Quid fēcit . . . ? What did . . . do?

VERBS: *Perfect Tense I*

Compare the following pairs of sentences:

Caupō **mussat.**	*The innkeeper* **mutters.**
Caupō **mussāvit.**	*The innkeeper* **muttered.**
Dāvus servōs **iubet** canēs dūcere.	*Davus* **orders** *the slaves to lead the dogs.*
Caupō servōs **iussit** cēnam parāre.	*The innkeeper* **ordered** *the slaves to prepare dinner.*
Marcus **gemit.**	*Marcus* **groans.**
Aurēlia **gemuit.**	*Aurelia* **groaned.**
Marcus nūntium in vīllam **dūcit.**	*Marcus* **leads** *the messenger into the house.*
Cornēliam ad cubiculum **dūxit.**	*He* **led** *Cornelia to the bedroom.*
Cornēlius vōcēs hominum **audit.**	*Cornelius* **hears** *men's voices.*
Cornēlius vōcēs hominum **audīvit.**	*Cornelius* **heard** *men's voices.*

In each of the pairs of examples listed above, the verb in the first example is in the present tense and the verb in the second example is in the *perfect tense.*

The perfect tense refers, not to something that *is happening* (present tense) or *was happening* (imperfect tense), but to something that *happened* in the past (see examples above). It may also refer to something that *has happened*, e.g.:

Servus meus alium lectum tibi **parāvit.**	*My slave* **has prepared** *another bed for you.*

or to something that *did* or *did* not *happen*, e.g.:

Aurēlia nōn **cēnāvit.**	*Aurelia* **did** *not* **eat dinner.**

17

In the perfect tense, the ending of the 3rd person singular is **-it**; the ending of the 3rd person plural is **-ērunt**.

In many verbs, the stem for the perfect tense ends in **-v-** or **-s-** or **-u-** or **-x-**, e.g.:

> mussāv- iuss- gemu- dūx- audīv-

The perfect endings are then added to the perfect stem, e.g.:

> mussāv*it*   iuss*it*   gemu*it*   dūx*it*   audīv*it*
> mussāv**ērunt**   iuss**ērunt**   gemu**ērunt**   dūx**ērunt**   audīv**ērunt**

Here are some more examples:

	Singular		**Plural**
Present	*Perfect*	*Present*	*Perfect*
exclāmat	exclāmāvit	exclāmant	exclāmāvērunt
habet	habuit	habent	habuērunt
rīdet	rīsit	rīdent	rīsērunt
cōnspicit	cōnspexit	cōnspiciunt	cōnspexērunt

Exercise 18b

Give the missing forms and meanings to complete the following table:

Perfect Tense		Infinitive	Meaning
Singular	*Plural*		
intrāvit	intrāvērunt	intrāre	to enter
	custōdīvērunt		
timuit			
	cēnāvērunt		
	traxērunt		
mīsit			
	īvērunt		
spectāvit			
doluit			
	mānsērunt		
	voluērunt		
haesit			

18

Exercise 18c

Read the following passage and answer the questions in full Latin sentences:

Cornēliī per viam ad caupōnam lentē ambulābant.
Sextus, "Nōnne ille tabellārius equōs vehementer incitāvit, Marce?"
Cui respondit Marcus, "Ita vērō! Eōs ferōciter verberāvit. Equī cisium
celeriter traxērunt. Raedārius noster, 'Cavē, sceleste!' magnā vōce exclāmāvit.
Tum raedam dēvertēbat, sed frūstrā. Tabellārius tamen neque cisium dēvertit   5
neque raedam vītāvit. Itaque equī raedam in fossam traxērunt. Gemuit raedārius; gemuērunt pater et māter; lacrimāvit Cornēlia."
    "Pater tuus certē īrātus erat," interpellāvit Sextus. "Statim virgam arripuit
et miserum raedārium verberābat. Cornēlia, ubi hoc vīdit, iterum lacrimāvit.
'Pater! Pater!' inquit. 'Nōlī miserum hominem verberāre!'"   10
    "Tum pater," inquit Marcus. "Cornēliam tacēre iussit. Omnēs sollicitī
caelum spectāvērunt quod iam advesperāscēbat. Pater igitur Eucleidem nōs
ad caupōnam dūcere iussit."
    Mox caupōnam cōnspexērunt. Intrāvērunt Cornēliī et brevī tempore cē-
nāvērunt.   15

> **vehementer incitāre,** to drive hard
> **cui,** to whom, to him, to her
> **certē,** certainly
> **arripuit,** he seized
> **hoc,** this

1. What did the driver shout?
2. Where did the horses drag the coach?
3. What did Cornelius and Aurelia do when the coach went into the ditch?
4. What did Cornelia do?
5. What did Cornelius seize?
6. What did Cornelia say when Cornelius beat the coachman?
7. What did Cornelius order Cornelia to do?
8. What did Cornelius do when he saw that it was getting dark?

Exercise 18d

Read aloud and translate:

Dum Cornēliī ad caupōnam lentē ībant, raedārius equōs custōdiēbat. Miser
erat quod Cornēlium timēbat. Mox adveniunt duo servī caupōnis.
"Salvē!" inquiunt. "Quid accidit? Quid faciēbās? Raedamne ferōciter agē-
bās? Cūr nōn dīligenter viam spectābās? Dormiēbāsne?"
Sed raedārius miser, "Minimē vērō!" respondet. "Raedam magnā arte 5
agēbam. Puerī mē vexābant; tacēre nōlēbant. Ego certē nōn dormiēbam. Sed
cūr vōs adestis? Vultisne mē adiuvāre? Potestisne raedam ex fossā extrahere?"
Tum omnēs diū labōrābant, sed raedam neque servī neque equī extrahere
poterant. Tandem dēfessī ad caupōnam redeunt.
"Raedam movēre nōn poterāmus," inquiunt. "Necesse est magnum nu- 10
merum servōrum mittere."

accidit, (it) happened	**adsum, adesse** (*irreg.*), to be present
dīligenter, carefully	**adiuvō, adiuvāre** (1), to help

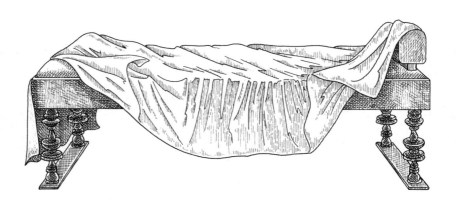

Bed reconstructed from fragments in the
National Roman Museum.

20

Graffiti from Ancient Inns

I

Assibus hīc bibitur; dīpundium sī dederis, meliōra bibēs;
quattus sī dederis, vīna Falerna bibēs.

*A drink is had here for one as; if you pay two, you'll drink better (wines);
if you pay four, you'll drink Falernian.*

II

Viātor, audī. Sī libet, intus venī: tabula est aēna quae tē cūncta
perdocet.

*Traveler, listen. Come inside if you like: there's a bronze tablet which
gives you all the information.*

III

Tālia tē fallant utinam mendācia, caupō:
tū vēndis aquam et bibis ipse merum.

*I hope these deceptions get you into trouble, innkeeper:
you sell water and drink the pure wine yourself.*

IV

Mīximus in lectō. Fateor, peccāvimus, hospes.
Sī dīcēs, "Quārē?" Nūlla matella fuit.

*I wet the bed. I have sinned, I confess it, O host.
If you ask why: there was no chamber-pot.*

V

"Caupō, computēmus."
"Habēs vīnī (sextārium) I, pānem a. I, pulmentār. a. II."
"Convenit."
"Puell. a. VIII.'
"Et hoc convenit."
"Faenum mūlō a. II."
"Iste mūlus mē ad factum dabit!"

*"Innkeeper, let's reckon up (the bill)."
"You have 1 pint of wine, 1 as-worth of bread, 2 asses-worth of food."
"Right."
"Girl, 8 asses."
"That's right, too."
"Fodder for the mule, 2 asses."
"That darn mule is going to bankrupt me!"*

21

Horace's Journey

This account of Horace's journey from Rome to Brundisium describes some of the hazards with which travelers might be faced:

After I had left great Rome, I put up in Aricia in a humble inn. My companion was Heliodorus, a teacher of rhetoric. From there we went to Forum Appii, a town packed with boatmen and grasping innkeepers. We were idle enough to take this part of the journey in two stages; for the more energetic it is only one; the Appian Way is less tiring for leisurely travelers. Here, because of the water, which is very bad, I suffered an upset stomach; and it was in a bad temper that I waited for my companions to finish their evening meal. As we were about to go on board, the boatmen began to argue. A whole hour went past while the fares were being collected and the mule harnessed. The vicious mosquitoes and marsh-frogs made sleep impossible while the boatman, who had drunk too much cheap wine, sang of his absent girlfriend, and a passenger joined in the singing.

At last the weary passengers fell asleep; and the idle boatman turned the mule out to graze, fastened its halter to a stone, and lay on his back snoring.

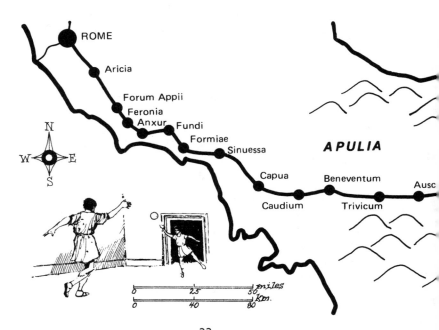

22

At dawn we realized we weren't moving. A hot-tempered passenger leapt up and beat the boatman and the mule with a stick. When at last we disembarked, it was almost ten o'clock. With due reverence and ceremony we washed our hands and faces in the fountain of Feronia. After lunch we "crawled" the three miles * to Anxur, which is perched on rocks that shine white in the distance. There our very good friend Maecenas was due to meet us. As my eyes were giving me trouble, I smeared black ointment on them. Meanwhile, Maecenas arrived with that perfect gentleman, Fonteius Capito. We were glad to leave Fundi behind, with its self-appointed "praetor" Aufidius Luscus. How we laughed at the official get-up of the ambition-crazy clerk, his toga praetexta and the tunic with the broad stripe. At last, tired out, we stayed in the city of Formiae, where Murena provided accommodation and Capito a meal.

The next day we reached Sinuessa and were met by Varius, Plotius, and Vergil—friends to whom I was most attached. Then a small villa next to the Campanian bridge gave us shelter; and the official purveyors, as they were obliged to do, provided us with wood and salt. After we left here, our pack-mules were unsaddled early at Capua. Maecenas went to play ball, Vergil and I to sleep; for ball games are bad for a man with sore eyes and an upset stomach. After Capua, Cocceius received us in a house with ample provisions built above the inns of Caudium.

* about two and three-fourths modern English miles or four and a half kilometers.

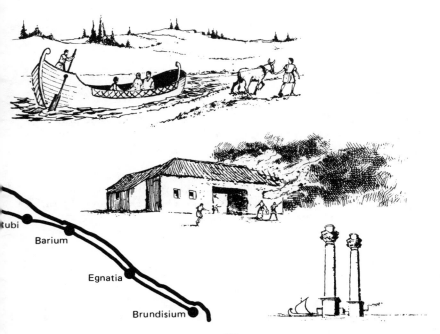

ubi
Barium
Egnatia
Brundisium

From here we made our way right on to Beneventum, where the over-worked innkeeper nearly burned the place down while roasting lean thrushes on a spit. Soon after leaving Beneventum, I saw again the familiar mountains of my native Apulia. We would never have struggled over those mountains if we had not found lodgings at Trivicum. There the smoke made our eyes water, for they put green branches on the fire, leaves and all. There also I waited until midnight for a deceitful girl who never showed up. What a fool I was!

From here we sped on twenty-four miles * in carriages, intending to lodge in the small town of Ausculum. Here they charge for the cheapest of all commodities—water. The bread, however, is very good indeed, so that the experienced traveler usually takes some away in his bag; for the bread at Canusium is as hard as a stone, and the water supply is no better.

From here we arrived at Rubi, tired out—as was to be expected—for the stage was long and the road conditions difficult because of heavy rain. After this the weather was better, but the road worse as far as Barium, a fishing town. Then Egnatia provided us with laughter and amusement: the people tried to convince us that in the temple there frankincense melts without a flame. I don't believe it!

Brundisium is the end of my long account and of my long journey.

Horace, *Satires* I.5 (abridged)

* about 22 modern English miles or 36 kilometers.

Although the following account given by Cicero of how one provincial governor traveled is probably exaggerated, there is no doubt that the rich and powerful often went to great lengths to avoid the discomforts of travel:

Verres traveled in a litter carried by eight bearers. In the litter was a cushion of transparent Maltese linens stuffed with roseleaves. He held to his nose a close-mesh bag filled with rosepetals. Whenever he reached a town, he was carried, still in his litter, direct to his bedroom.

Cicero, *in Verrem* II.27

Travel by Land

Gaius Cornelius and his family traveled from Baiae to Rome along a section of the Via Appia, which ran south from Rome to Brundisium—a distance of 358 miles or 576 kilometers. It was part of a network of major highways that radiated from the Golden Milestone (**mīliārium aureum**), in the Forum at Rome, to all parts of the Empire. These roads, originally built by the legions to make easy movement of troops possible, were laid on carefully made foundations with drainage channels at both sides and were usually paved with slabs of basalt. Although travel was safer and easier than at any time before the "Railway Age," it was nevertheless extremely slow by modern standards. The **raeda** seldom averaged more than five miles or eight kilometers per hour; a man walking might manage twenty-five miles or forty kilometers a day; an imperial courier on urgent business might, with frequent changes of horse, manage to cover over 150 miles or 240 kilometers in twenty-four hours. Since carriage wheels had iron rims and vehicles lacked springs, a journey by road was bound to be uncomfortable. Moreover, since the vehicles were open or, at best, had only a canopy, the travelers often had to endure both clouds of dust and attacks from insects.

The following passage illustrates these discomforts:

> When I had to make my way back from Baiae to Naples, to avoid the experience of sailing a second time, I easily convinced myself that a storm was raging. The whole road was so deep in mud that I might as well have gone by sea. That day I had to endure what athletes put up with as a matter of course: after being anointed with mud, we were dusted with sand in the Naples tunnel. Nothing could be longer than that prison-like corridor, nothing dimmer than those torches that do not dispel the darkness but merely make us more aware of it. But even if there were light there, it would be blacked out by the dust which, however troublesome and disagreeable it may be in the open, is, as you can imagine, a thousand times worse in an enclosed space where there is no ventilation and the dust rises in one's face. These were the two entirely different discomforts which we suffered. On the same day and on the same road we struggled through both mud and dust.
>
> Seneca, *Epistulae Morales* LVII

19
Chance Encounter

Ubi Cornēlia et māter cubitum īvērunt, Marcus et Sextus cum Cornēliō
mānsērunt. Cum Cornēliō cēnāre et post cēnam ad mediam noctem vigilāre
in animō habuērunt, nam omnia vidēre et omnia audīre voluērunt.
Marcus, "Ēsuriō, pater," inquit. "Ēsurīsne tū quoque, Sexte?"
"Ita vērō!" respondit Sextus.   5
"Semper ēsurītis, tū et Marcus!" exclāmāvit Cornēlius.
"Licetne nōbīs," inquit Marcus, "hīc cēnāre?"
Paulīsper tacēbat pater, sed tandem, "Estō!" inquit. "Tibi et Sextō licet
hīc cēnāre. Post cēnam tamen necesse est statim cubitum īre."
Rīsērunt puerī quod laetī erant. "Gaudēmus, pater," inquit Marcus,   10
"quod nōs in cubiculum nōn statim mīsistī. Voluimus enim hīc manēre et
aliōs viātōrēs spectāre."
Tum Cornēlius caupōnem iussit cibum parāre. Brevī tempore servus
cibum ad eōs portāvit. Dum puerī cibum dēvorant, subitō intrāvit mīles
quīdam. Cornēlium attentē spectāvit. "Salvē, vir optime!" inquit. "Salvēte,   15
puerī! Cūr vōs in hanc caupōnam intrāvistis? Cūr nōn ad vīllam hospitis
īvistis? Nōnne tū es senātor Rōmānus?"
"Senātor Rōmānus sum," respondit Cornēlius. "Nōs in hanc caupōnam
intrāvimus quod raeda nostra in fossā haeret immōbilis. In agrīs nocte manēre
nōlēbāmus, sed numquam anteā in caupōnā pernoctāvimus. Certē in agrīs   20
pernoctāre est perīculōsum."
Tum mīles, "Etiam in caupōnā pernoctāre saepe est perīculōsum."
"Cūr hoc nōbīs dīcis?" rogāvit Cornēlius. "Estne hic caupō homō scelestus? Dē Apollodōrō quid audīvistī?"
"Dē Apollodōrō nihil audīvī, sed semper est perīculōsum in caupōnā   25
pernoctāre. Vōsne audīvistis illam fābulam dē caupōne nārrātam? Ille caupō
hospitem necāvit."
"Minimē!" inquit Cornēlius. "Illam fābulam nōn audīvī. Cūr igitur nōbīs
illam nōn nārrās dum cēnāmus?"

mānsērunt, (they) stayed	**mīsistī,** you have sent
post (+ *acc.*), after	**voluimus,** we wanted
media nox, midnight	**enim,** for
vigilō, vigilāre (1), to stay awake	**mīles quīdam,** a certain soldier
in animō habēre, to intend	**mīles, mīlitis** (*m*), soldier
licet nōbīs, we are allowed, we may	**vir optime!** sir!
paulīsper, for a short time	**optimus, -a, -um,** best, very good
Estō! All right!	**in hanc caupōnam,** into this inn

numquam, never
anteā, before
dīcō, dīcere (3), to say
dē (+ abl.), about
audīvī, I have heard

illam fābulam dē caupōne nārrātam, that famous story told about
the innkeeper
necō, necāre (1), to kill
nārrō, nārrāre (1), to tell (a story)

Exercise 19a

Respondē Latīnē:

1. Quid fēcērunt Marcus et Sextus ubi Cornēlia et Aurēlia cubitum īvērunt?
2. Quid puerī facere voluērunt?
3. Ēsuriuntne puerī?
4. Licetne Marcō et Sextō in caupōnā cēnāre?
5. Cūr puerī laetī sunt?
6. Quis intrāvit dum puerī cibum dēvorant?
7. Quid rogat?
8. Cūr Cornēlius in agrīs pernoctāre nōlēbat?
9. Quid mīles dē Apollodōrō audīvit?
10. Quid fēcit caupō in fābulā?

Exercise 19b

Using story 19 as a guide, give the Latin for:

1. Marcus and Sextus wished to stay awake until midnight.
2. Cornelius ordered the slave to bring food.
3. Soon a soldier entered and suddenly looked at Cornelius.
4. Cornelius said, "I came into this inn because my carriage is stuck in a ditch."
5. Cornelius has never before spent the night in an inn.
6. What has the soldier heard about Apollodorus?
7. Cornelius has not heard that famous story told about the innkeeper.

VERBS: Perfect Tense II

You have now met all the endings of the perfect tense.

Singular	1	*-ī*		1	*-imus*
	2	*-istī*	Plural	2	*-istis*
	3	*-it*		3	*-ērunt*

These are the endings of the perfect tense of *all* Latin verbs, e.g.:

Singular	1	mīs*ī*		1	mīs*imus*
	2	mīs*istī*	Plural	2	mīs*istis*
	3	mīs*it*		3	mīs*ērunt*

28

Exercise 19c

With proper attention to the new perfect tense endings, read aloud and translate:

1. Marcus et Sextus ad mediam noctem vigilāre in animō habuērunt.
2. Ego et tū cubitum īre nōluimus.
3. Mīlesne Cornēlium spectāvit?
4. Cūr voluistī hīc pernoctāre, Marce?
5. Cūr in caupōnā pernoctāvistis, puerī? Licetne fīliō senātōris in caupōnam intrāre?
6. Cornēlius in cubiculum servum īre iussit.
7. Puerī laetī fuērunt quod ad mediam noctem vigilāvērunt.
8. Dum Cornēlius et puerī cēnant, mīles fābulam nārrāvit.
9. Ego et Cornēlius in agrīs manēre timēbāmus.
10. Omnia vidēre et audīre volunt quod numquam anteā in caupōnā pernoctāvērunt.

fuī, I was (perfect of sum)

Exercise 19d

Supply the appropriate perfect tense endings, read aloud, and translate:

1. Ego līberōs in hortō petīv_____; tū eōs in silvā invēn_____.
2. Ubi tunica Sextī in rāmīs haerēbat, nōs omnēs rīs_____.
3. Quō īvistī, Cornēlia? Ego et Marcus patrem hoc rogāv_____, sed ille nihil respond_____.
4. Quamquam Sextus fu_____ molestus, servī eum nōn verberāv_____.
5. Ubi heri fu_____, Marce et Cornēlia? Pater et māter nōs iuss_____ hīc manēre.
6. Postquam vōs cēnāv_____, cubitum īre volu_____.
7. Heri nōs ad urbem īv_____, sed mātrem ibi nōn vīd_____.
8. "Unde vēn_____, amīcī?" rogā_____ caupō. "Quō nunc ītis?"
9. Tūne Cornēlium vīd_____, ubi tū Rōmam advēn_____? Ego certē eum nōn vīd_____.
10. Ille, postquam hoc audīv_____, ē caupōnā sē praecipitāv_____.

ille, he
heri, yesterday
postquam, after

29

Roman Hospitality

Because inns were dirty and often dangerous, well-to-do Romans tried to avoid staying in them. Instead, they tried to plan their journey so that they could stay at the **vīlla** of a **hospes.** This word means "host" or "guest," but it is also translated as "friend," although in this special sense it has no exact equivalent in English. It describes a relationship established between two families in the past and kept up by every succeeding generation. As a result of such a relationship, a traveler could go to the house of his "family friend"—whom in some cases he personally might never have met—and claim **hospitium** for the night, producing, if need be, some token such as a coin that had been halved as proof of the link between the two families. Members of the host's family, if they happened to be traveling in a district in which their guest's family owned a **vīlla,** could claim similar rights of hospitality. It could extend to other situations. For instance, if a Roman had business interests in one of the provinces, someone residing there might look after them for him. In return, he might have some service done for him in Rome. Cornelius, you may remember, is responsible for Sextus' education while his father is in Asia.

VERBS: Principal Parts

When we refer to a Latin verb, we normally give the four *principal parts,* from which all forms of that verb may be derived. These principal parts are:
   the 1st person singular of the present tense
   the present infinitive
   the 1st person singular of the perfect tense
   the supine.

	Present	*Infinitive*	*Perfect*	*Supine*	*Meaning*
1st Conj.	parō	parāre (1)	parāvī	parātum	*to prepare*
2nd Conj.	habeō	habēre (2)	habuī	habitum	*to have*
3rd Conj.	mittō	mittere (3)	mīsī	missum	*to send*
	iaciō	iacere (3)	iēcī	iactum	*to throw*
4th Conj.	audiō	audīre (4)	audīvī	audītum	*to hear*

Be sure to learn the above forms thoroughly.

Notes

1. The perfect stem is found by dropping the -ī from the end of the third principal part of the verb. The perfect endings are then added directly to this stem.

2. The principal parts of most verbs in the 1st, 2nd, and 4th conjugations follow the patterns on the opposite page. There is no set pattern for 3rd conjugation verbs.

3. In vocabulary lists from this point on, the verbs in the 1st, 2nd, and 4th conjugations which follow the set patterns will appear as follows:

> clāmō (1), to shout
> appāreō (2), to appear
> pūniō (4), to punish

When they do not follow the pattern, they will be given in full, e.g.:

> lavō, lavāre (1), lāvī, lavātum, to wash
> veniō, venīre (4), vēnī, ventum, to come

Third conjugation verbs will be given in full, e.g.:

> dūcō, dūcere (3), dūxī, ductum, to lead

Exercise 19e

Read aloud and translate each verb form given at the left below. Then deduce and give the first three principal parts for each verb:

	1st Sing. Present	Present Infinitive	1st Sing. Perfect
necāmus, necāvimus	necō	necāre (1)	necāvī
intrant, intrāvērunt			
errās, errāvistī			
tenēs, tenuistī			
mittunt, mīsērunt			
manēmus, mānsimus			
iubet, iussit			
discēdimus, discessimus			
haeret, haesit			
dormiunt, dormīvērunt			
petunt, petīvērunt			
custōdīmus, custōdīvimus			
gemitis, gemuistis			

Can you give the principal parts for the following?

estis, fuistis			

20
Murder

Mīles hanc fābulam nārrāvit.

Duo amīcī, Aulus et Septimus, dum iter in Graeciā faciunt, ad urbem Megaram vēnērunt. Aulus in caupōnā pernoctāvit, in vīllā hospitis Septimus. Mediā nocte, dum Septimus dormit, Aulus in somnō eī appāruit et clāmāvit, "Age, Septime! Fer mihi auxilium! Caupō mē necāre parat." 5
Septimus, somniō perterritus, statim surrēxit et, postquam animum recuperāvit, "Nihil malī," inquit. "Somnium modo fuit."
Deinde iterum obdormīvit. Iterum tamen in somnō Aulus suō amīcō appāruit; iterum Septimō clāmāvit, "Ubi ego auxilium petīvī, tū nōn vēnistī. Nēmō mē adiuvāre nunc potest. Caupō enim mē necāvit. Postquam hoc 10 fēcit, corpus meum in plaustrō posuit et stercus suprā coniēcit. In animō habet plaustrum ex urbe crās movēre. Necesse est igitur crās māne plaustrum petere et caupōnem pūnīre."
Iterum surrēxit Septimus. Prīmā lūce ad caupōnam īvit et plaustrum petīvit. Ubi plaustrum invēnit, stercus remōvit et corpus extrāxit. Septimus, 15 ubi amīcum mortuum vīdit, lacrimāvit. Caupō scelestus quoque lacrimāvit, nam innocentiam simulābat. Septimus tamen caupōnem statim accūsāvit. Mox cīvēs eum pūnīvērunt.

Postquam mīles fābulam fīnīvit, silentium fuit. Subitō Cornēlius exclāmāvit, "Agite, puerī! Nōnne vōs iussī post cēnam cubitum īre? Cūr ad 20 cubiculum nōn īvistis?"
Sed Marcus, "Pater, nōs quoque fābulam mīlitis audīre voluimus. Nōn dēfessī sumus. Nōn sērō est."
Hoc tamen dīxit Marcus quod cubitum īre timēbat. Dum enim fābulam mīlitis audiēbat, caupōnem spectābat. Cōgitābat, "Quam scelestus ille caupō 25 vidētur! Certē in animō habet mediā nocte mē necāre. Necesse est vigilāre."
Etiam Sextus timēbat. Cōgitābat tamen, "Sī hic caupō est scelestus, gaudeō quod mīles in caupōnā pernoctat. Eucleidēs certē nōs adiuvāre nōn potest."
Invītī tandem puerī cubitum īvērunt, vigilāre parātī. Mox tamen sēmi- 30 somnī fuērunt. Brevī tempore obdormīvit Marcus.

somnus, -ī (m), sleep
eī, to him
somnium, -ī (n), dream
animum recuperāre, to regain one's
senses, be fully awake
Nihil malī. There is nothing wrong.
obdormiō (4), to go to sleep
corpus, corporis (n), body
stercus, stercoris (n), dung, manure

suprā, above, on top
prīmā lūce, at dawn
mortuus, -a, -um, dead
simulō (1), to pretend
finiō (4), to finish
sērō, late
cōgitō (1), to think
vidētur, (he) seems
invītus, -a, -um, unwilling

surgō, surgere (3), surrēxī, surrēctum, to rise, get up
sum, esse (irreg.), fuī, to be
adiuvō, adiuvāre (1), adiūvī, adiūtum, to help
pōnō, pōnere (3), posuī, positum, to place, put
coniciō, conicere (3), coniēcī, coniectum, to throw
eō, īre, (irreg.), īvī, itum, to go
petō, petere (3), petīvī, petītum, to look for, seek
inveniō, invenīre (4), invēnī, inventum, to come upon, find
removeō, removēre (2), remōvī, remōtum, to remove
extrahō, extrahere (3), extrāxī, extractum, to drag out
videō, vidēre (2), vīdī, vīsum, to see
iubeō, iubēre (2), iussī, iussum, to order, bid
volō, velle (irreg.), voluī, to wish, want, be willing
dīcō, dīcere (3), dīxī, dictum, to say, tell

Exercise 20a

Respondē Latīnē:

1. Ubi est Megara?
2. Ubi pernoctāvit Aulus? Ubi erat amīcus Aulī?
3. Quandō Aulus Septimō appāruit?
4. Quid fēcit Septimus postquam animum recuperāvit?
5. Ubi caupō corpus Aulī posuit? Quid in animō habuit?
6. Quid Septimus prīmā lūce fēcit?
7. Quandō lacrimāvit Septimus?
8. Cūr lacrimāvit caupō?
9. Quid cīvēs fēcērunt?
10. Quid Marcus timēbat?
11. Quōmodo puerī cubitum īvērunt?
12. Quid Marcus et Sextus in animō habuērunt?

Quandō. . . ? When. . . ?

33

Exercise 20b

The following sentences contain errors of fact in the light of the last story you read. Explain these errors and give new Latin sentences which correct them:

1. Duo puerī, Aulus et Septimus, urbem Rōmam intrāvērunt.
2. Aulus et Septimus frātrēs Marcī erant.
3. Septimus mediā nocte surrēxit quod ēsuriēbat.
4. Aulus auxilium petīvit quod lectus sordidus erat.
5. Cīvēs, postquam Septimum necāvērunt, corpus sub stercore cēlāvērunt.
6. Caupō Septimum accūsāvit postquam cīvem mortuum invēnit.
7. Septimus cīvēs pūnīre in animō habuit quod scelestī erant.
8. Cīvēs corpus in caupōnā sub lectō invēnērunt.
9. Marcus cubitum īre timuit quod silentium erat.
10. Cornēlius caupōnem pūnīvit quod Marcus eum accūsāvit.

Exercise 20c.

Using the list of principal parts given in the vocabulary on page 33, give the Latin for:

1. What did you want, boys?
2. They got up suddenly.
3. The boys went to bed at last.
4. Septimus looked for the wagon.
5. What have you seen?
6. We went to the inn.
7. What did you say, Marcus?
8. We ordered Cornelia to go to sleep.
9. What have they found?
10. He placed the body in the wagon.

Vēnī, vīdī, vīcī. *I came, I saw, I conquered.* (Julius Caesar, after the battle of Zela, 47 B.C.; reported in Suetonius, *Julius Caesar* XXXVII)

Nihil sub sōle novum. *There's nothing new under the sun.* (Vulgate, *Ecclesiastes* I.10)

Mēns sāna in corpore sānō. *A sound mind in a sound body.* (Juvenal X.356)

VERBS: Perfect and Imperfect

The imperfect tense describes an action in the past which
a. went on for a time, or
b. was repeated, or
c. was beginning to happen.

The perfect tense describes an action in the past which *happened* or *was completed* on one occasion, e.g.:

> Hoc dīxit Marcus quod cubitum īre timēbat.
> *Marcus said this because he was afraid to go to bed.*

> Virgam arripuit et raedārium verberābat.
> *He grabbed the stick and beat the driver repeatedly.*

> Corneliī sollicitī caelum spectāvērunt quod iam advesperāscēbat.
> *The Cornelii looked anxiously at the sky because it was already getting dark.*

Exercise 20d

Read aloud and translate, paying particular attention to the tenses of the verbs:

1. Marcus sub arbore sedēbat, sed subitō surrēxit.
2. Iam advesperāscēbat ubi viātōrēs aedificia urbis cōnspexērunt.
3. Caupōnam nōn intrāvimus quod ibi pernoctāre timēbāmus.
4. Caupō prope portam labōrābat ubi clāmōrem audīvit.
5. Ubi Aurēlia cubiculum intrāvit, Cornēlia adhūc dormiēbat.
6. "Tacēte, omnēs!" exclāmāvit Dāvus, nam dominus appropinquābat.
7. Postquam Aurēlia rem explicāvit, Eucleidēs quoque dolēbat.
8. Tū, Sexte, mox obdormīvistī, sed ego diū vigilābam.
9. Caupō mussābat quod servōs alium lectum petere iussistī.
10. Sextus caupōnam statim petīvit quod canēs lātrābant.

Quid hōc somniō dīcī potest dīvīnius? *What can be said to be more divinely inspired than this dream?* (Cicero, *On Divination* I.57, after telling the story of Aulus and Septimus)

Versiculī: *"Murder," page 99.*

Review IV

Exercise IVa

Supply Latin nouns or adjectives to match the English cues. Be sure to give the correct endings. Read each sentence aloud and translate it.

1. Puellae _____ ad cubiculum īvērunt, quod dormīre nōlēbant. (unwilling)
2. Multī servī _____ lectōs ē cubiculīs portāvērunt. (all)
3. Corpora _____ amīcōrum _____ _____ vīdimus. (of all) (our dead)
4. Servī scelestī _____ _____ in plaustrō posuērunt. (all the bodies)
5. Cīvis caupōnem _____ necāvit. (fat)
6. Lectī _____ sunt in _____ caupōnā. (dirty) (every)
7. Caupō fābulam dē _____ scelestō nārrāvit. (innkeeper)
8. Mīles longam fābulam dē _____ _____ nārrāvit. (all the innkeepers)
9. Corpus hominis _____ in plaustrō posuimus. (dead)
10. In _____ caupōnam prope urbem intrāvistis. (every)

Exercise IVb

Identify the tense, person, and number of each of the following verb forms. Then give the principal parts of the verb:

	Tense	Person	Number
1. veniēbātis	_____	_____	_____
2. cōgitāvistis	_____	_____	_____
3. coniciēbam	_____	_____	_____
4. iussērunt	_____	_____	_____
5. surrēxī	_____	_____	_____
6. removēbās	_____	_____	_____
7. clāmāvistī	_____	_____	_____
8. obdormiēbāmus	_____	_____	_____

Exercise IVc

Give the requested forms of the following verbs in the present, imperfect, and perfect tenses:

	Present	Imperfect	Perfect
1. dīcere (2nd sing.)	_____	_____	_____
2. īre (3rd pl.)	_____	_____	_____
3. appārēre (1st pl.)	_____	_____	_____
4. iacere (1st sing.)	_____	_____	_____
5. lavāre (3rd sing.)	_____	_____	_____
6. pūnīre (2nd pl.)	_____	_____	_____

Exercise IVd

Give the imperatives of the following verbs:

	Singular	Plural
1. īre	_____	_____
2. pōnere	_____	_____
3. ferre	_____	_____
4. explicāre	_____	_____
5. nōlle	_____	_____
6. esse	_____	_____
7. dolēre	_____	_____
8. venīre	_____	_____

Exercise IVe

Change the following verbs to the present tense and the perfect tense where requested. Keep the same person and number.

	Present	Perfect
1. poterat	_____	
2. volēbam	_____	_____
3. ferēbās	_____	
4. erāmus	_____	_____
5. nōlēbās	_____	_____
6. ībant	_____	_____
7. volēbātis	_____	_____
8. erās	_____	_____
9. ferēbātis	_____	
10. nōlēbat	_____	_____

Exercise IVf

Read aloud and translate:

Sextus tamen nōn obdormīvit, nam dē mīlitis fābulā cōgitābat. Itaque diū vigilābat et dē Aulō mortuō cōgitābat. Tandem, "Marce!" inquit. "Tūne timuistī ubi illam fābulam audīvistī?"

Sed Marcus nihil respondit. Iterum, "Marce!" inquit. "Tūne caupōnem spectābās?" Iterum silentium! Deinde Sextus, iam timidus, "Marce! Marce!" 5 inquit. "Cūr tū obdormīvistī? Cūr tū nōn vigilāvistī?"

Subitō sonitum in cubiculō audīvit Sextus. "Ō mē miserum! Audīvitne sonitum Aulus ille miser ubi caupō eum necāre parābat? Quālis sonitus fuit?"

Sonitum Sextus iterum audīvit. "Ō Eucleidēs!" inquit. "Cūr ad cubiculum nōndum vēnistī? Ō pater! Ō māter! Cūr mē in Italiam mīsistis? Voluistisne 10 ita mē ad mortem mittere? In Asiam ego redīre volō. Ibi enim nūllum est perīculum, sed perīculōsum est hīc in Italiā habitāre."

Multa sē rogābat Sextus, nam, quamquam puer temerārius esse solēbat, nunc mediā nocte sōlus in cubiculō tremēbat.

Itaque Sextus, per tōtam noctem vigilāre parātus, diū ibi sedēbat. "Quō- 15 modo iam ē manibus caupōnis scelestī effugere possum? Suntne omnēs cau- pōnēs scelestī? Fortasse caupō mē, fīlium cīvis praeclārī, necāre in animō habet. Quamquam Aulus aurum habuit, ego tamen nihil habeō, neque aurum neque pecūniam."

Ita cōgitābat Sextus. Iterum sonitum audīvit. Timēbat sed tandem surrēxit 20 invītus, nam omnēs cubiculī partēs īnspicere volēbat. Mox tamen rīsit. Ecce! Sub lectō erat fēlēs, obēsa et sēmisomna. Prope fēlem Sextus mūrem mortuum vīdit. Mussāvit Sextus, "Nōn necesse est hoc corpus sub stercore cēlāre!"

sonitum, sound	**ē manibus,** from the hands
ita, in this way	**aurum, -ī** (*n*), gold
mors, mortis (*f*), death	**pecūnia, -ae** (*f*), money
sē rogābat, (he) asked	**fēlēs, fēlis** (*f*), cat
himself, wondered	**mūs, mūris** (*m*), mouse
tōtus, -a, -um, whole	

tremō, tremere (3), **tremuī,** to tremble
īnspiciō, īnspicere (3), **īnspexī, īnspectum,** to examine

Exercise IVg

In the above passage, locate the following in sequence:

1. All verbs in the present tense.
2. All verbs in the imperfect tense.
3. All verbs in the perfect tense.
4. All infinitives.

Eavesdropping

It was quite dark. Cornelia was still wide awake. All kinds of exciting sounds were floating up from the inn downstairs, inviting her to go down and have a look. She slipped out of bed, put a shawl around her shoulders, and tiptoed into the corridor where Eucleides was on guard.

"Take me downstairs, Eucleides," she wheedled. "I've never seen the inside of an inn before." This was quite true, because a Roman away from home preferred to stay in a friend's villa and avoided inns if possible.

Eucleides took a lot of persuading, but Cornelia could always get around him; he soon found himself downstairs, looking into the main room, with Cornelia peering from behind his arm.

It was pretty dark inside, despite the lamps. The atmosphere was thick with smoke and reeked of garlic. On the far side Cornelia could see her father; and nearer were other customers seated on stools at rough tables, and an evil-looking group they were.

"Stay away from them, Cornelia," whispered Eucleides. "Those rogues would murder their own mothers for a silver **dēnārius.**

But Eucleides needn't have worried because they were all absorbed in what was going on at the far end of the low room, where a girl was dancing. Above the hum of conversation her singing could be heard to the accompaniment of a rhythmic clacking noise she seemed to be making with her fingers. "Makes that noise with castanets," whispered Eucleides. "Dancing girl from Spain, probably Gades."

But one person was not paying much attention to the entertainment— the **tabellārius,** whose reckless driving had ditched them. He had not come out of the incident unscathed. One of his horses had gone lame, and he was making the most of the enforced delay, drinking the innkeeper's best Falernian.

As Cornelia and Eucleides entered, the innkeeper was bringing forward a young man to introduce him to the imperial courier. "This is Decimus Junius Juvenalis, Sir, a soldier like yourself." The **tabellārius,** unbending slightly as a rather haggard young man came forward wearing the insignia of a junior officer, dismissed the innkeeper with a look and said pleasantly enough, "Greetings, young man! Where are you from?"

"I'm on my way back from service in Britain, sir. What a place! They don't have any climate there, just bad weather! Mist, rain, hail, snow—the lot! Hardly a blink of sunshine!"

"Perhaps he knows our Davus," whispered Cornelia.

"Let me see!" said the **tabellārius.** "Who's governor of Britain these days? A chap called Agricola, I hear."

"That's right!" replied Juvenalis. "A madman, if you ask me. He's not content with conquering the bit of Britain that's near Gaul, where you can get something profitable, like silver or wool or hides or those huge hunting dogs. Before I left he had gone to the very edge of the world where the Caledonii live. They say that there, in the middle of winter, the sun doesn't shine at all! But I can't vouch for that myself!"

"I've been to Britain too," said the **tabellārius,** much interested. "I'm not an ordinary **tabellārius,** you know. I'm really in charge of a section of the **cursus pūblicus.** I personally carry dispatches only if they are confidential messages from—"

And here he whispered something in Juvenalis' ear which Cornelia could not catch.

The innkeeper sidled up again with some more wine.

"We get lots of interesting people stopping here on the Via Appia," he confided. "Not only military gentlemen like yourselves, or that scum of humanity there"—jerking his thumb towards the dancer's audience—"but special envoys to the Emperor himself. When Nero was Emperor, we had one of this new Jewish religious sect who lodged here on a journey all the way from Judaea, to be tried by the Emperor himself no less! He was called Paul or something—"

Suddenly Cornelia felt her ear seized between finger and thumb and looked around into the eyes of a very angry Aurelia. She found herself upstairs and back in bed before she knew what had happened.

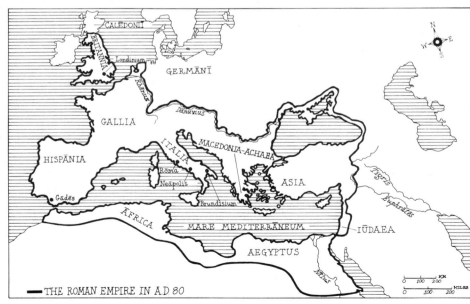

THE ROMAN EMPIRE IN A.D 80

21
From the Inn to Rome

Iam diēs erat. Prīmā lūce raedārius auxiliō servōrum caupōnis raedam ē
fossā extrāxit et ad caupōnam admōvit. Tum servī cistās Cornēliōrum raedāriō trādidērunt. Intereā in caupōnā, dum omnēs sē parābant, Sextus, iam
immemor terrōris nocturnī, mīlitis fābulam Cornēliae nārrābat; Eucleidēs
mandāta servīs dabat. Cornēlius ipse Aurēliae et līberīs clāmābat, "Agite, 5
omnēs! Nōlīte cessāre! Tempus est discēdere."
  Tandem cūnctī ē caupōnā vēnērunt et in raedam ascendērunt.
  "Valē!" clāmāvērunt puerī.
  "Valēte!" respondit caupō, quī in viā stābat. "Nōlīte in fossam iterum
cadere! Nōn in omnibus caupōnīs bene dormīre potestis." 10
  Tum raedārius habēnās sūmpsit et equōs verberāvit. Tandem Rōmam
iterum petēbant.
  In itinere Sextus omnia dē mūre mortuō Marcō explicāvit, Cornēlius
mīlitis fābulam uxōrī nārrāvit. Iam urbī appropinquābant, cum subitō puerī
ingēns aedificium cōnspexērunt. 15
  Marcus patrem, "Quid est illud?" rogāvit.
  Atque Sextus, "Quis in illō aedificiō habitat?"
  Cui Cornēlius, "Nēmō ibi habitat," cum rīsū respondit. "Est sepulcrum
Messallae Corvīnī quī erat ōrātor praeclārus. Hīc sunt sepulcra multōrum
et praeclārōrum cīvium quod Rōmānīs nōn licet intrā urbem sepulcra 20
habēre."
  Mox alterum aedificium magnum vīdērunt.
  "Estne id quoque sepulcrum, pater?" rogāvit Marcus.
  "Ita vērō!" Cornēlius respondit. "Est sepulcrum Caeciliae Metellae. Nōnne
dē Caeciliā Metellā audīvistī?" 25
  Sed Marcus patrī nihil respondit. Iam enim urbem ipsam vidēre poterat.
"Ecce Rōma!" clāmāvit.
  "Ecce Rōma! Ecce Rōma!" clāmāvērunt Sextus et Cornēlia.
  Tum Cornēlius, "Brevī tempore ad Portam Capēnam adveniēmus et
Titum, patruum vestrum, ibi vidēbimus. Epistulam enim per servum mīsī 30
et omnia eī explicāvī. Titus mox nōs prope Portam excipiet."

auxiliō, with the help
raedāriō, to the coachman
sē parāre, to prepare oneself, get ready
immemor, immemoris, forgetful
nocturnus, -a, -um, during the night
Cornēliae, to Cornelia
mandātum, -ī (n), order, instruction
bene, well
habēnae, -ārum (f pl), reins
mūs, mūris (m), mouse
uxōrī, to his wife

cum, wnen
ingēns, ingentis, huge
illud, that
atque, and
sepulcrum, -ī (n), tomb
intrā (+ acc.), inside
adveniēmus, we will come
patruus, -ī (m), uncle
vester, vestra, vestrum, your (pl)
vidēbimus, we will see
excipiet, (he) will welcome

admoveō, admovēre (2), admōvī, admōtum, to move towards
trādō, trādere (3), trādidī, trāditum, to hand over
dō, dare (1), dedī, datum, to give (note short a)
ascendō, ascendere (3), ascendī, ascēnsum, to climb
respondeō, respondēre (2), respondī, respōnsum, to reply
cadō, cadere (3), cecidī, cāsum, to fall
sūmō, sūmere (3), sūmpsī, sūmptum, to take, take up
cōnspiciō, cōnspicere (3), cōnspexī, cōnspectum, to catch sight of
excipiō, excipere (3), excēpī, exceptum, to welcome, receive

NOUNS: Cases and Declensions
Dative Case

Look at the following sentences:

1. Fābulam **Cornēliae** nārrābat.
2. Omnia **Marcō** explicāvit.
3. Mandāta **servīs** dabat.
4. Marcus **patrī** nihil respondit.
5. Aulus **eī** appāruit.
6. Lectum **tibi** parāvērunt.

He was telling a story **to Cornelia**.
He explained everything **to Marcus**.
He was giving orders **to the slaves**.
Marcus made no reply **to his father**.
Aulus appeared **to him**.
They have prepared a bed **for you**.

The Latin words in bold type are all in the *dative case*.

Amīcus omnibus amīcus nēminī. *A friend to everyone is a friend to no one.*

42

Here is a table showing the groups of nouns and cases, including the dative:

Number Case	1st Declension Fem.	2nd Declension Masc.	2nd Declension Masc.	2nd Declension Neut.	3rd Declension Masc.	3rd Declension Fem.	3rd Declension Neut.
Singular							
Nom.	puell*a*	serv*us*	puer	bacul*um*	pater	vōx	nōmen
Gen.	puell*ae*	serv*ī*	puer*ī*	bacul*ī*	patr*is*	vōc*is*	nōmin*is*
Dat.	puell*ae*	serv*ō*	puer*ō*	bacul*ō*	patr*ī*	vōc*ī*	nōmin*ī*
Acc.	puell*am*	serv*um*	puer*um*	bacul*um*	patr*em*	vōc*em*	nōmen
Abl.	puell*ā*	serv*ō*	puer*ō*	bacul*ō*	patre	vōc*e*	nōmine
Plural							
Nom.	puell*ae*	serv*ī*	puer*ī*	bacul*a*	patr*ēs*	vōc*ēs*	nōmin*a*
Gen.	puell*ārum*	serv*ōrum*	puer*ōrum*	bacul*ōrum*	patr*um*	vōc*um*	nōmin*um*
Dat.	puell*īs*	serv*īs*	puer*īs*	bacul*īs*	patr*ibus*	vōc*ibus*	nōmin*ibus*
Acc.	puell*ās*	serv*ōs*	puer*ōs*	bacul*a*	patr*ēs*	vōc*ēs*	nōmin*a*
Abl.	puell*īs*	serv*īs*	puer*īs*	bacul*īs*	patr*ibus*	vōc*ibus*	nōmin*ibus*

Notes

1. In each declension dative and ablative plurals have the same endings.

2. The datives of the pronouns are as follows:

Singular		Plural	
Nominative	Dative	Nominative	Dative
ego	mihi	nōs	nōbīs
tū	tibi	vōs	vōbīs
is, ea, id	eī	eī, eae, ea	eīs

The dative endings of the adjectives are:

	1st and 2nd Declension Masc.	Fem.	Neut.	3rd Declension Masc.	Fem.	Neut.
Singular	magn*ō*	magn*ae*	magn*ō*	omn*ī*	omn*ī*	omn*ī*
Plural	magn*īs*	magn*īs*	magn*īs*	omn*ibus*	omn*ibus*	omn*ibus*

Be sure to learn the new dative forms thoroughly.

43

Exercise 21a

Translate the following sentence:

Cornēlius fābulam uxōrī nārrāvit.

Now reword the sentence to show that Cornelius told the story to each of the following in turn. (Remember that you must check the declension of each noun before you can produce the correct ending.):

**Septimus, Flāvia, puellae, mīles, puerī,
raedārius, senātōrēs, caupō, viātōrēs.**

Exercise 21b

The sentence **Eucleidēs mandāta servīs dabat** can be translated
Eucleides was giving orders to the slaves.

or

Eucleides was giving the slaves orders.

Translate each of the following sentences in two ways:

1. Patruus pecūniam puerīs dat.
2. Māter fābulam puellae nārrāvit.
3. Ōrātōrēs fābulās cīvibus nārrāvērunt.
4. Ancilla invīta caupōnī cibum trādit.
5. Caupōnēs rārō cēnam senātōribus dant.   rārō, seldom
6. Omnia patrī meō semper dīcō.
7. Nihil lēgātō prīncipis dīxit.

Note

The dative case is also found with **licet** and **appropinquāre**, e.g.:

Mihi licet exīre.	*It is permissible for me to go out.*
	I am allowed to go out. I may go out.
Urbī appropinquābant.	*They were coming near to the city.*
	They were approaching the city.

Exercise 21c

Read aloud and translate:

1. Mātrēs līberōrum multa eīs dīcunt.
2. Dāvus Cornēliī mandāta servīs dedit.
3. Cornēliī mox urbis portīs appropinquābant.
4. Cornēlius epistulam ad Titum mīsit et omnia eī explicāvit.
5. Puerīs nōn licēbat sōlīs per viās errāre.
6. Marcus, "Tacē, Sexte!" inquit. "Nōbīs nōn licet hīc clāmāre."
7. Dum Cornēliī urbī appropinquābant, Titus omnia eīs parābat.

44

Building Up the Meaning IV
NOUNS: Dative or Ablative?

You will have noticed that the dative and ablative cases often have identical endings, e.g., **servō, puellīs, mīlitibus.** How are you to tell which case is used in a particular sentence? The Latin will usually provide clues to help you decide correctly:

a. Is the noun preceded by a preposition? If it is, the noun will be in the ablative case because no preposition governs the dative case.

b. If there is no preposition, does the noun refer to a *person*? If it does, it will normally be in the dative because nouns referring to persons are usually governed by a preposition if they are in the ablative. If the noun refers to a *thing*, it is more likely to be ablative than dative.

Consider the following sentences, noting the clues provided by each word and group of words as you meet them:

1. Canem nostrum puerō dedit.
The words **canem nostrum** are obviously accusative. When we reach **puerō,** knowing that **puer** refers to a person, we can say that it must be in the dative case because it would be governed by a preposition if it was in the ablative case. A Roman reading as far as **puerō** would have known before he reached the verb that someone was transferring "our dog" in some way or other "to the boy."

2. Puerō canem nostrum dedimus.
The fact that **puerō** comes first in the sentence does not alter the reasoning. Since it refers to a person and is not governed by a preposition, it must be in the dative case and, again, some transfer is taking place.

3. Canem nostrum baculō verberat.
When we come to **baculō,** knowing that **baculum** refers to a thing, we can be sure because of the sense that it is in the ablative case. A Roman would have understood as soon as he reached **baculō** that someone was "doing" something to our dog *with* a stick.

4. Baculō canem nostrum verberat.
Again, the fact that **baculō** appears as the first word makes no difference. We again know that **baculō** must be in the ablative case because it refers to a thing, and when we come to **canem** we know that someone is "doing" something to our dog *with* a stick.

Exercise 21d

*Look carefully for the type of clue mentioned in the preceding discussion
to help you with the words which could be dative or ablative. Identify
each as dative or ablative and then translate the entire sentence.*

1. Caupō viātōribus cibum dedit.
2. Servus mūrem baculō necāvit.
3. Raedārius equōs habēnīs dēvertēbat.
4. Amīcō captīvī aurum trādidī.
5. Puellae lupum virgīs repellunt.
6. Necesse erat pecūniam praedōnibus trādere.
7. Puerī pontem in rīvō rāmīs faciēbant.
8. Epistulās prīncipis tabellāriīs dedistī.
9. Aurīga habēnās manibus arripuit.
10. Senātor filiīs fābulās narrat.
11. Servus nōmina virōrum dominō dīxit.
12. Bovēs clāmōribus incitāmus.
13. Vīlicus bovem ē rīvō manibus extrāxit.
14. Frāter meus captīvōs aurō adiūvit.
15. Mercātōrēs togās et tunicās cīvibus mōnstrant.

> captīvus, -ī (m), captive
> aurum, -ī (n), gold
> pecūnia, -ae (f), money
> praedō, praedōnis (m), robber
> pōns, pontis (m), bridge
> mercātor, mercātōris (m), merchant
> mōnstrō (1), to show

CAECILIAE
Q·CRETICI·F
METELLAE·CRASSI

I

Caeciliae
  Q. Crēticī f(īliae)
Metellae Crassī

(the tomb) of Caecilia Metella, daughter of Q(uintus Caecilius Metellus) Creticus, (wife) of Crassus

II

D. M. S. CRISPINAE CONIUGI DIVINAE, NUTRICI SENATORUM DUUM, ALBUS CONIUNX, C. Q. F. AN. XVII, H. VIX. AN. XXX M. II.B. M. F.

D(īs) m(ānibus) s(acrum) Crispīnae coniugī dīvīnae, nūtrīcī senātōrum du(ōr)um, Albus coniunx, c(um) q(uō) f(ēlīciter) an(nōs) XVII (vīxit), h(oc monumentum fēcit). Vīx(it) an(nōs) XXX m(ēnsēs) II. B(ene) m(erentī) f(ēcit).

Sacred to the deified spirits of Crispina, divine wife, nurse of two senators; Albus her husband, with whom she lived happily seventeen years, (set up this monument). She lived thirty years, two months. He made (this for her) who well deserved it.

III

D(īs) M(ānibus) Iūliae Velvae piētissimae. Vīxit an(nōs) L. Aurēl(ius) Mercuriālis hēr(ēs) faciundum cūrāvit. Vīvus sibi et suīs fēcit.

To the deified spirits of Julia Velva, a most dutiful woman. She lived 50 years. Aurelius Mercurialis, her heir, had this (tomb) made. He made it for himself and his family while he was still alive.

Word Study VI

The Supine Stem

The stem of the supine (fourth principal part) of a Latin verb may be the source of other Latin words and English derivatives. This stem is found by dropping the -um from the supine, e.g., the supine stem of **vīsum** is **vīs-**. Here are some common types of words formed from the supine stem:

1. No suffix.
   The supine stem may form an English word with no change:
   invent (**inventum**)   fact (**factum**)

2. Silent -e.
   An English word may be formed by adding silent -e to the supine stem:
   narrate (**nārrātum**)   finite (**fīnītum**)

3. Suffix -or.
   When added to the supine stem, the Latin suffix -or creates a 3rd declension, masculine noun, which means "one who does" the action of the verb. These nouns are often borrowed into English with no change in spelling, although there is sometimes a change in meaning:

Supine	Latin Noun & Meaning	English Word
nārrātum (nārrāre)	**nārrātor, nārrātōris** (*m*), *story-teller*	narrator
spectātum (spectāre)	**spectātor, spectātōris** (*m*), *onlooker, observer*	spectator
āctum (agere)	**āctor, āctōris** (*m*), *driver, doer, actor*	actor

4. Suffix -iō.
   The Latin suffix -iō, when added to the supine stem, forms a 3rd declension, feminine noun, which means the "act of," "state of," or "result of" the action of the verb. The genitive singular of these nouns ends in -iōnis, and the base has -iōn-, which is the source of English words ending in -sion and -tion. The meaning of the English word is similar or identical to that of the Latin noun, which takes its meaning from the Latin verb:

Supine	Latin Noun & Meaning	English Word
vīsum (vidēre)	**vīsiō, vīsiōnis** (*f*), act of viewing	vision
nārrātum (nārrāre)	**nārrātiō, nārrātiōnis** (*f*), act of telling (a story)	narration

   Note that whether the English word ends in -sion or -tion depends on whether the supine from which it is derived ends in -sum or -tum.

48

Exercise 1

Using the above information, give a 3rd declension Latin noun and an English derivative for each of the following supines. Check in a Latin dictionary to verify the existence of each noun and compare its meaning with that of its English derivative.

1. audītum (audīre)   4. factum (facere)   7. petītum (petere)
2. cautum (cavēre)   5. mānsum (manēre)   8. positum (pōnere)
3. exclāmātum (exclāmāre) 6. missum (mittere)   9. statum (stāre)

Exercise 2

Give the meaning of each English word below. Then give the supine, infinitive, and the meaning of the verb from which the English word is derived.

1. apparition   4. habitation   7. session
2. cogitate   5. inventor   8. state
3. diction   6. motor   9. tacit

Latin Expressions in English

Latin phrases and expressions are often used in English. Some are very familiar, such as **et cetera** (etc.), *and the rest*. Others are more specialized, such as **ipso facto**, *by the fact itself*, a legal expression used to describe an assumption that has obvious truth, e.g., "A slave, ipso facto, had no right to vote."

While Latin expressions may sometimes be used in English as mere affectations, there are occasions when they are very effective in summarizing an idea succinctly. For example, the term *de facto segregation* refers to a long history of racial segregation which occurred *in fact*, even though no legal measures were taken to achieve it. **De jure** segregation, on the other hand, was achieved *by law*. These two Latin phrases capsulize these notions in a minimum of words, thereby making communication more efficient.

Exercise 3

Look up the following Latin expressions in an English dictionary. Use each expression in a sentence which illustrates its special use in English.

1. ad hoc   4. non sequitur   7. quid pro quo
2. ad infinitum   5. per capita   8. sine qua non
3. modus operandi   6. per se   9. status quo

22
At the Porta Capena

Intereā Titus, patruus Marcī et Cornēliae, eōs prope Portam Capēnam
exspectābat. Cīvēs, mercātōrēs, servī per portam ībant atque hūc illūc currēbant. Titus tamen in lectīcā sedēbat. Ubi Cornēliōs cōnspexit, ē lectīcā
dēscendit. Ē raedā dēscendērunt Cornēliī. Interdiū enim raedās intrā urbem
agere Rōmānīs nōn licēbat.   5
Stupuit Sextus ubi multitūdinem cīvium, servōrum turbam vīdit. Undique erat strepitus plaustrōrum, undique clāmor mercātōrum, viātōrum,
raedāriōrum.
Titus Cornēlium et Aurēliam et līberōs maximō cum gaudiō salūtāvit.
"Quam laetus," inquit, "vōs omnēs excipiō! Nōnne estis itinere dēfessī?"   10
"Valdē dēfessī," respondit Cornēlius. "Mihi necesse est celeriter ad Cūriam īre, sed prīmum Aurēliam et Cornēliam domum dūcam."
"Ita vērō!" inquit Titus. "Ecce! Lectīcāriī, quōs vōbīs condūxī, vōs domum ferent. Ego puerōs cūrābō. Multa et mīra vidēbunt puerī, atque ego
omnia eīs explicābō."   15
Itaque per viās urbis lectīcāriī patrem, mātrem, fīliam celeriter domum
tulērunt. Postquam eō advēnērunt, Aurēlia et Cornēlia, itinere dēfessae, sē
quiētī dedērunt. Cornēlius tamen sē lāvit, togam pūram induit, iterum in
lectīcā cōnsēdit.
"Ad Cūriam celeriter!" inquit.   20

hūc illūc, this way and that
lectīca, -ae (f), litter
interdiū, during the day
stupeō (2), to be amazed, gape
turba, -ae (f), crowd, mob
undique, on all sides
strepitus, noise, clattering
maximō cum gaudiō, with very great
   joy
Cūria, -ae (f), Senate House

prīmum, first
domum, homeward, home
dūcam, I will take
ferent, (they) will carry
cūrābō, I will take care of
multa et mīra, many wonderful things
vidēbunt, (they) will see
eō, there, to that place
quiēs, quiētis (f), rest
pūrus, -a, -um, clean

50

curr**ō**, **currere** (3), **cucurrī**, **cursum**, to run
sedeō, **sedēre** (2), **sēdī**, **sessum**, to sit
dēscendō, **dēscendere** (3), **dēscendī**, **dēscēnsum**, to climb down
agō, **agere** (3), **ēgī**, **āctum**, to do, drive
condūcō, **condūcere** (3), **condūxī**, **conductum**, to hire
ferō, **ferre**, **tulī**, **lātum**, to carry, bring, bear
induō, **induere** (3), **induī**, **indūtum**, to put on
cōnsīdō, **cōnsīdere** (3), **cōnsēdī**, to sit down

Slaves carrying a **lectīca**.

Exercise 22a

Respondē Latīnē:

1. Quis Cornēliōs prope Portam Capēnam exspectābat?
2. Quī hūc illūc currēbant per portam?
3. Ubi sedēbat Titus?
4. Cūr Cornēliī ē raedā dēscendērunt?
5. Quid Sextus prope portam vīdit et audīvit?
6. Quōmodo Titus Cornēliōs salūtāvit?
7. Suntne Cornēliī itinere dēfessī?
8. Quō necesse est Cornēliō īre?
9. Quis lectīcāriōs condūxit?
10. Quis puerīs multa et mīra explicābit?
11. Quid fēcit Cornēlius postquam domum Cornēliī advēnērunt?

51

VERBS: Future Tense I

Look at these sentences:

Ego omnia eīs **explicābō**.	I **will explain** *everything to them.*
Multa et mīra **vidēbunt** puerī.	*The boys* **will see** *many wonderful things.*
Ego Cornēliam domum **dūcam**.	I **will take** *Cornelia home.*
Brevī tempore ad Portam Capēnam **adveniēmus**.	*In a short time* **we will arrive** *at the Porta Capena.*

The words in bold type are examples of the *future tense*. The endings of the future tense are shown in the table below:

			1st and 2nd Conjugations	3rd and 4th Conjugations
Singular		1	**-bō**	**-am**
		2	**-bis**	**-ēs**
		3	**-bit**	**-et**
Plural		1	**-bimus**	**-ēmus**
		2	**-bitis**	**-ētis**
		3	**-bunt**	**-ent**

Note that in the future tense the endings of verbs in the 3rd and 4th conjugations are quite different from the endings of verbs in the 1st and 2nd conjugations.

Note also that the e of the ending in the 3rd and 4th conjugations is short before final **-t** and **-nt.**

Learn the forms of the future tense, as follows:

		1st Conjugation	2nd Conjugation	3rd Conjugation		4th Conjugation
Infinitive		par**āre**	hab**ēre**	mitt**ere**	iac**ere (-iō)**	aud**īre**
Singular	1	parā**bō**	habē**bō**	mitt**am**	iaci**am**	audi**am**
	2	parā**bis**	habē**bis**	mitt**ēs**	iaci**ēs**	audi**ēs**
	3	parā**bit**	habē**bit**	mitt**et**	iaci**et**	audi**et**
Plural	1	parā**bimus**	habē**bimus**	mitt**ēmus**	iaci**ēmus**	audi**ēmus**
	2	parā**bitis**	habē**bitis**	mitt**ētis**	iaci**ētis**	audi**ētis**
	3	parā**bunt**	habē**bunt**	mitt**ent**	iaci**ent**	audi**ent**

Exercise 22b

Read aloud and translate:

1. Titus nōs prope Portam Capēnam exspectābit; omnēs maximō cum gaudiō salūtābit.
2. Hodiē sepulcra magna Rōmānōrum praeclārōrum vīdimus; crās Cūriam et alia aedificia Rōmāna vidēbimus.
3. Fortasse patruus noster nōs ad Cūriam dūcet.
4. Cornēliī omnēs sē parant; brevī tempore ad urbem iter facient.
5. Multa et mīra vident puerī; lectīcāriī eōs mox domum portābunt.
6. Cornēlius ē raedā dēscendet, nam raedam intrā urbem agere nōn licet.
7. Quam diū in urbe manēbis, pater?
8. Bene dormiētis, puerī. Longum enim iter hodiē fēcistis.
9. Cornēlia, itinere longō dēfessa, sē quiētī dabit.
10. Puerī multa rogābunt dē aedificiīs quae in urbis viīs vidēbunt.
11. Crās, ubi surgētis, puerī, strepitum plaustrōrum audiētis.
12. Titus, ubi puerōs domum dūcet, omnia eīs explicābit.

> **maneō, manēre** (2), **mānsī, mānsum,** to remain, stay
> **faciō, facere** (3), **fēcī, factum,** to make, do

Note that in sentences 11 and 12 the verbs in the clauses introduced by **ubi** are in the future tense. English, however, requires the present tense here.

Exercise 22c

Add one of the following adverbs to each sentence, according to the tense of the verb: **hodiē** *(present),* **heri** *(perfect), or* **crās** *(future). Read aloud and translate:*

1. Mīlitēs ad urbem _____ veniunt.
2. Puerōs parentēs ad cubiculum _____ mīsērunt.
3. Multī hominēs in viā _____ stābunt.
4. Lectīcāriī ad portam _____ venient.
5. Multae mātrēs līberōs _____ expectāvērunt.
6. Senātōrēs mīlitēs _____ cōnspiciunt.
7. Aedificia multa _____ vīdimus.
8. Cūr nōn caupōnem _____ petēmus?
9. Nōs omnēs in raedā _____ sedēmus.
10. Vōs in lectīs _____ dormiētis.

> **Quandō cadet Rōma, cadet et mundus.** *When Rome falls, the world will fall, too.* (Medieval pilgrims' proverb; Venerable Bede)

53

Exercise 22d

Take parts, read aloud, and translate:

Intereā Eucleidēs et puerī cum Titō extrā Portam Capēnam stābant.

TITUS: Salvēte, puerī! Quid in itinere vīdistis? Vīdistisne rūsticōs in agrīs? Agrōsne colēbant?

SEXTUS: Rūsticōs vīdimus. Agrōs nōn colēbant, sed sub arboribus quiēscēbant. At caupōnam vīdimus; nostra raeda in fossā haerēbat et nōbīs necesse 5 erat in caupōnā pernoctāre.

MARCUS: Ita vērō! Gaudēbam quod pater meus in illā caupōnā pernoctāre cōnstituit. Caupō erat vir Graecus, amīcus Eucleidis.

SEXTUS: Ego quoque gaudēbam, nam mīles bonam fābulam nōbīs narrāvit. In illā fābulā caupō quīdam hospitem necāvit. Tālēs fābulās amō.   10

MARCUS: Sed quid nunc faciēmus, patrue? Ego volō Cūriam et Forum vidēre.

SEXTUS: Quandō Circum Maximum vīsitābimus? Ecce! Nōnne Circum Maximum suprā mūrōs urbis exstantem vidēre possum?

MARCUS: Ita vērō! Est Circus Maximus. Nōn procul abest.

TITUS: Nōn possumus omnia hodiē vidēre. Crās satis temporis habēbimus.   15

SEXTUS: Sed quid est illud aedificium? Nōnne pontem ingentem suprā portam videō?·

MARCUS: Nōn pontem hīc vidēs, ō stulte! Est aquaeductus, Aqua Marcia. Per illum aquaeductum Rōmānī aquam in urbem ferunt. Cavē imbrem, Sexte!   20

SEXTUS: Sed nōn pluit.

TITUS: Semper hīc pluit, Sexte. Rīmōsa enim est Aqua Marcia.

extrā (+ *acc.*), outside
at, but
tālis, -is, -e, such
Circus Maximus, a stadium in Rome
  maximus, -a, -um, very great, greatest, very large
suprā (+ *acc.*), above
mūrus, -ī (*m*), wall

exstantem, standing out, towering
satis temporis, enough time
stultus, -a, -um, stupid
aqua, -ae (*f*), water
Cavē imbrem! Watch out for the rain!
rīmōsus, -a, -um, full of cracks, leaky

colō, colere (3), coluī, cultum, to cultivate
quiēscō, quiēscere (3), quiēvī, quiētum, to rest, keep quiet
cōnstituō, cōnstituere (3), cōnstituī, cōnstitūtum, to decide
pluit, pluere (3), pluit, it rains (usually found only in 3rd person singular and infinitive)

54

Exercise 22e

Give the appropriate form of the future tense for each verb in parentheses:

1. Nōs in Viā Appiā nōn (pernoctāre).
2. Mox vōs urbī (appropinquāre) et patruum (cōnspicere).
3. Titus multās fābulās dē aedificiīs Rōmae puerīs (nārrāre).
4. Ego prīmum Aurēliam et Cornēliam domum (dūcere).
5. Puerī multa et mīra in urbe crās (vidēre).
6. Quandō Cornēlius ad Cūriam (venīre)?
7. Tū cēnam bonam in illā caupōnā (habēre).
8. Nōs in lectīs sordidīs nōn (dormīre).
9. Crās Marcus et Sextus māne (surgere).
10. Cornēlius Titum frātrem (petere); mox eum (invenīre).

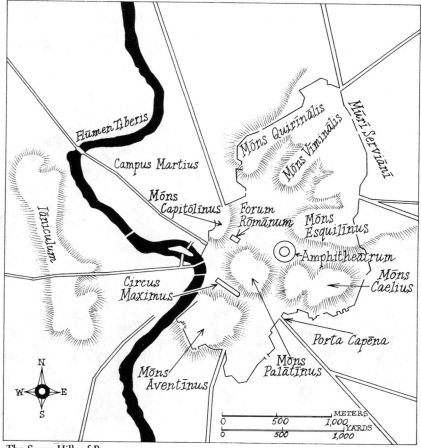

The Seven Hills of Rome

Aqueducts

One feature of the city which the Cornelii would notice as they approached Rome was the evidence of the Romans' passion for water. Abundant water for baths and fountains and lakes was an utter necessity to the Roman, so that it had to be brought in by the aqueducts whose arches strode into Rome from all directions. By A.D. 80, nine aqueducts were in use, carrying water across the plain to Rome from sources up to fifty-six miles or ninety kilometers distant.

The illustration shows the arches supporting the water-channel and a cross-section of the channel itself. To maintain the downhill flow, experts recommended a fall of six inches or fifteen centimeters in every ninety-eight feet or thirty meters. Tunnels, with inspection shafts built into them, were driven through hills which it was impossible to by-pass. Sometimes, by using the principle that water rises to its own level, a U-shaped arrangement of the tunnel allowed an uphill flow. Responsibility for maintaining and cleaning the whole vast system rested with the **cūrātor aquārum** and his staff.

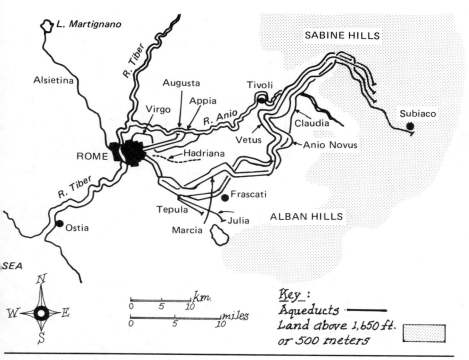

Routes of the Roman aqueducts.

The first aqueduct, the **Aqua Appia,** went underground. Since a gravity system was employed, later ones had to be higher to serve the hillier districts of the town. The Romans then hit on the idea of using arches to support the water-channel. The arches turned out to be beautiful structures in themselves, but the Romans had adopted them for quite different reasons. They stood up better to earthquakes, always a hazard in Italy; the wind could blow through them, where a solid wall would invite disaster; and they could be easily repaired, as workmen could take the building materials from one side to the other.

Admiring comments about the aqueducts abound from native and foreigner alike. "Just as impressive," says one writer, "as the pyramids, but how much more useful!" Not only so, but we also have an astonishing book, *De aquis urbis Romae,* by Frontinus, Superintendent of Aqueducts, written about A.D. 97, describing the system in detail and the difficulties of organizing and maintaining it. He reports that, through bribery of watermen, supplies were sometimes diverted into private estates and never reached Rome at all. Householders in Rome itself often succeeded in bribing inspectors (who were, after all, slaves) to replace a narrow pipe by one of wider bore, while they continued to pay at the old rate!

According to the latest available figures, the daily consumption of water in a large city today is about 120 gallons or 455 liters per person. According to Frontinus, in his day the Roman aqueducts could deliver over 264 million gallons or one billion liters in twenty-four hours, providing a daily allowance of about 240 gallons or 900 liters per person! The aqueducts leaked dreadfully, as the Cornelii found at the Porta Capena, and what with water thieves and corrupt inspectors, all this water did not actually reach Rome. For all that, the Roman citizen still had a lot of water at his disposal. Did he use it all? The answer is "Yes," because as one Roman writer put it, "The waters, having provided the city with the life-giving element, passed on into the sewers." The Roman, you see, hardly ever turned the tap off. For him, running water was simply running water!

A Roman Contemplates the Aqueducts

We must now describe marvels which are unsurpassed for their genuine value. Quintus Marcius Rex (praetor 144–143 B.C.), having been ordered by the senate to repair the channels of the **Aqua Appia** (the earliest aqueduct, built by Appius Claudius Caecus in 312 B.C.), the **Aniō Vetus** (begun in 272 B.C.), and the **Tepula,** drove underground passages through the mountains and brought to Rome a new water-supply named after himself (the **Aqua Marcia**) and completed within the period of his praetorship.

Agrippa, moreover, as aedile added to these the **Aqua Virgō** (completed in 19 B.C.), repaired the channels of the others and put them in order, and constructed 700 basins, not to speak of 500 fountains and 130 reservoirs for distribution of water, many of the latter being richly decorated. On these works he erected 300 bronze or marble statues and 400 marble pillars marking the course taken by the channels. All of this he did in a year. In the memoirs of his aedileship he adds that in celebration of these achievements games lasting 59 days were held and that the bathing establishments were opened to the public free of charge—all 170 of them, a number which at Rome has now been infinitely increased.

All of these previous aqueducts have been surpassed by the most recent and very costly work inaugurated by the Emperor Gaius (A.D. 37–41) and completed by Claudius (A.D. 41–54), who made the Curtian and Caerulean Springs and the **Aniō Novus** flow into Rome from the 40th milestone at such a high level as to supply water to all the seven hills of the city. 350,000,000 sesterces were spent on this work.

If we carefully consider the abundant supplies of water in public buildings, baths, pools, open channels, private houses, gardens, and country estates near the city; if we consider the distances traversed by the water before it arrives, the raising of arches, the tunneling of mountains, and the building of level routes across deep valleys, we shall readily admit that there has never been anything more remarkable in the whole world.

Pliny, *Natural History* XXXVI.121–123

VERBS: *Future Tense II*

The following are the future tenses of the irregular verbs you have met:

Infinitive			esse	posse	velle	nōlle	īre	ferre
Number and Person	*Singular*	1	erō	poterō	volam	nōlam	ībō	feram
		2	eris	poteris	volēs	nōlēs	ībis	ferēs
		3	erit	poterit	volet	nōlet	ībit	feret
	Plural	1	erimus	poterimus	volēmus	nōlēmus	ībimus	ferēmus
		2	eritis	poteritis	volētis	nōlētis	ībitis	ferētis
		3	erunt	poterunt	volent	nōlent	ībunt	ferent

Note that **velle, nōlle, īre,** and **ferre** have future tense endings like those of regular verbs. Note also where long vowels occur in the endings of these verbs.

Exercise 22f

Read aloud and translate:

1. Ībisne ad Cūriam, pater? Ita vērō! Ad Cūriam celeriter ībō.
2. Quandō domum redībis, pater? Nesciō.
3. Fortasse Cornēlius domum redīre brevī tempore poterit.
4. Eucleidēs ad amphitheātrum īre nōlet.
5. Necesse erit diū in urbe manēre.
6. Nocte vehicula magna onera in urbe ferent.
7. Puerī Circum Maximum crās vidēre volent.
8. Ubi līberī māne erunt? Tū līberōs nōn vidēbis, nam domō mox exībunt.
9. Sī equī strēnuē labōrābunt, raedam ē fossā extrahere poterunt.
10. Sī pluet, ad silvam ambulāre nōlam.
11. Ferēsne cistam meam in caupōnam? Minimē! Tū ipse eam fer!
12. Redībitisne ad vīllam rūsticam? Fortasse redīre poterimus.
13. Volētisne crās ad Circum Maximum īre? Ita vērō! Crās illūc īre volēmus.
14. "Ego īre nōlam," inquit Aurēlia.
15. Post cēnam puerī cubitum īre nōlent.

> **domō**, out of the house
> **exeō, exīre** (*irreg.*), **exiī, exitum,** to go out

Note that in sentences 9 and 10 the verbs in the clauses introduced by **sī** are in the future tense. English, however, requires the present tense here.

23
Always Tomorrow

Simulac Titus et puerī et Eucleidēs urbem per Portam Capēnam intrāvērunt, clāmāvit Sextus, "Quid nōs prīmum faciēmus? Quō ībimus? Vīsi-
tābimusne — ?"
"Quō tū nōs dūcēs, patrue?" interpellāvit Marcus. "Vidēbimusne Cūriam
et Forum?"   5
Titus, "Tacēte! Tacēte!" inquit. "Forum crās vīsitābimus. Crās, Eu-
cleidēs, tibi licēbit puerōs eō dūcere. Tum erit satis temporis. Hodiē tamen,
puerī, vōs domum per urbem dūcam et omnia in itinere vōbīs dēmōnstrābō."
Iam advēnerant ad Circum Maximum, quī nōn procul aberat. Stupuit
Sextus ubi mōlem Circī Maximī vīdit. Stupuit quoque Marcus, quamquam 10
Circum anteā vīderat. Stupuit Titus, attonitus nōn mōle, sed silentiō Circī.
"Ēheu! Ēheu!" inquit Titus. "Hodiē Circus est clausus. Tribus diēbus
tamen prīnceps ipse lūdōs magnificōs faciet."
"Nōnne tū nōs eō dūcēs?" rogāvit Marcus.
"Ēheu! Ego nōn poterō vōs dūcere," inquit Titus. "Fortasse Eucleidēs 15
vōs dūcet."
"Minimē!" respondit Sextus. "Librōs, nōn lūdōs amat Eucleidēs."
"Agite, puerī!" interpellāvit Titus. "Nunc circumībimus Montem Palā-
tīnum et Forum intrābimus ad arcum Tiberiī. Ibi fortasse patrī tuō occur-
rēmus, Marce. Mox senātōrēs ē Cūriā exībunt."   20
Itaque Circum relīquērunt et Palātīnum circumiērunt. Titus in itinere
mōnstrāvit puerīs mīra aedificia quae prīncipēs in Palātīnō aedificāverant.
Tandem ad arcum Tiberiī advēnērunt, iam labōre et aestū dēfessī.
"Hic est arcus," inquit Titus, "quem — "
"Omnia vidēre poteritis crās," interpellāvit Cornēlius, quī eō ipsō tempore 25
ad arcum ē Cūriā advēnerat. "Eucleidēs omnia vōbīs explicābit. Iam sērō
est. Agite! Iam domum ībimus."

simulac, as soon as
advēnerant, they had arrived
mōlēs, mōlis (f), mass, huge bulk
vīderat, he had seen
attonitus, -a, -um, astonished, as-
  tounded
clausus, -a, -um, closed
lūdī, -ōrum (m pl), games

liber, librī (m), book
Mōns Palātīnus, Montis Palātīnī (m),
  the Palatine Hill
arcus, arch
aedificō (1), to build
aestū, by the heat
quem (acc.), which

60

licet, licēre (2), licuit, it is allowed (usually found only in 3rd person singular and infinitive)

possum, posse (*irreg.*), potuī, to be able

circumeō, circumīre, circumiī, circumitum, to go around

occurrō, occurrere (3), occurrī, occursum (+ *dat.*), to meet, encounter

relinquō, relinquere (3), relīquī, relictum, to leave

Tantae mōlis erat Rōmānam condere gentem! *It was such a vast undertaking to found the Roman nation!* (Vergil, *Aeneid* I.33)

Cūriam et continēns eī Chalcidicum . . . fēcī. *I built the Curia and the Chalcidicum next to it.* (Augustus, *Res gestae* XIX)

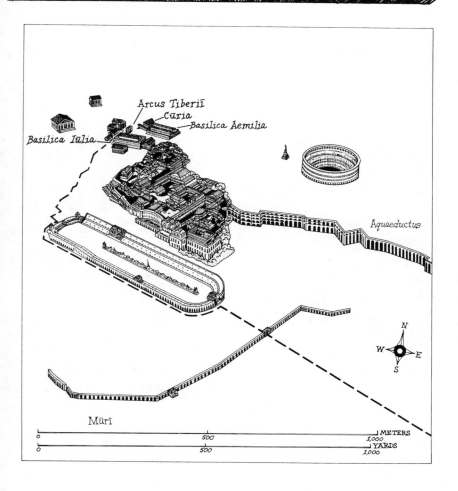

Exercise 23a

Respondē Latīnē:

1. Quid facere volēbant Sextus et Marcus postquam urbem intrāvērunt?
2. Quis puerōs crās ad Forum dūcet?
3. Quid Titus hodiē facere vult?
4. Vīderatne Sextus anteā Circum Maximum?
5. Stupuitne Marcus ubi Circum Maximum vīdit?
6. Eratne Titus attonitus mōle Circī?
7. Cūr Circum hodiē puerī nōn intrant?
8. Quid faciet prīnceps tribus diēbus?
9. Dūcetne Titus puerōs ad lūdōs?
10. Quid amat Eucleidēs?
11. Ubi occurrent puerī Cornēliō?
12. Quī mīra aedificia in Palātīnō aedificāverant?
13. Dēfessīne puerī ad arcum Tiberiī advēnērunt?
14. Quis puerīs prope arcum Tiberiī occurrit?
15. Quō Cornēlius puerōs hodiē dūcet?

Roman Magistrates and Lictors; an oil painting by Jean Lemaire (1598–1659). Montreal Museum of Fine Arts.

62

VERBS: Pluperfect Tense

Look at these sentences:

Iam **advēnerant** ad Circum.	*They* **had** *already* **reached** *the Circus.*
Circum anteā **vīderat.**	*He* **had seen** *the Circus before.*
Mīra aedificia **aedificāverant.**	*They* **had built** *marvelous buildings.*

The verbs in these sentences are all in the *pluperfect tense,* which can nearly always be translated into English by the word "had."

The endings of the pluperfect tense are the same for *all* Latin verbs:

	1	*-eram*	1	*-erāmus*
Singular	2	*-erās*	Plural 2	*-erātis*
	3	*-erat*	3	*-erant*

These endings are added to the perfect stem, which is found by dropping the ī from the end of the third principal part, e.g., **relīquī**, stem **relīqu-**.

	1	relīqu*eram*	1	relīqu*erāmus*
Singular	2	relīqu*erās*	Plural 2	relīqu*erātis*
	3	relīqu*erat*	3	relīqu*erant*

Exercise 23b

Read aloud and translate:

1. Eucleidēs puerōs ad urbem dūxerat et omnia eīs dēmōnstrāverat.
2. Aurēlia sollicita erat quod servī cēnam nōndum parāverant.
3. Hodiē librum diū legēbam quem mihi heri dedistī.
4. Dēfessus eram quod multās epistulās iam scrīpseram.
5. Vix domum advēnerātis, puerī, cum Eucleidēs in hortum intrāvit.

> **scrībo, scrībere** (3), **scrīpsī, scrīptum,** to write
> **vix,** scarcely

Exercise 23c

Substitute the corresponding pluperfect form for each verb in parentheses, read the sentence aloud, and translate:

1. Tantum sonitum numquam anteā (audīmus) _____.
2. Marcus laetus fuit quod patrī prope Cūriam (occurrit) _____.
3. Via erat plēna hominum quī ad urbem (veniunt) _____.
4. Lectīcāriī, quī Cornēlium per urbis viās (ferunt) _____, extrā Cūriam eum exspectābant.
5. Titus, quod Circum (invēnit) _____ clausum, puerōs domum dūcēbat.

> **tantus, -a, -um,** so great, such a big
> **sonitus,** sound

Building Up the Meaning V
VERBS: Present or Future?

Look at these sentences:

Cornēlius multōs servōs habet.	*Cornelius* **has** *many slaves.*
Scelestōs servōs ad vīllam mittet.	*He* **will send** *the wicked slaves to the farm.*
Hodiē in caupōnā manēmus.	*Today we* **remain** *in the inn.*
Crās Rōmam adveniēmus.	*Tomorrow we* **will reach** *Rome.*

The endings -ēs, -et, -ēmus, -ētis, -ent can denote the present tense of verbs of the 2nd conjugation or the future tense of verbs of the 3rd and 4th conjugations. If there is an *i* before the *e*, the verb will be the future tense of a 3rd conjugation -iō verb or the future tense of a 4th conjugation verb.

Exercise 23d

Following the examples, identify the remainder of the verb forms below:

Verb	Conjugation	Tense	Meaning
habent	2	present	they have
mittent	3	future	they will send
vident			
iubent			
ascendent			
admovent			
dormient			
timent			
dūcent			
rīdent			
facient			

Exercise 23e

Look carefully at the verbs in the following sentences. Decide the conjugation number first (this will help you to get the tense right) and then read aloud and translate:

1. Puerī Eucleidem nōn vident, sed vōcem eius audient.
2. Vidēsne senātōrēs in viīs? Quandō Cornēlius veniet?
3. Servī celeriter current, nam Cornēlium timent.
4. Sextus māne surget; in animō habet exīre.
5. Ego et Cornēlia tacēmus; patrem timēmus.

Versiculī: *"Procrustes," pages 100–102.*

Review V

Exercise Va

Supply Latin words to match the English cues. Be sure to give the right endings. Read each sentence aloud and translate it.

1. Sextus fābulam dē caupōne _____ _____ nārrābat. (wicked) (to Cornelius)
2. Eucleidēs mandāta _____ et _____ dabat. (to the slaves) (to the slave-women)
3. Cūnctī Cornēliī ē _____ vēnērunt. (the inn)
4. Viātōrēs nōn in _____ caupōnīs bene cēnāre possunt. (all)
5. Raedārius habēnīs _____verberāvit. (the horses)
6. Sextus _____ dē _____ _____ _____ nārrāvit. (everything) (the dead mouse) (to Marcus)
7. Dum Cornēlius fābulam _____ nārrat, _____ appropinquāvērunt. (to his wife) (the city)
8. Prope viam sunt sepulcra _____ _____ _____ _____. (of many famous Romans)
9. Titus _____ prope Portam Capēnam exspectābat. (them)
10. Interdiū raedās intrā urbem agere _____ nōn licēbat. (to or for them)
11. "Quam laetus _____ _____ videō!" exclāmat Titus. (all of you = you all)
12. "_____ sumus valdē dēfessī," respondet Cornēlius. (We)
13. "_____ necesse est ad Cūriam īre." (For me)
14. Titus respondet, "_____ lectīcāriōs condūxī." (For you)
15. "Ego multa et mīra _____ et _____ explicābō," inquit Titus. (to you) (to Sextus)
16. Postquam domum advēnit, Cornēlius _____ lāvit. (himself)
17. "_____ in caupōnā pernoctāre necesse erat," inquit Sextus. (For us)
18. Sextus _____ _____ suprā portam videt. (a huge aqueduct)
19. Crās Forum vīsitāre _____ licēbit. (to or for the boys)
20. Hodiē _____ dormīre licet. (to or for Cornelia)
21. _____ diēbus prīnceps lūdōs _____ faciet. (In three) (for the Romans)
22. _____ _____ Titus Marcum et Sextum dūcet. (To them, i.e., the games)
23. Cornēlius ē Cūriā mox exībit. _____ Marcus et Sextus occurrent. (Him)
24. Titus mīra aedificia _____ mōnstrāvit. (to the boys)
25. Crās multa alia aedificia _____ mōnstrābit. (to them)

65

Exercise Vb

Give the requested forms of the following verbs in the present, imperfect,
future, perfect, and pluperfect tenses:

		Present	Imperfect	Future	Perfect	Pluperfect
1.	circumīre (3rd pl.)	_____	_____	_____	_____	_____
2.	dēscendere (2nd sing.)	_____	_____	_____	_____	_____
3.	ferre (2nd pl.)	_____	_____	_____	_____	_____
4.	dare (1st pl.)	_____	_____	_____	_____	_____
5.	esse (3rd sing.)	_____	_____	_____	_____	_____
6.	respondēre (1st sing.)	_____	_____	_____	_____	_____
7.	surgere (3rd pl.)	_____	_____	_____	_____	_____
8.	cōgitāre (2nd sing.)	_____	_____	_____	_____	_____
9.	conicere (1st sing.)	_____	_____	_____	_____	_____
10.	venīre (1st pl.)	_____	_____	_____	_____	_____

Exercise Vc

Read the following passage and answer the questions below with full
sentences in Latin:

Cornēlius, postquam in triclīnium intrāvit, Cornēliam vīdit. Cornēlia
pictūram, quae in mūrō erat, spectābat.
"Quid tū facis, mea filia?" inquit Cornēlius.
Cui Cornēlia, "Hanc pictūram valdē amō, pater. Nōnne hic vir est Herculēs? Eucleidēs nōbīs multa dē Hercule dīxit, sed ego omnia audīre volō." 5
Respondit Cornēlius, "Herculēs, ut bene scīs, erat vir Graecus. Ōlim, ubi
īnfāns erat et in lectō dormiēbat, subitō duo serpentēs lectō appropinquāvērunt
et Herculem dormientem necāre volēbant. Sed Herculēs, ē somnō excitātus,
serpentēs sōlus strangulāvit."
Cornēlia tamen rogāvit, "Sed cūr in pictūrā est canis triformis? Cūr Herculēs 10
hunc canem trahit?"
Eī respondit Cornēlius, "Herculēs, quod dēmēns filiōs suōs ōlim necāverat,
miser erat et sē pūnīre cōnstituit. Itaque factus est servus dominī cuiusdam
scelestī quī eum valdē timēbat et multōs labōrēs perficere iussit. Ille canis,
quem in pictūrā vidēs, est Cerberus quī portās Īnferōrum custōdit. In hāc 15
pictūrā Herculēs ex Īnferīs dūcit Cerberum invītum. Dominus enim Herculis
eum in Īnferōs dēscendere iusserat, quod ita cōgitābat: 'Herculēs numquam
ex Īnferīs redībit. Cerberus certē eum necābit.' Sed tandem exiit ex Īnferīs
Herculēs cum cane, nam omnia perficere solēbat. Itaque dominus perterritus
Herculem canem ad Īnferōs statim redūcere iussit." 20
At iam Cornēlia et pater vōcem Aurēliae audīvērunt. "Ēheu!" clāmāvit
Cornēlia. "Māter nōs vocat. Mox erit cēnae tempus."

66

"Ita vērō!" respondit Cornēlius. "Senātōrēs quīdam apud nōs cēnābunt. Necesse est mihi mātrem tuam cōnsulere. Crās tamen de aliīs Herculis labōribus tibi nārrābō."

25

triclīnium, -ī (n), dining room
ut bene scīs, as you know well
excitātus, -a, -um, wakened,
    aroused
triformis, -is, -e, three-headed
dēmēns, in a fit of madness

factus est, became
cuiusdam, genitive of quīdam
Īnferī, -ōrum, (m pl), the
    underworld
apud nōs, at our home

perficiō, perficere (3), perfēcī, perfectus, to accomplish

1. What does Cornelia love?
2. What does Cornelia want to hear?
3. What did the snakes do?
4. What is Hercules doing with the dog in the picture?
5. Why did Hercules decide to punish himself?
6. Who is Cerberus?
7. Why did the master order Hercules to descend into the underworld?
8. What did the master do when Hercules brought Cerberus to him?
9. Why does Cornelius have to consult with Aurelia?
10. When will Cornelia hear about other labors of Hercules?

Exercise Vd

1. *In the passage above, locate in sequence all of the verbs in the imperfect, perfect, pluperfect, and future tenses and translate them.*
2. *Locate all of the words in the dative case and translate the sentences in which they occur.*

24
First Morning in Rome

Iam diēs erat. Magnus erat clāmor in urbe. Iam canēs in viīs lātrābant,
iam hominēs clāmābant et per viās currēbant. Servī ad Forum magnō
tumultū onera ferēbant. Undique clāmor et strepitus! Sed nihil clāmōris,
nihil strepitūs ad Marcum pervēnit. Neque clāmōrēs hominum neque lā-
trātūs canum eum excitāverant. In lectō stertēbat nam dēfessus erat.   5
Sextus quoque in lectō manēbat sed dormīre nōn poterat. Numquam
anteā urbem tantam vīsitāverat. Clāmōribus et strepitū excitātus, iam cōgitābat dē omnibus rēbus quās Titus heri narrāverat. "Quid hodiē vidēbimus?
Fortasse cum Titō ībimus quī omnia nōbīs dēmōnstrābit. Cornēliusne nōs
in Forum dūcet? Ego certē Forum et Cūriam et senātōrēs vidēre volō."   10
    Intereā Eucleidēs, quī prīmā lūce exierat, iam domum redierat. Statim
cubiculum puerōrum petīvit et, "Eho, puerī!" inquit. "Cūr nōndum sur-
rēxistis? Abhinc duās hōrās ego surrēxī. Quod novum librum emere volēbam,
in Argīlētum māne dēscendī ad tabernam quandam ubi in postibus nōmina
multōrum poētārum vidēre potes. Catullus, Flaccus—"   15
    At puerī celeriter interpellāvērunt quod Eucleidēs, ut bene sciēbant,
semper aliquid novī docēre volēbat. "Quid in viā vīdistī?"
    Eucleidēs, "Nihil," inquit, "nisi miserum hominem lapidibus oppres-
sum. Bovēs lapidēs quadrātōs in plaustrō trahēbant ad novum aedificium
quod Caesar prope Domum Auream aedificat. Illud aedificium est ingēns   20
amphitheātrum et mox—"
    At puerī in cubiculō nōn iam manēbant, nam Eucleidēs, quī erat semper
verbōsus, multa dē aedificiīs urbis narrāre solēbat; neque tamen puerī eum
audīre volēbant.

---

magnō tumultū, with a great uproar
excitātus, -a, -um, aroused
dē omnibus rēbus, about all the
    things, about everything
Eho! Hey!
abhinc duās hōrās, two hours ago
novus, -a, -um, new
taberna, -ae (f), shop
ad tabernam quandam, to a certain
    shop
postis, postis (m), door-post

poēta, -ae (m), poet
ut, as
sciō (4), to know
aliquid, something
lapis, lapidis (m), stone
    lapidibus oppressum, crushed by
    stones
    lapidēs quadrātī, squared stones
quod, which
Domus Aurea, (Nero's) Golden House
neque tamen, but . . . not

perveniō, pervenīre (4), **pervēnī, perventum,** to arrive (at), reach
stertō, stertere (3), **stertuī,** to snore
redeō, redīre (*irreg.*), **rediī, reditum,** to return, go back
emō, emere (3), **ēmī, ēmptum,** to buy
doceō, docēre (2), **docuī, doctum,** to teach
trahō, trahere, (3), **trāxī, tractum,** to drag, pull

NOUNS: 4th and 5th Declensions

Most Latin nouns belong to the 1st, 2nd, or 3rd declensions. There are two other declensions to which a few nouns belong:

Number Case	4th Declension	5th Declension
Singular		
Nominative	man**us**	di**ēs**
Genitive	man**ūs**	di**ēī**
Dative	man**uī**	di**ēī**
Accusative	man**um**	di**em**
Ablative	man**ū**	di**ē**
Plural		
Nominative	man**ūs**	di**ēs**
Genitive	man**uum**	di**ērum**
Dative	man**ibus**	di**ēbus**
Accusative	man**ūs**	di**ēs**
Ablative	man**ibus**	di**ēbus**

Be sure to learn these forms thoroughly.

Nouns of the 4th and 5th declensions will appear in vocabularies as follows:

4th Declension
aestus, -ūs (*m*), heat
aquaeductus, -ūs (*m*), aqueduct
arcus, -ūs (*m*), arch
domus, -ūs (*f*), house
lātrātus, -ūs (*m*), barking
manus, -ūs (*f*), hand
rīsus, -ūs (*m*), smile, laugh
sonitus, -ūs (*m*), sound
strepitus, -ūs (*m*), noise, clattering
tumultus, -ūs (*m*), uproar, commotion

5th Declension
diēs, -ēī (*m*), day
rēs, reī (*f*), thing, matter, situation

Most 4th declension nouns are masculine; most 5th declension nouns are feminine.

69

Latin Phrases Used in English

ante meridiem, *before noon*
post meridiem, *after noon*
per diem, *a daily allowance for expenses*
in medias res, *into the middle of things*
in situ, *in its original place*

Exercise 24a

Read aloud and translate:

1. Mediā nocte tumultum magnum audīvī. Quae erat causa huius tumultūs?
   Magnō cum strepitū bovēs plaustra per viās trahēbant. Prīmum strepitus
   procul aberat; deinde in viā nostrā erat tumultus.
   huius, of this
   absum, abesse (*irreg.*), **āfuī,** to be away, absent, be distant

2. Multās rēs manibus nostrīs facimus. Eucleidēs manū stilum tenēbat, nam
   puerōs scrībere docēbat. Puerī arborēs manibus et pedibus anteā ascen-
   derant. Manūs igitur eōrum sordidae erant. Eucleidēs eōs iussit manūs
   statim lavāre.
   stilus, -ī (*m*), pen   **eōrum,** their

3. Abhinc multōs diēs illa domus incēnsa est. Itaque dominus, quod mūrī
   domūs īnfirmī erant, domum novam ibi aedificāre cōnstituit. Ille dominus
   est senātor quī multās domūs in urbe habet. Omnēs eius domūs sunt
   magnae, sed domus nova erit omnium maxima. In hāc domō senātor ipse
   habitābit.
   incēnsa est, was burned

4. Multōs diēs in vīllā manēbāmus. Vēnit tamen diēs reditūs. Necesse erat
   iter septem diērum facere quod ad urbem celerrimē redīre volēbāmus. Eō
   diē discessimus. Sex diēs per Viam Appiam iter faciēbāmus. Septimō diē
   Rōmam pervēnimus.
   reditus, -ūs (*m*), return   **eō diē,** on that day
   discēdō, discēdere, (3), **discessī, discessum,** to go away, depart

5. Titus rem mīram nōbīs nārrāvit. Servus, quī nocte per viās urbis ambulābat,
   subitō fūgit perterritus. Quae erat causa huius reī? In viā occurrerat canī
   quī, ut ipse dīxit, tria capita habēbat. Dē tālibus rēbus in librīs saepe
   legimus sed numquam tālem rem ipsī vīdimus. Dē hāc rē omnēs cīvēs
   multās fābulās nārrant.
   caput, capitis (*n*), head
   fugiō, fugere (3), **fūgī, fugitum,** to flee
   legō, legere (3), **lēgī, lēctum,** to read

70

Selections from Catullus and Horace

I

Vīvāmus, mea Lesbia, atque amēmus,
rūmōrēsque senum sevēriōrum
omnēs ūnius aestimēmus assis!
Sōlēs occidere et redīre possunt;
nōbīs cum semel occidit brevis lūx,
nox est perpetua ūna dormienda.

Let us live, my Lesbia, and let us love,
and let us value all the gossips of the stern old men
as worth but a penny.
The sun is able to set and rise again;
for us when once our brief light has set,
one eternal night must be slept.

(Catullus, V.1–6)

II

Tū nē quaesieris—scīre nefās—quem mihi, quem tibi
fīnem dī dederint, Leuconoē, . . . Dum loquimur, fūgerit invida
aetās: carpe diem, quam minimum crēdula posterō.

Don't inquire—it's wrong to know—what length of life the gods
have granted to you and to me, Leuconoe, . . . While we are talking, envious
time has fled; seize the day, putting as little trust as possible in the future.

(Horace, *Odes* I.11–2 and 7–8)

III

Sunt quōs curriculō pulverem Olympicum
collēgisse iuvat mētaque fervidīs
ēvītāta rotīs palmaque nōbilis
terrārum dominōs ēvehit ad deōs.

Some people take pleasure in gathering
Olympic dust on the racetrack. When they narrowly
avoid the turning posts with their hot wheels, the noble
palm of victory exalts them as masters of the earth to the level of the gods.

(Horace, *Odes* I.1.3–6)

Rome

Impressions of Rome

What nation is so far distant, Caesar, or so barbarous that it does not have a representative at the games here in your city? Here come farmers from the Balkans, natives of South Russia nurtured on horse's blood, people from the banks of the Nile, as well as those from the Atlantic's farthest shores. Here too are Arabs, men from Southern Turkey, German tribesmen, and Ethiopians—all so different in dress and in appearance. Their speech too sounds all different; yet it is all one when you are hailed, Caesar, as the true father of our country.

Martial, *De spectaculis* III

72

Caecilius, in your own eyes you are a polished gentleman, but take my word
for it, you are not. What are you then? A clown! You are like the hawker
from across the Tiber who trades pale brimstone matches for broken glass
or the man who sells to the idle bystanders soggy pease-pudding; like the
keeper and trainer of snakes or the cheap slaves of the salt-sellers; like the
hoarse-voiced seller of smoking sausages with his hot trays or a third-class
street poet.

Martial, *Epigrams* I.41

If duty calls, the crowd gives way and the rich man is borne along rapidly
over their heads by stout Liburnian bearers. On the way he will read, write,
or sleep, for with the windows shut the litter induces sleep. Even so, he will
get there before us. Though we hurry, the sea of humanity in front hinders
us, and the great throng following jostles our backs. One man strikes us
with his elbow, another with a hard pole; one knocks a beam against our
heads, another a barrel. Our legs are plastered with mud, we are trampled
on all sides by great feet, a soldier's hob-nailed boot crushes my toe. Newly
patched togas are torn. A tall fir tree sways as the wagon rumbles on. Other
carts carry pine trees, a nodding menace over the heads of the crowd. If the
cart carrying Ligurian stone tilts forward and pours its overturned pile on
the crowds, what remains of their bodies?

Juvenal, *Satires* III.239

The Streets of Rome

Roman houses were neither named nor numbered. Hence the very complicated instructions given to those wishing to reach a certain "address":

> Every time you meet me, Lupercus, you ask, "May I send a slave to fetch your book of poems? I'll return it as soon as I've read it." Lupercus, it's not worth troubling your slave. It's a long journey to the Pear Tree, and I live up three flights of steep stairs. You can find what you want closer to home. No doubt you often go down to the Argiletum. There's a shop opposite Caesar's Forum with both door-posts covered with advertisements so that you can in a moment read the names of all the poets. Look for me there.
>
> Martial, *Epigrams* I.117

SYRUS: I don't know the man's name, but I know where he lives.

DEMEA: Then tell me where.

SYRUS: Down here. You know the colonnade by the butcher's?

DEMEA: Of course I do.

SYRUS: Go straight up the street that way; a bit along there's a slope facing you; down there and after that, on this side here, there's a shrine with an alley beside it.

DEMEA: Where?

SYRUS: Near where the big wild fig-tree grows.

DEMEA: I've got it.

SYRUS: Down there.

DEMEA: But that's a dead end!

SYRUS: Ugh! What an idiot I am! I've made a mistake. Come right back to the colonnade again. Here's a much quicker and more direct route. Do you know the house of rich Cratinus?

DEMEA: Yes.

SYRUS: Go past it, down a street to the left; turn right at Diana's temple. Before you reach the gate, near the pool, there's a bakery with a carpenter's opposite. He's there.

> Terence, *Adelphi* 571

Domitian, who followed Titus as Emperor of Rome, issued an edict forbidding shopkeepers to display their wares on the streets. This, according to Martial, was a vast improvement:

> The aggressive shopkeepers had taken the whole city away from us and never kept to the limits of their thresholds. But you, Domitian, ordered our narrowed streets to expand and what had been but a path has now become a street. No longer do they chain wine bottles to the pillars in front of their shops, and no longer are officials forced to walk in the middle of the mud. No longer does the barber blindly draw his razor in a dense crowd, and no longer do the greasy fast-food shops take up the whole street. The barbers, bartenders, cooks, and butchers now keep to their own thresholds. Now Rome is a city again, whereas before it was just one big shop.
>
> Martial, *Epigrams* VII.61

Columns and Porticos

The column was one of the main features of Roman architecture. Sometimes a single column was used to support a statue; more often, columns were used to support the roofs or to form the entrance-porches of temples and other buildings.

From the idea of the porch, there developed the portico or long covered walk which afforded the citizens protection from sun and dust, while allowing them to enjoy the fresh air. In the shelter of the portico various activities took place. The Portico of Minucius was used as a corn-exchange; in another a vegetable market was held. In the porticos philosophers lectured, poets recited, schoolmasters held their classes, lawyers met their clients, entertainers performed, snacks were sold, and business deals were concluded. In fact, porticos became so common that it was eventually possible to walk from one end of the city to the other without coming out into the open at all!

According to one writer, porticos covered more than a quarter of the total area of the Campus Martius, the number of columns supporting them being about 2000. Halls built in the shelter of these housed wall-maps of Rome and the Roman world, exhibitions of wonders from the Far East, natural marvels such as a snake 23 yards or 21 meters long, and, in the Portico of Philippus, a display of wigs and the latest in ladies' hairstyles.

Exercise 24b

Take parts, read aloud, and translate:

SEXTUS: Quam dēfessus sum, Marce! Nam hodiē māne dormīre nōn poteram.
Tantus clāmor in viīs erat.
MARCUS: Quālem clāmōrem audīvistī? Ego certē nihil clāmōris audīvī.
SEXTUS: Quid? Nōnne audīvistī illōs canēs in viīs lātrantēs? Multās hōrās lātrā-
bant. Numquam audīvī tantum strepitum. Audīvī etiam clāmōrem mul- 5
tōrum hominum quī per viās currēbant.
MARCUS: Quid clāmābant?
SEXTUS: Id audīre nōn poteram, nam omnēs simul clāmābant. Certē tamen īrātī
erant. Erat quoque strepitus plaustrōrum. Nōs in urbe heri plaustra nōn
vīdimus. Unde vēnērunt plaustra? 10
MARCUS: Interdiū nōn licet plaustra intrā urbem agere. Nocte igitur necesse est
labōrāre. Servī in urbem ferēbant cibum, vīnum, lapidēs —
SEXTUS: Cūr lapidēs intrā urbem tulērunt?
MARCUS: Caesar cōnstituit ingēns amphitheātrum in urbe aedificāre.
SEXTUS: Nōs illud aedificium vīdimus? 15
MARCUS: Heri illud cōnspexistī, ubi ad Forum cum patre meō dēscendēbāmus.
Heri nōn satis temporis erat id īnspicere quod pater domum festīnābat.
Sed mox amphitheātrum iterum vīsitābimus atque id īnspiciēmus. For-
tasse Eucleidēs nōs dūcet.
SEXTUS: Dum hoc mihi dīcis, multī hominēs in domum vēnērunt. Quī sunt? 20
MARCUS: Nōnne heri in urbe vīdistī multōs cīvēs post senātōrem sequentēs? Hic
erat patrōnus, illī erant clientēs. Pater meus est patrōnus multōrum
cīvium. Tū audīvistī clientēs domum intrantēs.
SEXTUS: Ēheu! Eucleidēs quoque intrāvit!

> vīnum, -ī (n), wine   sequentēs, following
> īnspiciō, īnspicere (3), īnspexī, īnspectum, to examine

Patrōnī were wealthy men who gave food or money to their dependents
(**clientēs**). The **clientēs** came to the patron's home early in the morning to
receive this dole and then escorted him to the Forum and performed other
services for him. Here is Juvenal's satirical comment:

> Now the meager dole sits on the outer edge of the threshold of the patron's
> house to be snatched up by the clients in their togas. But first the patron
> inspects each face, fearing that someone might come and claim his due
> under a false name. Once he recognizes you, you'll get your share.
>
> Juvenal, *Satires* I.95–99

Eucleides
the Statistician

Marcus had always visualized himself showing Sextus around the city of Rome, but he should have realized that Cornelius would never allow Sextus and himself to wander around Rome unsupervised. If neither Cornelius nor Titus was free to act as guide, Eucleides was bound to be their companion. He certainly knew a lot; the trouble was, there was no stopping him.

"Rome," Eucleides was now saying in that affected Greek voice of his, "is built on seven hills, the most famous being the Capitol and the Palatine. By now, of course, it has far outstripped these petty limits. Augustus divided it into fourteen regions, which are in turn subdivided into 265 **vīcī** or wards. At the last census the population numbered 1,284,602, living in 1,797 **domūs** and 46,602 **īnsulae.**"

"I can't see any islands!" complained Sextus, in all seriousness.

"**Īnsulae,**" explained Eucleides, "are those ramshackle tenements where all the riff-raff live."

"And **Īnsula Feliculae** is the biggest in the world," said Marcus.

"There are," said Eucleides, "64 miles of streets, using your Roman measurements."

"Not very wide, are they?" commented Sextus.

"Maximum width according to *The Twelve Tables* was only 17 feet."

"And some of them are not even paved!" cried Sextus, peering along the dark tunnel they were now traversing between the **īnsulae.**

"Watch out!" yelled Marcus, pulling Sextus and Eucleides close to the wall to dodge a deluge of slops from a third-floor window.

"We'll have the law on you for that!" shouted Marcus up at the unseen law-breaker. But Eucleides, not anxious to linger bandying threats, hustled the boys off through the labyrinth of shadowy alleys.

Suddenly they emerged into the blinding sun of the open Forum.

"This," said Eucleides impressively, pointing to a massive column, "is the center of the universe, the *Golden Milestone*. Erected by Augustus, it bears upon it in letters of gilt bronze the distances to all the cities of the Empire."

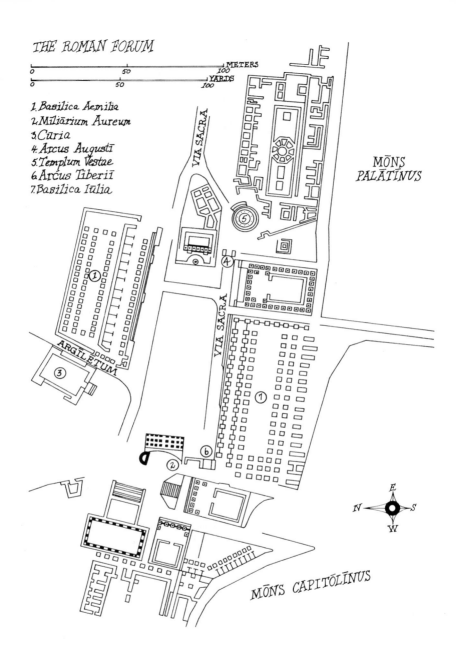

THE ROMAN FORUM

1. Basilica Aemilia
2. Miliārium Aureum
3. Cūria
4. Arcus Augustī
5. Templum Vestae
6. Arcus Tiberiī
7. Basilica Iūlia

METERS
YARDS

VIA SACRA

VIA SACRA

ARGILETUM

MŌNS PALĀTĪNUS

MŌNS CAPITŌLĪNUS

N E S W

But it was not the *Golden Milestone* the boys were looking at, nor was it the splendor of the Capitol behind them. They were gazing down at the **Forum Rōmānum** which glittered with marble and bronze and gold. Senators and businessmen with their slaves were hurrying in and out of the **basilicae** that flanked the Forum. The noise was deafening. Cries of sausage-sellers and pastry-vendors mingled with the uproar of every language under heaven. White toga and tunic jostled with all kinds of colors of outlandish garb.

Eucleides, sensing their preoccupation, was just pursing his lips to launch out on a lecture on the Forum; but Marcus and Sextus were off, scampering along the **Via Sacra.**

"Come and tell us what's going on here!" they shouted, running to the far end of the Forum where their attention had been caught by the feverish activity of an army of masons engaged, amidst mountains of rubble and building stone, in some mammoth task of demolition or construction—it was hard to tell which.

"The Emperor Nero—" began Eucleides breathlessly as he caught up with them.

"I know," said Marcus. "He's the one that set Rome on fire for fun."

"The Emperor Nero," Eucleides repeated, "on the space cleared of unsightly hovels by a quite accidental fire, built the wonderful **Domus Aurea.**"

"And they're still working at it by the look of it!" said Sextus, grinning.

"No, you idiot!" said Marcus. "Vespasian and Titus pulled down parts of Nero's folly and are putting up things for the citizens of Rome to enjoy, baths, for instance, and—"

"And that terrific statue over there?" pointed Sextus.

"That was a statue of Nero himself," Marcus went on, "but Vespasian put rays around its head and made it into a statue of the sun-god."

"It is 118 feet high," began Eucleides, but his hearers were gone again, towards an immense building under construction.

"What's this?" they asked, as an exhausted Eucleides caught up with them.

"This is the **Amphitheātrum Flāvium,**" he gasped. "The Emperor Titus is to dedicate it in June."

25

A Grim Lesson

Eucleidēs et puerī iam domum redierant. Post cēnam Cornēlius et Marcus
et Sextus in ātriō sedēbant.

"Quid hodiē vīdistis, puerī?" inquit Cornēlius.

"Nihil nisi aedificia antīqua," respondit Marcus. "Nōs in urbem exīre
volumus sōlī. Cūr nōn licet?"   5

Cui Cornēlius, "Est perīculōsum sine custōde exīre in viās huius urbis.
Sunt multī hominēs scelestī quī bona cīvium arripiunt. Nōnnumquam hī
hominēs cīvēs ipsōs necant. Vōbīs igitur nōn licet sine custōde exīre. Iam
sērō est. Nunc necesse est vōbīs cubitum īre. Nōlīte cessāre sed īte statim!"

Puerī, labōre diēī dēfessī, simulac cubitum īvērunt, obdormīvērunt.   10

Postrīdiē māne Marcus in lectō suō iacēbat et dē Circō Maximō ita
cōgitābat: "Quandō Circum Maximum vīsitābimus? Cūr pater meus nōs
exīre vetat? Herī nūllōs hominēs scelestōs in urbe vīdī. Interdiū certē praedōnēs nōbīs nōn nocēbunt. Meum patrem, quod est senātor Rōmānus,
praedōnēs timent. Nihil perīculī est."   15

Brevī tempore, ut Marcō vidēbātur, puerī ad Circum ībant. Mox mōlem
ingentem Circī Maximī Marcus cōnspexit.

"Ecce!" clāmāvit Marcus. "Est Circus. Ubi intrāverimus, tandem aurīgās
ipsōs spectābimus."

Subitō tamen in viam sē praecipitāvērunt trēs hominēs.   20

"Cavē illōs hominēs!" clāmāvit Sextus. "Illī certē nōs in domūs vīcīnās
trahent et ibi nōs necābunt."

Sed frūstrā, nam Marcus, metū commōtus, postquam Sextum audīvit
clāmantem, ad terram cecidit et iacēbat in lutō immōbilis.

"Eho!" clāmāvit ūnus ē praedōnibus. "Quō abīs, parvule? Quid est nōmen   25
tuum? Nōnne tū fīlius es senātōris? Nōnne nōmen tuum est Marcus Cornēlius?"

Cui Marcus, "Quid vultis, scelestī? Nihil pecūniae habeō. Nōlīte mē
verberāre! Sī mihi nocueritis, pater meus certē vōs pūniet."

Sed interpellāvit praedō, "Tacē, puer! Tū es captīvus noster neque ad   30
patrem redībis. Nēmō nunc poterit tē servāre. Ipse enim tē necābō."

Tum praedō gladium strīnxit. Marcus stābat perterritus et, "Fer auxilium!" clāmāvit. "Fer auxilium!" Sed nēmō clāmōrem audīvit. Nēmō auxilium tulit. Marcus oculōs clausit et mortem exspectābat.

Nihil accidit. Oculōs aperuit. In lectō erat suō. Somnium modo fuerat.   35
Hodiē tamen domī manēre cōnstituit Marcus. Exīre nōluit.

ātrium, -ī (n), atrium, central room
in a Roman house
nisi, unless, except
sine (+ abl.), without
custōs, custōdis (m), guard
bona, bonōrum (n pl), goods, pos-
sessions
nōnnumquam, sometimes
postrīdiē, on the following day
iaceō (2), to lie, be lying down
noceō (2) (+ dat.), to harm
ut Marcō vidēbātur, as it seemed to
Marcus, as Marcus thought
intrāverimus, we will have entered,
we enter

metū commōtus, moved by fear, in
a panic
terra, -ae (f), earth, ground
lutum, -ī (n), mud
parvulus, -a, -um, little
nocueritis, you will have harmed,
you harm
neque, and . . . not
servō (1), to save
gladius, -ī (m), sword
oculus, -ī (m), eye
mors, mortis (f), death
domī, at home

arripiō, arripere (3), arripuī, arreptum, to snatch, seize
vetō, vetāre (1), vetuī, vetitum, to forbid
stringō, stringere (3), strīnxī, strictum, to draw
claudō, claudere (3), clausī, clausum, to shut
accidit, accidere (3), accidit, (it) happens
aperiō, aperīre (4), aperuī, apertum, to open
nōlō, nōlle (irreg.), nōluī, to be unwilling, not to wish, refuse

Exercise 25a

Respondē Latīnē:

1. Quid puerī in urbe hodiē vīdērunt?
2. Cūr nōn licet puerīs exīre in urbem sōlīs?
3. Quid faciunt hominēs scelestī in viīs urbis?
4. Quōcum puerīs licet exīre in urbem?
5. Quid Cornēlius puerōs statim facere iubet?
6. Quā dē rē Marcus postrīdiē in lectō cōgitābat?
7. Timetne Marcus interdiū in urbem exīre?
8. Praedōnēsne Marcō et Sextō interdiū nocēbunt?
9. Quem praedōnēs timēbunt?
10. Quō ībant puerī?
11. Quid Marcus cōnspexit?
12. Quī sē in viam praecipitāvērunt?
13. Quid fēcit Marcus postquam Sextum clāmantem audīvit?
14. Quid pater Marcī faciet sī praedōnēs Marcō nocuerint?
15. Cūr praedō gladium strīnxit?
16. Quis vēnit ubi Marcus clāmāvit?

Quōcum . . . ? With whom . . . ?

DEMONSTRATIVE ADJECTIVES: **Hic** and **Ille**

Look at the following sentences:

Ille tabellārius equōs vehementer incitāvit.

That courier fiercely whipped the horses on.

Quis in **illō** aedificiō habitat?

Who lives in **that** building over there?

Hī canēs lātrant modo.

These dogs are only barking.

Est perīculōsum in viās **huius** urbis exīre.

It is dangerous to go out into the streets of **this** city.

Sextus, **hīs** clāmōribus et **hōc** strepitū excitātus, dormīre nōn poterat.

Roused by **these** shouts and **this** noise, Sextus could not sleep.

You will see from the above examples that both **hic** and **ille** are used to point out someone or something. **Hic** points to someone or something near at hand or near in time, while **ille** points to someone or something further away or "over there" or distant in time.

Here is a table showing all the cases of **hic** ("this," "these") and **ille** ("that," "those") in masculine, feminine, and neuter genders:

Number Case	Masc.	Fem.	Neut.	Masc.	Fem.	Neut.
Singular						
Nominative	hic	haec	hoc	ille	illa	illud
Genitive	huius	huius	huius	illīus	illīus	illīus
Dative	huic	huic	huic	illī	illī	illī
Accusative	hunc	hanc	hoc	illum	illam	illud
Ablative	hōc	hāc	hōc	illō	illā	illō
Plural						
Nominative	hī	hae	haec	illī	illae	illa
Genitive	hōrum	hārum	hōrum	illōrum	illārum	illōrum
Dative	hīs	hīs	hīs	illīs	illīs	illīs
Accusative	hōs	hās	haec	illōs	illās	illa
Ablative	hīs	hīs	hīs	illīs	illīs	illīs

Be sure you know all of the above forms.

Exercise 25b

Using story 25 as a guide, give the Latin for:

1. It is dangerous to go out into the streets of this city.
2. Why does my father forbid us to visit the Circus Maximus?
3. Watch out for those men!
4. You are our prisoner and no one will be able to save you.

Exercise 25c

Choose the proper form of **hic** *or* **ille** *to fill each blank, and then read the sentence aloud and translate:*

1. Cornēliī in _____ villā habitant.
2. "Spectāte _____ arcum, puerī!" clāmāvit Eucleidēs.
3. Ōlim _____ puellae in agrīs ambulābant.
4. Vīlicus cibum _____ servō nōn dabit.
5. "Vīdistīne _____ aedificium, Marce?" inquit Sextus.
6. Raeda _____ mercātōris prope tabernam manet.
7. Māne _____ canēs ferōciter lātrābant.
8. Bona _____ rūsticōrum in raedā erant.
9. Ūnus ex _____ praedōnibus gladium strīnxit.
10. Nōbīs _____ arborēs ascendere nōn licet.
11. _____ rem explicāre nōn possum.
12. _____ strepitus Marcum nōn excitāvit.

Exercise 25d

Read aloud and translate:

1. Hic puer in hāc viā, ille puer in illā viā habitat.
2. Illa puella in hāc vīllā habitat; hī puerī in illā vīllā habitant.
3. Nōnne illud aedificium mox ad terram cadet?
4. Sī in hāc caupōnā pernoctābimus, hic caupō nōbīs certē nocēbit.
5. Illī praedōnēs illōs viātōrēs sub hīs arboribus petunt.
6. Quandō illī servī haec onera in vīllam portābunt?
7. Nōlī illud plaustrum in hanc urbem interdiū agere!
8. Huic puerō multa dabimus, illī nihil.
9. Hīs rūsticīs licēbit agrōs huius vīllae colere.
10. Huic senātōrī ad Cūriam in lectīcā redīre necesse erat.
11. Illī aedificiō appropinquāre perīculōsum est, nam mūrī sunt īnfirmī.
12. Ūnus ex hīs praedōnibus aliquid illī servō dīcēbat.

VERBS: Future Perfect Tense

Look at these sentences:

Ubi **intrāverimus,** tandem aurīgās ipsōs spectābimus.
When we enter (**will have entered, have entered**), *we will finally watch the charioteers themselves.*
Sī mihi **nocueritis,** pater meus certē vōs pūniet.
If you harm (**will have harmed**) *me, my father will surely punish you.*

The verbs in boldface above are in the *future perfect tense.* The future perfect tense is used to express an action in the future which will be completed before another action will begin. Note that the Latin future perfect is often best translated by the present tense in English.

The endings of the future perfect tense are the same for *all* Latin verbs:

	1 -erō		1 -erimus
Singular	2 -eris	Plural	2 -eritis
	3 -erit		3 -erint

Note that, except for the third person plural, these endings are the same as the forms of the future tense of **esse.** These endings are added to the perfect stem, which is found by dropping the -ī from the end of the third principal part of the verb, e.g., **nocuī,** stem **nocu-.**

	1 nocu*erō*		1 nocu*erimus*
Singular	2 nocu*eris*	Plural	2 nocu*eritis*
	3 nocu*erit*		3 nocu*erint*

Exercise 25e

Read aloud and translate:

1. Sī illud baculum coniēceris, hī canēs ferōciter lātrābunt.
2. Ubi ad Portam Capēnam advēnerimus, ē raedā dēscendēmus.
3. Sī equī raedam ē fossā extrāxerint, Cornēliī ad urbem iter facere poterunt.
4. Nisi caupō alium lectum in cubiculum mōverit, Aurēlia ibi dormīre nōlet.
5. Crās puerī, ubi surrēxerint, strepitum plaustrōrum audient.

moveō, movēre (2), **mōvī, mōtum,** to move

26
A Visit to the Races

Chariot-racing (**lūdī circēnsēs**) was perhaps the most popular spectacle in ancient Rome. It was held in the **Circus Maximus,** a huge open-air stadium in the valley between the Palatine and the Aventine hills. It could hold about 200,000 spectators, seated in tiers around the long course (**arēna**).

It has been estimated that at one time some 90 holidays (**fēriae**) were given over to games at public expense. On these days the citizens were "celebrating a holiday" (**fēriātī**).

A barrier (**spīna**) ran down the center of the course, and the chariots (**quadrīgae**), each pulled by four horses, had to complete seven laps, about five miles or eight kilometers in all. Fouling was permitted, and collisions were frequent, especially at the turning posts (**mētae**). A race began when the Emperor or presiding official gave the signal (**signum**) by dropping a white cloth (**mappa**).

The charioteers, some of whom won great popularity and very high salaries, were employed by four companies (**factiōnēs**), each with its own color—the "Reds" (**russātī**), the "Whites" (**albātī**), the "Greens" (**prasinī**), and the "Blues" (**venetī**). Rival groups of spectators were accustomed to show their support (**favēre**) for each color vociferously.

One charioteer we hear about, Gaius Apuleius Diocles, drove chariots for the Red Stable for twenty-four years, ran 4,257 starts, and won 1,462 victories.

No wonder Marcus, Cornelia, and Sextus are eager to go to the races! As we return to our story, three days after the Cornelii arrived in Rome, Sextus is sitting alone when suddenly Marcus rushes in.

MARCUS:	Sexte! Sexte! Hodiē nōbīs licet ad lūdōs circēnsēs īre. Eucleidēs mē et tē et Cornēliam ad Circum dūcet.
SEXTUS:	Lūdōs circēnsēs amō. Sed nōnne Circus clausus erit?
MARCUS:	Minimē! Circus nōn erit clausus, nam hodiē cīvēs omnēs fēriātī sunt. Viae erunt plēnae hominum. Virī, mulierēs, 5 līberī Circum celerrimē petent.
SEXTUS:	Sed cūr nōn nunc discēdimus? Ego sum iam parātus.
MARCUS:	Simulac Cornēlia ē somnō surrēxerit, statim ībimus.

mulier, mulieris (*f*), woman

(Much to the boys' disgust, Cornelia was rather late in waking up from her siesta, but soon they were all ready to leave.)

85

EUCLEIDĒS: Agite! Iam tandem ad Circum īre tempus est. Estisne parātī,
             puerī? Esne parāta, Cornēlia?   10

             *(Eucleides takes Cornelia and the boys quickly through
             the streets; they can now hear the noise of the Circus
             crowds.)*

EUCLEIDĒS: Iam ā Circō nōn procul absumus. Nōnne strepitum audītis?
             Ecce! Omnēs ad Circum festīnant. Brevī tempore nōs ipsī
             intrābimus.

             (They enter the Circus.)

CORNĒLIA: Quam ingēns est turba hominum! Tōtus Circus est plēnus
             spectātōrum.   15

EUCLEIDĒS: Ita vērō! Semper multī spectātōrēs in Circō sunt. Hīc cōn-
             sīdēmus?

MARCUS: Minimē! Prope arēnam sedēre necesse est quod ibi omnia
             vidēre poterimus.

             tōtus, -a, -um, all, the whole

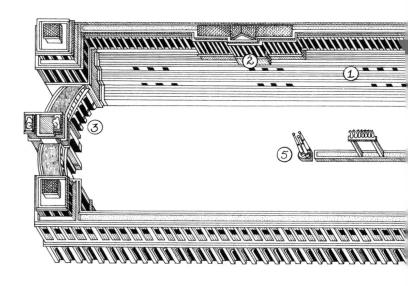

EUCLEIDĒS:	At prope arēnam sedēre perīculōsum est. Pater vester multa	20
	dē perīculō dīxit.	
MARCUS:	Nihil perīculī est, nam Titus, patruus meus, cum amīcīs	
	prope arēnam sedēre solet.	
SEXTUS:	Ecce! Caesar ipse iam surrēxit; signum dare parat. Ego	
	russātīs favēbō.	25
MARCUS:	Ego albātīs.	
CORNĒLIA:	Ego venetīs.	
MARCUS:	Ecce! Mappa! Signum est!	
CORNĒLIA:	Quam ferōciter equōs verberant illī aurīgae! Quam celeriter	
	equōs agunt! Quam temerāriī sunt! Nōnne mortem timent?	30
SEXTUS:	Ecce! Russātus meus certē victor erit, nam equōs magnā	
	arte agit.	

faveō, favēre (2), fāvī, fautum (+ *dat.*), to favor, support

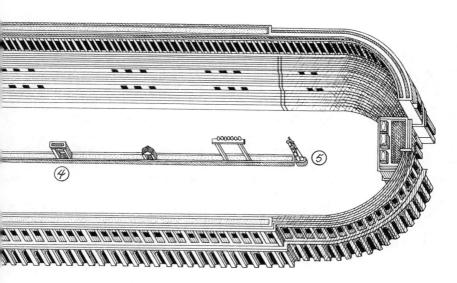

1. *Spectators' seats*
2. *Emperor's and distinguished guests' seats*
3. *Carcerēs (stalls)*
4. *Spina (low platform)*
5. *Metae (turning posts)*

MARCUS:	Ō mē miserum! Aurīga meus equōs dēvertit. Cavē mētam! Cavē mētam! Esne sēmisomnus, fatue? Cūr mētam nōn vītāvistī?	35
CORNĒLIA:	Ēheu! Ille aurīga cecidit. In arēnā iacet. Estne mortuus?	
SEXTUS:	Minimē! Minimē! Ecce! Animum recuperāvit. Iam surgit.	
CORNĒLIA:	Audīvistisne clāmōrēs hōrum spectātōrum? Magnā vōce nōmina aurīgārum et equōrum semper clāmant! Undique ingēns est strepitus! Tantum strepitum ego numquam au-dīvī.	40
MARCUS:	Russātī hanc victōriam habent, sed mox etiam albātī ha-bēbunt victōriam. Glōria albātōrum erit immortālis.	
EUCLEIDĒS:	Hoc fortasse accidet, sed Caligula ipse, ut dīcunt, prasinōs amābat.	

dēvertō, dēvertere (3), **dēvertī, dēversum,** to turn aside

88

(They watch a few more races, but it is not Marcus' lucky day. Eucleides becomes a little anxious as it grows later. He had been caught once before in a crush at the gates.)

EUCLEIDĒS: Iam sērō est. Nunc domum redībimus.
SEXTUS: Nōndum tempus est domum redīre. Ecce! Aurīgae habēnās sūmpsērunt et signum exspectant.
EUCLEIDĒS: Nisi mox discēdēmus, turbam ingentem vītāre nōn poterimus. Agite! Domum!

PREFIXES: *Compound Verbs*

Compare the following sentences:

1. Equī raedam **trahunt**.
   The horses **pull** *the coach.*
2. Servī lectum **ferēbant**.
   The slaves **were carrying** *the bed.*

1. Equī raedam **extrahunt**.
   The horses **pull out** *the coach.*
2. Servī lectum **referēbant**.
   The slaves **were carrying back** *the bed.*

In the right-hand column a prefix has been added to the beginning of the verb to give it a more specific meaning. Verbs with prefixes attached to them are called *compound verbs.* Common prefixes are:

ab-, abs-, ā-, away, from
ad-, towards, to
circum-, around
con-, along with, together (or simply to emphasize)
dē-, down, down from
dis-, dī-, apart, in different directions
ex-, ē-, out, out of
in-, into, in, on

inter-, between
per-, through (or simply to emphasize)
prae-, in front, ahead
praeter-, past, beyond
prō-, prōd-, forward
re-, red-, back, again
sub-, under, below
trāns-, trā- across

Note that many of these are common prepositions.

Be sure to learn these prefixes thoroughly.

Exercise 26a

Give the meaning of:

1. abesse, adesse, inesse, praeesse, subesse, interesse.
2. abīre, adīre, praeterīre, trānsīre, redīre, exīre, inīre, praeīre, subīre, circumīre.
3. referre, trānsferre, cōnferre, īnferre, praeferre, dēferre.
4. discēdere, excēdere, incēdere, recēdere, prōcēdere, intercēdere, praecēdere.

cēdo, cēdere (3), **cessī, cessum,** to come, go

Exercise 26b

Read aloud and translate:

1. Pater līberōs ē vīllā ēdūxit et trāns viam trādūxit.
2. Cornēlius Eucleidem iussit līberōs abdūcere.
3. Eucleidēs līberōs ad hortum redūxit.
4. Servī togās et tunicās in cistīs repōnunt.
5. Ubi ad Portam Capēnam veniunt, servī onera dēpōnunt.

90

6. Ubi plaustrum invēnit, stercus remōvit et corpus extrāxit.
7. Cornēliī Rōmam heri advēnērunt.
8. Homō per viam it. Mox viam transībit et ad vīllam redībit.
9. Ubi urbem intrāmus, necesse est Aquam Marciam subīre.
10. Puerī Circum relīquērunt et Palātīnum circumiērunt.
11. Nihil clāmōris, nihil strepitūs ad Marcum pervēnerat.
12. Puerōs, quod praecurrēbant, identidem revocābat Cornēlius.

Honorary Inscription

P. Aelius, Marī Rogātī fīl(ius), Gutta Calpurniānus equīs hīs vīcī in factiōne venetā: Germinātōre n(igrō) Ā(frō) LXXXXII, Silvānō r(ūfō) Āf(rō) CV, Nitid(ō) gil(vō) Āf(rō) LII, Saxōne n(igrō) Āf(rō) LX, et vīcī praemia m(aiōra) L̄ I, X̄L IX, X̄X̄X̄ XVII.

I, Publius Aelius Gutta Calpurnianus, son of Marius Rogatus, won for the Blue stable with the following horses: Germinator, African black, 92 (times); Silvanus, African chestnut, 105 (times); Glossy, African sorrel, 52 (times); Saxon, African black, 60 (times); and I won major purses of 50,000 sesterces (1), of 40,000 sesterces (9), and of 30,000 sesterces (17).

Sepulchral Inscription

D. M. Epaphrodītus agitātor f(actiōnis) r(ussātae), vīc(it) CLXXVIII, et ad purpureum līber(ātus) vīc(it) VIII. Beia Felicula f(ēcit) coniugī suō b(ene) merentī.

To the deified spirits (of) Epaphroditus, driver for the Red stable; he won 178 (times), and after being manumitted to the Purples he won 8 (times). Beia Felicula made (this monument) for her deserving husband.

Curses against Charioteers and Their Horses

Adiūrō tē daemōn quīcumque es et dēmandō tibi ex hāc hōrā ex hāc diē ex hōc mōmentō, ut equōs Prasinī et Albī cruciēs occīdās, et agitātōrēs Clārum et Fēlīcem et Prīmulum et Rōmānum occīdās collīdās, neque spīritum illīs relinquās.

I adjure you, demon, whoever you are, and I ask of you from this hour, from this day, from this moment, that you torture and kill the horses of the Green and the White, and that you kill and smash their drivers Clarus and Felix and Primulus and Romanus, and leave no breath in them.

Versiculī: "Medea," pages 103–105.

Word Study VII

Prefixes

Knowledge of Latin prefixes will help not only with the meanings of Latin compound verbs but also with the meanings of many English words derived from them. For example, when the Latin simple verb **portāre** is combined with various prefixes, the resulting compound verbs provide English with several words, e.g.:

deport (from **dēportāre**)	report (from **reportāre**)
export (from **exportāre**)	transport (from **trānsportāre**)

Relying on your knowledge of prefixes, can you tell the meaning of each of the English words above?

Some English words are derived from the infinitive stem of the Latin compound verb, e.g., *transport* (from **trānsportāre**). Others are derived from the supine stem, e.g., *transportation* (from **trānsportātum**). (For the suffix *-tion* see Word Study VI.)

Exercise 1

After each Latin simple verb below is a group of English verbs which are derived from Latin compounds of that simple verb. (The Latin compound verbs are in parentheses.) Give the meaning of each English verb:

dūcō, dūcere (3), dūxī, ductum

1. to conduct (**condūcere**)	4. to reduce (**redūcere**)
2. to induct (**indūcere**)	5. to produce (**prōdūcere**)
3. to deduct (**dēdūcere**)	6. to adduce (**addūcere**)

pōnō, pōnere (3), posuī positum

1. to propose (**prōpōnere**)	4. to depose (**dēpōnere**)
2. to dispose (**dispōnere**)	5. to transpose (**trānspōnere**)
3. to expose (**expōnere**)	6. to deposit (**dēpōnere**)

cēdō, cēdere (3), cessī, cessum

1. to precede (**praecēdere**)	*variant spelling:*
2. to recede (**recēdere**)	4. to proceed (**prōcēdere**)
3. to intercede (**intercēdere**)	5. to exceed (**excēdere**)

Note that **cēdere** can also mean *to yield*. From this meaning come the following English derivatives:

6. to cede (**cēdere**)	7. to concede (**concēdere**)

ferō, ferre *(irreg.)*, **tulī, lātum**

1. to refer (**referre**)
2. to infer (**īnferre**)
3. to defer (**dēferre**)
4. to transfer (**trānsferre**)
5. to confer (**cōnferre**)
6. to relate (**referre**)

Exercise 2

Give the infinitive of the Latin compound verb from which each of the following English nouns is derived. Use each English noun in a sentence which illustrates its meaning:

1. disposition
2. proponent
3. recess
4. inference
5. product
6. exposition
7. relation
8. procession
9. conference
10. precedent
11. translator
12. concession
13. deduction
14. referee
15. reference

Exercise 3

Each adjective in the pool below is derived from a Latin compound verb. Choose an adjective to fill each blank and give the Latin compound verb from which it is derived:

1. Eucleides provided an atmosphere for the boys that would lead them to learn. The atmosphere was _____ to learning.
2. The slave-woman, Syra, was shy and preferred not to socialize with the other slaves. Syra had a _____ personality.
3. Although the horses tried to pull the carriage out, their efforts brought forth no results. Their efforts were not _____.
4. Some masters treat their slaves with violence which goes beyond reasonable limits. Their use of violence is _____.
5. Davus was not unhappy, but he was not as happy as he might have been if he were not a slave. Davus enjoyed _____ happiness.
6. When Cornelius entered a shop, the merchant left the other customers and helped him immediately. Cornelius received _____ treatment.
7. After he considered all of the evidence, the overseer was certain which slave stole the money. The overseer used _____ reasoning to come to his conclusion.
8. When the emperor went by, all the citizens bowed respectfully. The emperor was greeted in a _____ manner.

relative	deferential	recessive	conducive
productive	excessive	preferential	deductive

93

Latin Abbreviations in English

Many abbreviations used in English are actually abbreviations of Latin words. For example, the common abbreviations for morning and afternoon, A.M. and P.M., stand for the Latin phrases **ante merīdiem** (*before noon*) and **post merīdiem** (*after noon*).

Exercise 4

With the aid of an English dictionary, give the full Latin words for the following abbreviations and explain how each is used in English:

1. etc.	4. i.e.	7. ad lib.	10. et al.
2. A.D.	5. e.g.	8. vs.	11. q.v.
3. P.S.	6. N.B.	9. cf.	12. ℞

Exercise 5

Replace the words in italics with abbreviations chosen from the list in Exercise 4 above:

1. The senators discussed the most critical problems first, *for example*, the revolt in Judea.
2. Titus was known for his ability to *speak at will* on almost any subject.
3. The eruption of Vesuvius occurred in *the year of our Lord* 79.
4. Titus pointed out the Curia, the Arch of Tiberius, *and the rest*, as they passed them.
5. The announcement of the chariot race read, "Reds *against* Blues."
6. Eucleides said that they would return early, *that is*, before the eleventh hour.
7. At the bottom of the letter Cornelius added an *afterthought*.
8. Cornelius had invited Titus, Messala, *and others*, to a dinner-party.
9. The abbreviation "B.C." is used to give dates before the birth of Christ. (*Compare* the abbreviation "A.D.")
10. A sign near the Porta Capena read, "*Note well:* It is forbidden to drive wagons or carriages within the city during the day."
11. "*Take this*" was written at the bottom of the doctor's prescription.
12. "*Which see*" is written after a word or topic which needs further explanation, and it directs the reader to find such explanation elsewhere in the book.

Find examples of Latin abbreviations in textbooks, newspapers, or magazines and bring them to class.

Review VI

Exercise VIa

From the list at the right select appropriate words to go with each of the following nouns. Give alternatives where requested.

1. _____ diem
2. _____ arbore
3. _____ lutum
4. _____ or _____ or _____ diēs
5. _____ fēminam
6. _____ terrās
7. _____ or _____ mandātō
8. _____ terra
9. _____ or _____ oculō
10. _____ arcuum
11. _____ somnia
12. _____ rīsū
13. _____ vōcum
14. _____ diē
15. _____ or _____ or _____ manūs
16. _____ capitum
17. _____ custōs
18. _____ or_____ reī
19. _____ or _____ or _____ tabernae
20. _____ rēbus
21. _____ caupōnī
22. _____ or _____ servī
23. _____ or _____ praedōnēs
24. _____ custōdum

hōs
hīs
hoc
huic
hunc
hōc
hās
huius
hārum
hāc
hic
hī
hanc
hae
haec
hōrum

Exercise VIb

From the pool of words below, choose an adjective to go with each noun in Exercise VIa above. Give the noun with the adjective in its proper form to modify the noun.

bonus, -a, -um	īrātus, -a, -um	parvulus, -a, -um
brevis, -is, -e	longus, -a, -um	pūrus, -a, -um
dēfessus, -a, -um	magnus, -a, -um	scelestus, -a, -um
prīmus, -a, -um	multī, -ae, -a	sēmisomnus, -a, -um
īnfirmus, -a, -um	novus, -a, -um	sordidus, -a, -um
ingēns, ingentis	omnis, -is, -e	vester, vestra, vestrum

Exercise VIc

Choose the correct form of the two choices in parentheses, read the sentence aloud, and translate it:

1. Sextus (illī, illō) arcuī appropinquāvit.
2. Mīles (illum, illud) gladium strīnxit.
3. Herculēs (illā, illō) manū Cerberum ex Īnferīs extrāxit.
4. Lātrātus (illum, illōrum) canum puerōs dormientēs excitāvit.
5. Cornēliī (illī, illō) diē Rōmam advēnērunt.

Exercise VId

Read the passage below and answer, in English, the questions that follow:

Porsinna, rēx Clūsīnōrum, urbem Rōmam iam diū obsidēbat. Rōmānī igitur, quod cibum in urbem afferre nōn poterant, fame perībant. Tum adulēscēns quīdam Rōmānus, Gāius Mūcius nōmine, quī cīvēs suōs servāre volēbat, Porsinnam necāre cōnstituit.

Itaque Mūcius, ubi Cūriam intrāvit, senātōribus, "Tiberim transīre," inquit, 5
"et castra hostium intrāre volō. Ibi Porsinnam petam et, sī dī adiuvābunt, eum necābō."

Cui senātōrēs, "Sī hoc facere vīs, nōs tē nōn vetāmus." Laetus domum rediit Mūcius. Gladium sūmpsit et intrā vestēs cēlāvit. Trāns Tiberim festīnāvit et in castra hostium clam intrāvit. Ibi magnam multitūdinem mīlitum vīdit. 10
Ad mēnsam sedēbant duo hominēs. Alter pecūniam mīlitibus dabat, alter spectābat. Sēcum cogitābat Mūcius, "Uter est rēx? Nōnne is est quī omnia facit? Illum necābō." Gladium strīnxit. Hominem necāvit. Stupuit turba adstantium. Ex castrīs paene effūgerat Mūcius cum custōdēs rēgis eum comprehendērunt. "Ō scelesti!" inquiunt. "Cūr scrībam rēgis necāvistī?" 15

"At rēgem," inquit Mūcius, "necāre voluī."

Rēx, ubi hoc audīvit, clāmāvit, "Ego tē gravissimē pūniam."

Superbē respondit Mūcius, "Cīvis sum Rōmānus. Mē Gāium Mūcium vocant. Cīvēs Rōmānī, quī magnam glōriam petunt, poenās nōn timent."

Forte Mūcius tum stābat prope ignem quī in altāribus erat. Subitō dextram 20
manum in ignem iniēcit. Statim rēx surrēxit et iussit custōdēs virum ab igne trahere. "Quamquam," inquit, "hostis es, tamen, quod vir fortissimus es, tē ad cīvēs tuōs iam remittō."

Postquam Mūcius Rōmam rediit, rem tōtam cīvibus narrāvit. Illī nōn modo Mūcium laudābant sed, quod iam sinistram modo manum habēbat, cognōmen 25
eī dedērunt Scaevolam.

rēx, rēgis (*m*), king
fame perīre, to die of hunger
adulēscēns, adulēscentis (*m*), young
  man
castra, -ōrum (*n pl*), camp
hostis, hostis (*m*), enemy
dī, deōrum (*m pl*), the gods
vestis, vestis (*f*), garment
clam, secretly
mēnsa, -ae (*f*), table
Uter . . . ? Utra . . . ?
  Utrum . . . ? Which . . . ?
  (of two)

paene, almost
scrība, -ae (*m*), clerk
gravissimē, very seriously
superbē, proudly
poena, -ae (*f*), punishment
forte, by chance
ignis, ignis (*m*), fire
altāria, altārium (*n pl*), altar
dexter, dextra, dextrum, right
fortissimus, -a, -um, very brave
sinister, sinistra, sinistrum, left
cognōmen, cognōminis (*n*), nickname, surname

obsideō, obsidēre (2), obsēdī, obsessum, to besiege
afferō, afferre (*irreg.*), attulī, allātum, to carry towards, bring
comprehendō, comprehendere (3), comprehendī, comprehēnsum, to seize,
  arrest
stupeō, stupēre (2), stupuī, to be astonished

1. What was the effect of King Porsinna's siege of Rome?
2. Who decided to kill Porsinna? Why?
3. What four things did he propose to do?
4. Did the senators grant permission? Quote the Latin words which support
  your answer.
5. Quote two words that show that Mucius was disguising his intentions as
  he went about his mission.
6. What was each of the two men at the table doing?
7. What made Mucius decide which of the two was the king?
8. Whom did the guards tell him he had killed?
9. Quote and translate the words which express the king's first reaction.
10. What boast did Mucius make about himself?
11. What boast did Mucius make about his fellow citizens?
12. What did he do to show he was not afraid?
13. What order did the king give the guards?
14. What reason did the king give for sending Mucius home?
15. Translate the clause **quod iam sinistram modo manum habēbat.**
16. What do you think is the meaning of the nickname "Scaevola"?

97

Exercise VIe

Give the appropriate future perfect form of each verb in parentheses, read the sentence aloud, and translate:

1. "Sī ego ad Cūriam sērō (advenīre), senātōrēs īrātī erunt," cōgitābat Cornēlius.
2. Ubi pater manūs (lavāre) et togam pūram (induere), ad Cūriam statim ībit.
3. "Nisi tū pecūniam nōbīs (dare), tē certē necābō," clāmāvit praedō.
4. Illōs praedōnēs, sī Marcō (nocēre), Cornēlius certē pūniet.
5. "Ubi fābulam mīlitis (audīre), pater, statim cubitum ībimus," inquit Marcus.

Exercise VIf

Give the requested forms of the following verbs in the present, imperfect, future, perfect, pluperfect, and future perfect tenses:

	Present	Imperfect	Future	Perfect	Pluperfect	Future Perfect
1. vetāre (1st pl.)						
2. aperīre (3rd pl.)						
3. stertere (2nd pl.)						
4. esse (3rd sing.)						
5. emō (3rd sing.)						
6. ferre (2nd sing.)						
7. arripere (1st sing.)						
8. docēre (1st sing.)						
9. posse (2nd sing.)						
10. velle (1st pl.)						

VERSICULĪ

10 Arrival at the Inn
(after Chapter 17)

Caupōnam petimus caupōque recēpit obēsus.
  "Hīc bene dormītur," dīcit, inīre iubēns.

recēpit, (he) welcomed (us)
bene dormītur, you'll sleep well
dīcō, dīcere (3), to say
ineō, inīre (*irreg.*), to come in
iubēns, bidding (us)

11 Murder
(after Chapter 20)

(i)

Septimus in somnō tē cōnspicit, Aule, necātum.
  Crās (ēheu!) in plaustrō trīste cadāver erit.

(ii)

"Fer, comes, auxilium!" clāmāvī, "Septime." Sed tū,
  "Somnia," dīxistī, "maesta fuēre modo."
Nunc, quod non illīs potuistī crēdere verbīs,
  nunc quaere in faenō corpus, amīce, meum!

(iii)

Cūr Marcus cubitum īre timet vigilatque etiam nunc?
  Quod puerum timidum fābula mīra movet.

erit, (it) will be
trīste cadāver, a wretched corpse
comes, comitis (*m/f*), companion
maestus, -a, -um, sad
fuēre = fuērunt
potuistī, you were able
illīs crēdere verbīs, to believe those words
quaerō, quaerere (3), **quaesīvī, quaesītum,** to look for
faenum, -ī (*n*), hay
mīrus, -a, -um, wonderful, strange

99

12 Procrustes

(after Chapter 23)

The young hero Theseus is making his way to Athens. During his journey, he has
met and overcome many giants, paying them in kind for their evil ways. He is almost
to the city when he encounters the last of the giants, Procrustes. The name means
"Stretcher." Why "Stretcher"? This the story reveals.

Longum iter est calidusque diēs. Stetit ille. Sinistrā
    parte videt magnam nōn procul inde domum.
"Rēx latrōnum habitat caupō-ne benignus in illā?"
    sē rogat. It propius. Iānua aperta manet.
In quā verba legit. "Salvē,"—sīc scrībitur—"hospes.   5
    Hīc bene dormītur. Hūc et adīre tibi—
sōlus sī veniēs—licet, hīc carnemque parātam
    sūmere et in lectō pōnere membra meō."
Intrāvit Thēseus. Carnem cōnsūmere multam
    audet et in lectō pōnere membra sua.   10
Mox obdormīvit. Parva est mora. Somnia vīdit:
    audent magna ambōs mōnstra tenēre pedēs!
Sollicitus somnīs sēsē excitat. Ecce, super sē
    cōnspexit hostem stāre minante manū.
Tālia quī magnā reprehendit vōce, "Viātor,   15
    sat iam audēs lectī, iam sat habēre cibī.
Quod dēbētur adest nōbīs iam solvere tempus!"
    Cui Thēseus, "Quid mē solvere, amīce, iubēs?"
"Tālia praebēbis," dīxit, "lūdibria nōbīs
    quālia iam hīc omnēs quī iacuēre prius.   20
Nam quōs inveniō prō lectīs esse minōrēs
    illōrum extendet māchina membra potēns.
Sed quī longa nimis praebēbit membra, necesse est
    aut illī caput aut ense secāre pedēs.
Haec in tē faciam!" dīxit gladiumque levābat.   25
    Quem Thēseus petiit corripuitque manū.
Nec longum sequitur certāmen membraque fiunt
    caupōnis lectīs ōcius apta suīs.

stō, stāre (1), stetī statum, to stand
sinister, sinistra, sinistrum, left (as opposed to right)
inde, from there
rēx, rēgis (m), king
latrō, latrōnis (m), thief
-ne, or
propius, nearer, closer
apertus, -a, -um, open
5 verbum, -ī (n), word
sīc scrībitur, thus it is written
bene dormītur, you'll sleep well
adeō, adīre (irreg.), adiī, aditum, to approach
carō, carnis (f), meat
membrum, -ī (n), limb
10 audeō, audēre (2), ausus sum, to dare
parvus, -a, -um, small, short
mora, -ae (f), delay, passage of time
ambō, -ae, -ō, both
mōnstrum, -ī (n), monster
pēs, pedis (m), foot
super (+ acc.), above
14 hostis, -is (m), enemy
minante manū, with threatening hand
quod dēbētur, what you owe
solvō, solvere (3), solvī, solūtum, to pay

tālia . . . quālia, such . . . as
praebeō (2), to offer, provide
lūdibrium, -ī (n), amusement, fun
20 iaceō (2), to lie, recline
(iacuēre = iacuērunt)
prius, before
prō (+ abl.), in relation to
minōrēs, smaller, shorter
māchina, -ae (f), machine
potēns, potentis, powerful
nimis, too
illī (dat.), for, of that (person)
caput, capitis (n), head
ensis, ensis (m), sword
secō, secāre (1), secuī, sectum, to cut
25 haec, these things
gladius, -ī (m), sword
levō (1), to raise
petiit = petīvit
corripiō, corripere (3), corripuī, correptum, to grab hold of, seize
sequitur, (it) follows
certāmen, certāminis (n), struggle, contest
fiunt, (they) become, are made
ōcius, quickly
aptus, -a, -um, fitted to, of a suitable length for (+ dat.)

101

Answer in Latin or English the following questions on Versiculī 12 (Procrustes):

1. Why do you think Theseus stopped (line 1)?
2. Where did he see a house?
3. What two questions does he ask himself (line 3)?
4. Is the house inviting (line 4)? How so?
5. What does the house promise (line 6)?
6. What restriction does the house place on its hospitality (line 7)?
7. What two things can a guest do in the house (lines 7–8)?
8. What four things does Theseus proceed to do (lines 9–11)?
9. What does he see in his dream (line 12)?
10. What does he see when he wakes up?
11. According to the speaker in line 16, of what two things has Theseus had enough?
12. What does Procrustes say it is time to do now (line 17)?
13. What must Theseus offer in payment for his food and rest (lines 19–20)?
14. What does Procrustes do with short people (lines 21–22)?
15. What does he do with people who are too tall (lines 23–24)?
16. Judging from line 25, were Theseus' limbs too short or too long?
17. What does Theseus do when Procrustes attacks him (line 26)?
18. What does Theseus do to Procrustes (lines 27–28)?

BONUS QUESTION: What clause early in the poem foreshadows trouble?

13 Medea
(after Chapter 26)

In order to win back the kingdom which was his by right, Jason was told to sail to the far land of Colchis and bring back the Golden Fleece which was guarded by a great and ever-watchful serpent. There the king, Aeëtes by name, was very unwilling to part with his priceless treasure and laid upon Jason a seemingly impossible task. He was to take two fire-breathing bulls, plough a field with them, and sow there a dragon's teeth, from which would immediately spring a nation of warriors bent on murdering him. King Aeëtes thought he had baffled Jason's attempt. Surely he would never face such a trial, or if he did there could be no doubt how things would turn out. But Aeëtes reckoned without the goddess of love, who put into his daughter's heart a fierce passion for the brave stranger. This daughter, Medea, was a sorceress and knew the secret powers of many herbs and spells. She smeared Jason with a magic ointment which provided an effective antidote to the bulls' fiery breath and told him, when the warriors sprang up to kill him, to throw a stone into their midst. They would be sure to blame one another and begin a fight which would end in their deaths at each other's hands. She used her magic also to charm the serpent and get away safely with Jason and the fleece in the good ship Argo.

Aeētae postquam audīvit crūdēlia verba
  hērōs, (heu!) stupuit conticuitque diū.
Verba patris nec nōn audīvit fīlia; nocte
  quae vēnit mediā, fīdaque verba dedit:
"Quod iubeō sī crās faciēs, et vīvus abīre   5
  aurea et incolumis vellera habēre potes.
Sed quamquam sēcūrus eris, simulāre timōrem
  dēbēbis multum fātaque flēre tua,
si tū mē, hospes, amās." Mīrō medicāmine corpus
  ūnxit amātōrī, mīraque multa docet.   10
Nōn magnus labor inde bovēs adiungere magnōs;
  illī flamma boum nūlla molesta fuit.
Parturiunt sulcī. Iam nascitur inde virōrum
  turba armātōrum magna. Nec ille fugit.
Saxa iacit. Socium culpābat quisque, sed ensem   15
  strīnxit. Mox mīles mortuus omnis erat.
Sed malus ingentī custōdit corpore serpēns,
  aurea nec quemquam vellera adīre sinit;
nam nōn clausa simul sunt omnia lūmina somnō:
  quot dormīre oculī, tot vigilāre solent.   20
At quid nōn, Mēdēa, potes medicāmine? Mōlēs
  serpentis somnō mox superāta iacet.

Aeētēs, -ae (m), King Aeëtes
crūdēlis, -is, -e, cruel
verbum, -ī (n), word
hērōs (the hero is Jason)
heu = ēheu
conticuit, (he) was silent
nec, and not
    nec nōn, also
quae, and she
fīdus, -a, -um, faithful, trustworthy
5 quod iubeō, what I tell you
vīvus, -a, -um, alive
vellera (n pl), fleece
sēcūrus, -a, -um, without fear
dēbēbis, you will have to
multus, -a, -um, much
fleō, flēre (3), flēvī, flētum,
    to lament over
mīrō medicāmine, with a strange
    ointment
corpus . . . amātōrī, her lover's
    body

10 unguō, unguere (3), ūnxī, ūnctum,
    to smear
inde, after that, from there
adiungō, adiungere (3), adiūnxī,
    adiūnctum, to yoke
boum, of the bulls
parturiunt sulcī, the furrows strain
    to give birth
nascitur, is born
armātus, -a, -um, armed
15 saxum, -ī (n), a boulder
socium culpābat quisque, each
    (of the armed men) began to
    blame his neighbor
ensis, ensis (m), sword
malus, -a, -um, evil
nec quemquam sinit, and does not
    allow anyone
lūmina, eyes
20 quot . . . tot, as many . . . so many
superātus, -a, -um, overcome

104

Answer in Latin or English the following questions on Versiculī 13 (Medea):

1. What was Jason's reaction to Aeetes' words (line 2)?
2. What word reveals the reason for this reaction?
3. What was the substance of these **crūdēlia verba** (see introductory paragraph)?
4. Why should Jason trust the words of Aeetes' daughter (see line 4 and introductory paragraph)?
5. Rewrite the Latin of lines 5–6 in English word order.
6. What does Medea ask Jason to do to prove his love for her (lines 7–9)?
7. In what ways did Medea help Jason (lines 9–10)?
8. What was the subsequent effect of this **medicāmen** (lines 11–12)?
9. What is the effect of the redundancy (anaphora) of **mīrus** in lines 9 and 10?
10. To whom or what does **illī** (line 12) refer?
11. What is the "crop" that the furrows strain to bear in line 13?
12. How does Jason react to this threat (lines 14–15)?
13. How does the situation resolve itself (lines 15–16)?
14. Of what poetic technique or device is **mox mīles mortuus** (line 16) an example? Find another example in this poem.
15. What is the effect of the placement of the words in line 17?
16. What do we learn about the dragon in lines 17–20?
17. Does **lūmina** (line 19) really mean "eyes"? Find its basic meaning in a Latin dictionary.
18. "Apostrophe" is a sudden break from the previous method of discourse and an address, in the second person, of some person or object, absent or present. Explain why line 21 is an apostrophe.
19. What do we learn about Medea from this apostrophe?
20. "Periphrasis" is a roundabout way of saying something. How else could you express the idea conveyed by **mōlēs serpentis** (lines 21–22)?
21. A particular sound can be used in poetry to create the effect of sleep. What is that sound and how is it effective in the last line of the poem?

FORMS

I. Nouns

Number / Case	1st Declension Fem.	2nd Declension Masc.	2nd Declension Masc.	2nd Declension Neut.	3rd Declension Masc.	3rd Declension Fem.	3rd Declension Neut.	4th Declension Fem.	4th Declension Neut.	5th Declension Masc.
Singular										
Nom.	puélla	sérvus	púer	báculum	páter	vōx	nómen	mánus	génū	díēs
Gen.	puéllae	sérvī	púerī	báculī	pátris	vócis	nóminis	mánūs	génūs	díēī
Dat.	puéllae	sérvō	púerō	báculō	pátrī	vócī	nóminī	mánuī	génū	díēī
Acc.	puéllam	sérvum	púerum	báculum	pátrem	vócem	nómen	mánum	génū	díem
Abl.	puéllā	sérvō	púerō	báculō	pátre	vóce	nómine	mánū	génū	díē
Plural										
Nom.	puéllae	sérvī	púerī	bácula	pátrēs	vócēs	nómina	mánūs	génua	díēs
Gen.	puellárum	servórum	puerórum	baculórum	pátrum	vócum	nóminum	mánuum	génuum	diérum
Dat.	puéllīs	sérvīs	púerīs	báculīs	pátribus	vócibus	nomínibus	mánibus	génibus	diébus
Acc.	puéllās	sérvōs	púerōs	bácula	pátrēs	vócēs	nómina	mánūs	génua	díēs
Abl.	puéllīs	sérvīs	púerīs	báculīs	pátribus	vócibus	nomínibus	mánibus	génibus	diébus

II. Adjectives

Number Case	1st and 2nd Declension			3rd Declension		
	Masc.	*Fem.*	*Neut.*	*Masc.*	*Fem.*	*Neut.*
Singular						
Nominative	mágnus	mágna	mágnum	ómnis	ómnis	ómne
Genitive	mágnī	mágnae	mágnī	ómnis	ómnis	ómnis
Dative	mágnō	mágnae	mágnō	ómnī	ómnī	ómnī
Accusative	mágnum	mágnam	mágnum	ómnem	ómnem	ómne
Ablative	mágnō	mágnā	mágnō	ómnī	ómnī	ómnī
Plural						
Nominative	mágnī	mágnae	mágna	ómnēs	ómnēs	ómnia
Genitive	magnórum	magnárum	magnórum	ómnium	ómnium	ómnium
Dative	mágnīs	mágnīs	mágnīs	ómnibus	ómnibus	ómnibus
Accusative	mágnōs	mágnās	mágna	ómnēs	ómnēs	ómnia
Ablative	mágnīs	mágnīs	mágnīs	ómnibus	ómnibus	ómnibus

Case	Masc.	Fem.	Neut.	Masc.	Fem.	Neut.	Masc.	Fem.	Neut.
Nominative	únus	úna	únum	dúo	dúae	dúo	trēs	trēs	tría
Genitive	úníus	úníus	úníus	duórum	duárum	duórum	tríum	tríum	tríum
Dative	únī	únī	únī	duóbus	duábus	duóbus	tríbus	tríbus	tríbus
Accusative	únum	únam	únum	dúōs	dúās	dúo	trēs	trēs	tría
Ablative	únō	únā	únō	duóbus	duábus	duóbus	tríbus	tríbus	tríbus

IV. Demonstrative Adjectives

Number / Case	Masc.	Fem.	Neut.	Masc.	Fem.	Neut.
Singular						
Nominative	hic	haec	hoc	ílle	ílla	íllud
Genitive	húius	húius	húius	illíus	illíus	illíus
Dative	húic	húic	húic	íllī	íllī	íllī
Accusative	hunc	hanc	hoc	íllum	íllam	íllud
Ablative	hōc	hāc	hōc	íllō	íllā	íllō
Plural						
Nominative	hī	hae	haec	íllī	íllae	ílla
Genitive	hórum	hárum	hórum	illórum	illárum	illórum
Dative	hīs	hīs	hīs	íllīs	íllīs	íllīs
Accusative	hōs	hās	haec	íllōs	íllās	ílla
Ablative	hīs	hīs	hīs	íllīs	íllīs	íllīs

V. Pronouns

Case	Singular					Plural				
	1st	2nd	3rd			1st	2nd	3rd		
			Masc.	Fem.	Neut.			Masc.	Fem.	Neut.
Nominative	égo	tū	is	éa	id	nōs	vōs	éī	éae	éa
Genitive	míhi	tíbi	éius	éius	éius	nóbis	vóbis	eórum	eárum	eórum
Dative	mē	tē	éī	éī	éī	nōs	vōs	éīs	éīs	éīs
Accusative	mē	tē	éum	éam	id	nóbis	vóbis	éōs	éās	éa
Ablative			éō	éā	éō			éīs	éīs	éīs

VI. Regular Verbs

		1st Conjugation	2nd Conjugation	3rd Conjugation	3rd (-iō)	4th Conjugation
Infinitive		paráre	habére	míttere	iácere (-iō)	audíre
Imperative		párā	hábē	mítte	iáce	aúdī
		paráte	habéte	míttite	iácite	audíte
Present	Singular 1	párō	hábeō	míttō	iáciō	aúdiō
	2	párās	hábēs	míttis	iácis	aúdīs
	3	párat	hábet	míttit	iácit	aúdit
	Plural 1	parámus	habémus	míttimus	iácimus	audímus
	2	parátis	habétis	míttitis	iácitis	audítis
	3	párant	hábent	míttunt	iáciunt	aúdiunt
Imperfect	Singular 1	parábam	habébam	mittébam	iaciébam	audiébam
	2	parábās	habébās	mittébās	iaciébās	audiébās
	3	parábat	habébat	mittébat	iaciébat	audiébat
	Plural 1	parābámus	habēbámus	mittēbámus	iaciēbámus	audiēbámus
	2	parābátis	habēbátis	mittēbátis	iaciēbátis	audiēbátis
	3	parábant	habébant	mittébant	iaciébant	audiébant

111

VI. Regular Verbs (continued)

		1st Conjugation	2nd Conjugation	3rd Conjugation		4th Conjugation
	Infinitive	paráre	habḗre	míttere	iácere (-iō)	audíre
Future	Singular 1	parábō	habḗbō	míttam	iáciam	aúdiam
	2	parábis	habḗbis	míttēs	iáciēs	aúdiēs
	3	parábit	habḗbit	míttet	iáciet	aúdiet
	Plural 1	parábimus	habḗbimus	mittḗmus	iaciḗmus	audiḗmus
	2	parábitis	habḗbitis	mittḗtis	iaciḗtis	audiḗtis
	3	parábunt	habḗbunt	míttent	iácient	aúdient
Perfect	Singular 1	parā́vī	hábuī	mī́sī	iḗcī	audī́vī
	2	parāvístī	habuístī	mīsístī	iēcístī	audīvístī
	3	parā́vit	hábuit	mī́sit	iḗcit	audī́vit
	Plural 1	parā́vimus	habúimus	mī́simus	iḗcimus	audī́vimus
	2	parāvistis	habuistis	mīsistis	iēcistis	audīvistis
	3	parāvḗrunt	habuḗrunt	misḗrunt	iēcḗrunt	audīvḗrunt

VI. Regular Verbs (continued)

			1st Conjugation	2nd Conjugation	3rd Conjugation		4th Conjugation
Infinitive			paráre	habére	míttere	iácere (-iō)	audíre
Pluperfect	*Singular*	1	paráveram	habúeram	míseram	iéceram	audíveram
		2	paráverās	habúerās	míserās	iécerās	audíverās
		3	paráverat	habúerat	míserat	iécerat	audíverat
	Plural	1	paráverámus	habuerámus	míserámus	iécerámus	audíverámus
		2	paráverátis	habuerátis	míserátis	iécerátis	audíverátis
		3	paráverant	habúerant	míserant	iécerant	audíverant
Future Perfect	*Singular*	1	paráverō	habúerō	míserō	iécerō	audíverō
		2	paráveris	habúeris	míseris	iéceris	audíveris
		3	paráverit	habúerit	míserit	iécerit	audíverit
	Plural	1	parávérimus	habuérimus	mīsérimus	iecérimus	audīvérimus
		2	parávéritis	habuéritis	mīséritis	iecéritis	audīvéritis
		3	paráverint	habúerint	míserint	iécerint	audíverint

113

VII. Irregular Verbs

		ésse	pósse	vélle	nólle	íre	férre
Infinitive		ésse	pósse	vélle	nólle	íre	férre
Imperative	2	es	—	—	nólī	ī	fer
	3	éste	—	—	nólīte	íte	férte
Present — *Singular*	1	sum	póssum	vólō	nólō	éō	férō
	2	es	pótes	vīs	nōn vīs	īs	fers
	3	est	pótest	vult	nōn vult	it	fert
Present — *Plural*	1	súmus	póssumus	vólumus	nólumus	ímus	férimus
	2	éstis	potéstis	vúltis	nōn vúltis	ítis	fértis
	3	sunt	póssunt	vólunt	nólunt	éunt	férunt
Imperfect — *Singular*	1	éram	póteram	volébam	nōlébam	íbam	ferébam
	2	érās	póterās	volébās	nōlébās	íbās	ferébās
	3	érat	póterat	volébat	nōlébat	íbat	ferébat
Imperfect — *Plural*	1	erámus	poterámus	volēbámus	nōlēbámus	ībámus	ferēbámus
	2	erátis	poterátis	volēbátis	nōlēbátis	ībátis	ferēbátis
	3	érant	póterant	volébant	nōlébant	íbant	ferébant
Future — *Singular*	1	érō	póterō	vólam	nólam	íbō	féram
	2	éris	póteris	vólēs	nólēs	íbis	férēs
	3	érit	póterit	vólet	nólet	íbit	féret
Future — *Plural*	1	érimus	potérimus	volémus	nōlémus	íbimus	ferémus
	2	éritis	potéritis	volétis	nōlétis	íbitis	ferétis
	3	érunt	póterunt	vólent	nólent	íbunt	férent

Note: perfect, pluperfect, and future perfect tenses are formed regularly from the perfect stem plus the regular endings.

114

Vocabulary

A

ā or ab (+ *abl.*)	by, from
ábeō, abíre (*irreg.*), ábiī, ábitum	to go away
24 abhínc	ago, previously
ábsum, abésse (*irreg.*), áfuī	to be away, absent, be distant
áccidit, accídere (3), áccidit	to happen
20 accúsō (1)	to accuse
ad (+ *acc.*)	to, towards, at, near
adhúc	still
18 ádiuvō, adiuváre (1), adiúvī, adiútum	to help
21 admóveō, admovére (2), admóvī, admótum	to move towards
18 ádsum, adésse (*irreg.*), ádfuī	to be present
advéniō, adveníre (4), advénī, advéntum	to reach, arrive at
advesperáscit, advesperáscere, advesperávit	to get dark
aedifícium, -ī (*n*)	building
23 aedíficō (1)	to build
23 aéstus, -ūs (*m*)	heat
Áge! Ágite!	Come on!
áger, ágrī (*m*)	field
17 agnóscō, agnóscere (3), agnóvī, ágnitum	to recognize
ágō, ágere (3), égī, áctum	to do, drive
Quid ágis?	How are you?
26 albátus, -a, -um	white
24 áliquid	something
álius, ália, áliud	other, another
álter, áltera, álterum	the other, an other, a second
ámbulō (1)	to walk
amícus, -ī (*m*)	friend
ámō (1)	to like, love
22 amphitheátrum, -ī (*n*)	amphitheater
ancílla, -ae (*f*)	slave-woman
19 ánimus, -ī (*m*)	mind
20 ánimum recuperáre	to regain one's senses, be fully awake
19 in ánimō habére	to intend
19 ánteā	previously, before
25 antíquus, -a, -um	ancient
25 apériō, aperíre (4), apéruī, apértum	to open
appáreō (2)	to appear
appropínquō (1) (+ *dat.* or ad + *acc.*)	to approach, draw near (to)
22 áqua, -ae (*f*)	water
22 aquaedúctus, -ūs (*m*)	aqueduct

	árbor, árboris (f)	tree
23	árcus, -ūs (m)	arch
26	arēna, -ae (f)	arena, sand
	arrípiō, arrípere (3), arrípuī, arréptum	to grab hold of, snatch, seize
	ars, ártis (f)	skill
	ascéndō, ascéndere (3), ascéndī, ascénsum	to climb, go up
22	at	but
21	átque	and, also
25	átrium, -ī (n)	atrium, central room in a house
19	atténtē	attentively, closely
23	attónitus, -a, -um	astonished, astounded
	aúdiō (4)	to hear, listen to
24	aúreus, -a, -um	golden
	auríga, -ae (m)	charioteer
21	aúrum, -ī (n)	gold
	auxílium, -ī (n)	help

B

	báculum, -ī (n)	stick
21	béne	well
25	bóna, -ōrum (n pl)	goods, possessions
	bónus, -a, -um	good
	bōs, bóvis (m/f)	ox, cow
	brévis, -is, -e	short

C

	cádō, cádere (3), cécidī, cásum	to fall
	caélum, -ī (n)	sky
	cánis, cánis (m/f)	dog
21	captívus, -ī (m)	prisoner
24	cáput, cápitis (n)	head
17	caúda, -ae (f)	tail
	caúpō, caupónis (m)	innkeeper
	caupóna, -ae (f)	inn
24	caúsa, -ae (f)	reason
	cáveō, cavére (2), cávī, caútum	to watch out, be careful
26	cédō, cédere (3), céssī, céssum	to come, go
	celériter	quickly
	celérrimē	very fast, quickly
	célō (1)	to hide
18	céna, -ae (f)	dinner
18	cénō (1)	to dine, eat dinner
18	cértē	certainly
	céssō (1)	to be idle, do nothing, delay
	cíbus, -ī (m)	food
26	circénsis, -is, -e	in the circus

116

23	circúmeō, circumíre (*irreg*.), circúmiī, circúmitum	to go around
22	Círcus, -ī (*m*)	Circus Maximus
	císium, -ī (*n*)	light two-wheeled carriage
	císta, -ae (*f*)	trunk, chest, box
	cívis, cívis (*m*)	citizen
	clámō (1)	to shout
	clámor, clāmóris (*m*)	shout, shouting
25	claúdō, claúdere (3), claúsī, claúsum	to shut
23	claúsus, -a, -um	shut, closed
24	clíēns, cliéntis (*m*)	client, dependent
20	cógitō (1)	to think
22	cólō, cólere (3), cóluī, cúltum	to cultivate
	commótus, -a, -um	moved
25	métū commótus	moved by fear, in a panic
22	condúcō, condúcere (3), condúxī, condúctum	to hire
20	conícīō, conícere (3), coniécī, coniéctum	to throw
22	cōnsídō, cōnsídere (3), cōnsédī	to sit down
	cōnspíciō, cōnspícere (3), cōnspéxī, cōnspéctum	to catch sight of
22	cōnstítuō, cōnstitúere (3), cōnstítuī, cōnstitútum	to decide
20	córpus, córporis (*n*)	body
	crās	tomorrow
	cubículum, -ī (*n*)	room, bedroom
18	cúbitum íre	to go to bed
18	cui	to whom, to him, to her
	cum (+ *abl*.)	with
21	cum	when
	cúnctī, -ae, -a	all
	Cūr . . . ?	Why . . . ?
22	Cúria, -ae (*f*)	Senate House
	cúrō (1)	to look after, attend to
	cúrrō, cúrrere (3), cucúrrī, cúrsum	to run
	custódiō (4)	to guard
25	cústōs, custódis (*m*)	guard

D

19	dē (+ *abl*.)	down from, concerning, about
	dēféssus, -a, -um	tired
	deínde	then, next
23	dēmónstrō (1)	to show
	dēscéndō, dēscéndere (3), dēscéndī, dēscénsum	to come or go down, climb down

117

	dēvértō, dēvértere (3), dēvértī, dēvérsum	to turn aside
19	dévorō (1)	to devour
19	dícō, dícere (3), díxī, díctum	to say, tell
	díēs, diḗī (m)	day
18	dīligénter	carefully
	discḗdō, discḗdere (3), discéssī, discéssum	to go away, depart
	díū	for a long time
21	dō, dáre, dédī, dátum	to give
24	dóceō, docḗre (2), dócuī, dóctum	to teach
17	dóleō (2)	to be sorry, sad
25	dómī	at home
	dómina, -ae (f)	mistress, lady of the house
	dóminus, -ī (m)	master, owner
22	dómō	out of the house
22	dómum	homeward, home
22	dómus, -ūs (f)	house
	dórmiō (4)	to sleep
	dū́cō, dū́cere (3), dū́xī, dúctum	to lead, take, bring
	dum	while, as long as
	dúo, dúae, dúo	two

E

	ē or ex (+ abl.)	from, out of
	Écce!	Look! Look at . . . !
	égo	I
	Éheu!	Alas!
24	Ého!	Hey!
20	éī	to him, her, it
21	éī, éae, éa	they
21	éīs	to them
	éius	his, her, its
24	émō, émere (3), ḗmī, ḗmptum	to buy
19	énim	for
	éō, íre (irreg.), ívī, ítum	to go
22	éō (adv.)	there, to that place
24	eórum	their
	éōs	them
	epístula, -ae (f)	letter
	équus, -ī (m)	horse
	érrō (1)	to wander, be mistaken
	ésse (see sum)	
19	Éstō!	All right!
18	ēsū́riō (4)	to be hungry
	et	and
	étiam	also, even

	éum	him, it
	ex or ē (+ *abl.*)	from, out of
	excípiō, excípere (3), excḗpī, excéptum	to welcome, receive
24	excitátus, -a, -um	wakened, aroused
	éxcitō (1)	to rouse, wake (someone) up
	exclámō (1)	to exclaim, shout out
	éxeō, exíre (*irreg.*), éxiī, éxitum	to go out
18	éxplicō (1)	to explain
	exspéctō (1)	to look out for, wait for
22	éxstāns, exstántis	standing out, towering
17	exténdō, exténdere (3), exténdī, exténtum	to hold out
22	éxtrā (+ *acc.*)	outside
	éxtrahō, extráhere (3), extráxī, extráctum	to pull out, drag out

F

19	fábula, -ae (*f*)	story
	fáciō, fácere (3), fḗcī, fáctum	to make, do
	fátuus, -a, -um	stupid
26	fáveō, favḗre (2), fávī, faútum (+ *dat.*)	to favor, support
26	fēriátus, -a, -um	celebrating a holiday
	férō, férre (*irreg.*), túlī, látum	to carry, bring, bear
	feróciter	fiercely
	festínō (1)	to hurry
	fília, -ae (*f*)	daughter
	fílius, -ī (*m*)	son
20	fíniō (4)	to finish
	fortásse	perhaps
22	Fórum, -ī (*n*)	the Forum (town center of Rome)
	fóssa, -ae (*f*)	ditch
	fráter, frátris (*m*)	brother
	frústrā	in vain
17	fúgiō, fúgere (3), fúgī, fúgitum	to flee
	fúī (see sum)	

G

	gaúdeō, gaudḗre (2), gavīsus sum	to be glad, rejoice
22	gaúdium, -ī (*n*)	joy
	gémō, gémere (3), gémuī, gémitum	to groan
25	gládius, -ī (*m*)	sword
25	gládium stríngere	to draw a sword
26	glória, -ae (*f*)	fame, glory
20	Graécia, -ae (*f*)	Greece
	Graécus, -a, -um	Greek

H

21	habḗnae, -árum (*f pl*)	reins
	hábeō (2)	to have, hold
	hábitō (1)	to live, dwell

	haéreō, haerére (2), haésī, haésum	to stick
19	héri	yesterday
17	hic, haec, hoc	this
	hīc (*adverb*)	here
	hódiē	today
17	hómō, hóminis (*m*)	man
22	hóminēs, hóminum (*m pl*)	people
	hốra, -ae (*f*)	hour
	hórtus, -ī (*m*)	garden
17	hóspes, hóspitis (*m*)	friend, host, guest
22	hūc illū́c	here and there, this way and that
24	húıus	genitive of hic

I
25	iáceō (2)	to lie, be lying down
	iáciō, iácere (3), iḗcī, iáctum	to throw
	iam	now, already
	iā́nua, -ae (*f*)	door
	íbi	there
	id (see is)	
	idéntidem	again and again, repeatedly
	ígitur	therefore
	ignā́vus, -a, -um	cowardly, lazy
	ílle, ílla, íllud	that, he, she, it; that famous
22	illū́c	there, to that place
22	ímber, ímbris (*m*)	rain
21	ímmemor, immémoris	forgetful
	immóbilis, -is, -e	motionless
26	immortā́lis, -is, -e	immortal
	in (+ *abl.*)	in, on
	in (+ *acc.*)	into
24	incéndō, incéndere (3), incéndī, incḗnsum	to burn, set on fire
	íncitō (1)	to spur on, urge on, drive
	índuō, indúere (3), índuī, indū́tum	to put on
	īnfírmus, -a, -um	weak, shaky
21	íngēns, ingéntis	huge
20	innocéntia, -ae (*f*)	innocence
	ínquit	(he, she) says, said
24	īnspíciō, īnspícere (3), īnspéxī, īnspéctum	to examine
22	intérdiū	during the day, by day
	intéreā	meanwhile
	interpéllō (1)	to interrupt
21	íntrā (+ *acc.*)	inside
	íntrō (1)	to enter, go in
	invéniō, invenī́re (4), invḗnī, invéntum	to come upon, find

120

20	invítus, -a, -um	unwilling, unwillingly
	ípse, ípsa, ípsum	-self, very
	īrátus, -a, -um	angry
	íre (see éō)	
	is, ea, id	he, she, it; this, that
	Íta vérō!	Yes!
	ítaque	and so, therefore
	íter, itíneris (n)	journey, road
	íterum	again, a second time
	iúbeō, iubére (2), iússī, iússum	to order, bid

L

23	lábor, labóris (m)	work, toil
	labórō (1)	to work
	lácrimō (1)	to weep, cry
	laétus, -a, -um	happy, glad
24	lápis, lápidis (m)	stone
17	látrāns, lātrántis	barking
24	lātrátus, -ūs (m)	a bark, barking
	látrō (1)	to bark
17	laúdō (1)	to praise
19	lávō, laváre (1), lávī, lavátum	to wash
22	lectíca, -ae (f)	litter
22	lectīcárius, -ī (m)	litter-bearer
18	léctus, -ī (m)	bed, couch
17	lēgátus, -ī (m)	envoy
	légō, légere (3), légī, léctum	to read
	léntē	slowly
23	líber, líbrī (m)	book
	líberī, -órum (m pl)	children
19	lícet, licére (2), lícuit	it is allowed
19	lícet nóbīs	we are allowed, we may
	lóngus, -a, -um	long
23	lúdī, -órum (m pl)	games
	lúpus, -ī (m)	wolf
25	lútum, -ī (n)	mud
20	lūx, lúcis (f)	light
20	príma lúce	at dawn

M

23	magníficus, -a, -um	magnificent
	mágnus, -a, -um	big, great, large, loud (voice)
21	mandátum -ī (n)	order, instruction
	máne	early in the day, in the morning
	máneō, manére (2), mánsī, mánsum	to remain, stay
17	mánus, -ūs (f)	hand
26	máppa, -ae (f)	napkin

121

	máter, mátris (f)	mother
22	máximus, -a, -um	very great, greatest, very large
	mē	me
19	médius, -a, -um	mid-, middle of
19	média nox	midnight
20	Mégara, -ae (f)	Megara (a city in Greece)
17	Mehércule!	By Hercules! Goodness me!
18	mélior, melióris	better
21	mercátor, mercātóris (m)	merchant
26	méta, -ae (f)	mark, goal, turning-post
25	métus, -ūs (m)	fear
	méus, -a, -um	my, mine
	míhi	for me, to me
19	míles, mílitis (m)	soldier
	Mínimē (vérō)!	Not at all! Not in the least! No!
22	mírus, -a, -um	wonderful, marvelous, strange
	míser, mísera, míserum	unhappy, miserable, wretched
	míttō, míttere (3), mísī, míssum	to send
17	módo	only
23	mólēs, mólis (f)	mass, huge bulk
	moléstus, -a, -um	troublesome, annoying
23	mōns, móntis (m)	mountain, hill
21	mónstrō (1)	to show
25	mors, mórtis, (f)	death
20	mórtuus, -a, -um	dead
	móveō, movére (2), móvī, mótum	to move
	mox	soon, presently
26	múlier, mulíeris (f)	woman
	múltī, -ae, -a	many
22	multitúdō, multitúdinis (f)	crowd
22	múrus, -ī (m)	wall
21	mūs, múris (m)	mouse
	mússō (1)	to murmur, mutter

N

	nam	for
19	nārrátus, -a, -um	told
19	nárrō (1)	to tell (a story)
	-ne	(indicates a question)
	necésse	necessary
19	nécō (1)	to kill
	némō, néminis	no one
25	néque	and . . . not
	néque . . . néque	neither . . . nor
24	néque támen	but . . . not

	nésciō (4)	to be ignorant, not know
	níhil	nothing
20	Níhil málī.	There is nothing wrong.
17	nísi	unless, if . . . not, except
	nóbīs	for us, to us
25	nóceō (2) (+ dat.)	to harm
	nócte	at night
21	noctúrnus, -a, -um	happening during the night
	nólō, nólle (irreg.), nóluī	to be unwilling, not to wish
	nómen, nóminis (n)	name
	nōn	not
	nóndum	not yet
18	Nónne . . . ?	(introduces a question that expects the answer "yes")
25	nōnnúmquam	sometimes
	nōs	we, us
24	nóster, nóstra, nóstrum	our
24	nóvus, -a, -um	new
	nox, nóctis (f)	night
	núllus, -a, -um	no, none
	númerus, -ī (m)	number
19	númquam	never
	nunc	now
	núntius, -ī (m)	messenger

O

20	obdórmiō (4)	to go to sleep
17	obésus, -a, -um	fat
23	occúrrō, occúrrere (3), occúrrī, occúrsum (+ dat.)	to meet
25	óculus, -ī (m)	eye
17	ólim	once (upon a time)
	ómnis, -is, -e	all, the whole, every, each
	ónus, óneris (n)	load, burden
24	oppréssus, -a, -um	crushed
19	óptimus, -a, -um	best, very good
19	Vir óptime!	Sir!
21	ōrátor, ōrātóris (m)	orator, speaker
17	os, óssis (n)	bone

P

23	Palātínus, -a, -um	belonging to the Palatine Hill
	parátus, -a, -um	ready, prepared
	párēns, paréntis (m/f)	parent
	párō (1)	to prepare
25	párvulus, -a, -um	small, little

123

	páter, pátris (m)	father
24	patrónus, -ī (m)	patron
21	pátruus, -ī (m)	uncle
19	paulísper	for a short time
21	pecúnia, -ae (f)	money
	per (+ acc.)	through, along
	perīculósus, -a, -um	dangerous
	perículum, -ī (n)	danger
	pernóctō (1)	to spend the night
	pertérritus, -a, -um	frightened, terrified
24	pervéniō, pervenīre (4), pervénī, pervéntum	to arrive (at), reach
	pēs, pédis (m)	foot
	pétō, pétere (3), petīvī, petītum	to seek, look for, aim at, attack
	plaústrum, -ī (n)	wagon, cart
	plénus, -a, -um	full
22	plúit, plúere (3), plúit	it is raining
24	poéta, -ae (m)	poet
	pónō, pónere (3), pósuī, pósitum	to put, place
21	pōns, póntis (m)	bridge
	pórta, -ae (f)	gate
	pórtō (1)	to carry
	póssum, pósse (irreg.), pótuī	to be able
19	post (+ acc.)	after
24	póstis, póstis (m)	door-post
19	póstquam	after
25	postrídiē	on the following day
17	(sē) praecipitáre	to hurl oneself, rush
	praeclárus, -a, -um	distinguished, famous
17	praecúrrō, praecúrrere (3), praecúrrī, praecúrsum	to run ahead
21	praédō, praedónis (m)	robber
26	prásinus, -a, -um	green
22	prímum	first, at first
20	prímus, -a, -um	first
20	prímā lúce	at dawn
	prínceps, príncipis (m)	emperor
	prócul	in the distance, far off
	própe (+ acc.)	near
	puélla, -ae (f)	girl
	púer, púerī (m)	boy
19	púniō (4)	to punish
22	púrus, -a, -um	spotless, clean

Q

24	quadrátus, -a, -um	squared

124

	Quális . . . ?	What sort of . . . ?
	Quam . . . !	How . . . !
	Quam . . . ?	How . . . ?
	quámquam	although
20	Quándō . . . ?	When . . . ?
24	quās	which
23	quem	whom, which
24	Quī . . . ?	Who . . . ? (pl.)
	quī, quae, quod	who, which
	quídam, quaédam, quóddam	a certain
22	quíēs, quiétis (f)	rest
22	sē quiétī dáre	to rest
	quiéscō, quiéscere (3), quiévī, quiétum	to rest, keep quiet
	Quis . . . ? Quid . . . ?	Who . . . ? What . . . ?
17	Quid ágis?	How are you?
	Quō . . . ?	Where . . . to?
25	Quócum . . . ?	With whom . . . ?
	quod	because
	quod (see quī, quae, quod)	
	Quómodo . . . ?	In what way . . . ? How . . . ?
	quóque	also

R

	raéda, -ae (f)	traveling carriage, coach
	raedárius, -ī (m)	coachman, driver
	rámus, -ī (m)	branch
21	rárō	seldom
20	recúperō (see ánimus)	
	rédeō, redíre (irreg.), rédiī, réditum	to return, go back
24	réditus, -ūs (m)	return
23	relínquō, relínquere (3), relíquī, relíctum	to leave
20	remóveō, removére (2), remóvī, remótum	to remove, move aside
	repéllō, repéllere (3), réppulī, repúlsum	to drive off, drive back
	reprehéndō, reprehéndere (3), reprehéndī, reprehénsum	to blame, scold
18	rēs, réī (f)	thing, matter, situation
18	rem explicáre	to explain the situation
	respóndeō, respondére (2), respóndī, respónsum	to reply
	révocō (1)	to recall, call back
	rídeō, rīdére (2), rísī, rísum	to laugh, smile
22	rīmósus, -a, -um	full of cracks, leaky
	rísus, -ūs (m)	laugh, smile
	rívus, -ī (m)	stream
	rógō (1)	to ask

125

	Rṓma, -ae (f)	Rome
	Rōmắnus, -a, -um	Roman
26	russắtus, -a, -um	red
	rū́sticus, -ī (m)	peasant

S

	saépe	often
	salū́tō (1)	to greet, welcome
	Sálvē! Salvḗte!	Greetings! Good morning! Hello!
22	sátis	enough
22	sátis témporis	enough time
	scelḗstus, -a, -um	wicked
24	scíō (4)	to know
	scrī́bō, scrī́bere (3), scrī́psī, scrī́ptum	to write
	sē	himself, herself, oneself, itself, themselves
	sed	but
	sédeō, sedḗre (2), sḗdī, séssum	to sit
	sēmisómnus, -a, -um	half-asleep
	sémper	always
	senắtor, senātṓris (m)	senator
	séptem	seven
	séptimus, -a, -um	seventh
21	sepúlcrum, -ī (n)	tomb
24	séquēns, sequéntis	following
20	sḗrō	late
25	sérvō (1)	to save
	sérvus, -ī (m)	slave
	sex	six
	sī	if
26	sígnum, -ī (n)	signal
	siléntium, -ī (n)	silence
	sílva, -ae (f)	woods, forest
	símul	together, at the same time
23	símulac	as soon as
20	símulō (1)	to pretend
25	síne (+ abl.)	without
	sóleō (2)	to be accustomed, in the habit of
	sollícitus, -a, -um	anxious, worried
	sṓlus, -a, -um	alone
20	sómnium, -ī (n)	dream
20	sómnus, -ī (m)	sleep
23	sónitus, -ūs (m)	sound
18	sórdidus, -a, -um	dirty
26	spectắtor, spectātṓris (m)	spectator
	spéctō (1)	to watch, look at

	státim	immediately
20	stércus, stércoris (n)	dung, manure
24	stértō, stértere (3), stértuī	to snore
24	stílus, -ī (m)	pen
	stō, stáre (1), stétī, státum	to stand
	strénuē	strenuously, hard
22	strépitus, -ūs (m)	noise, clattering
25	stríngō, stríngere (3), strínxī, stríctum	to draw
22	stúltus, -a, -um	stupid, foolish
22	stúpeō (2)	to be amazed, gape
	sub (+ abl.)	under, beneath
	súbitō	suddenly
	sum, ésse (irreg.), fúī	to be
21	súmō, súmere (3), súmpsī, súmptum	to take, take up, pick out
20	súprā (adv.)	above, on top
22	súprā (+ acc.)	above
	súrgō, súrgere (3), surréxī, surréctum	to get up, rise
	súus, -a, -um	his, her, its, their (own)
	tabellárius, -ī (m)	courier
24	tabérna, -ae (f)	shop
	táceō (2)	to be quiet
22	tális, -is, -e	such, like this, of this kind
	támen	however, nevertheless
	tándem	at last, at length
	tántum	only
23	tántus, -a, -um	so great, such a big
	tē (see tū)	
	temerárius, -a, -um	rash, reckless, bold
	témpus, témporis (n)	time
	téneō (2)	to hold
25	térra, -ae (f)	earth, ground
21	térror, terróris (m)	terror, fear
18	tíbi	to you, for you
	tímeō (2)	to fear, be afraid of
	tóga, -ae (f)	toga
26	tótus, -a, -um	all, the whole
	trádō, trádere (3), trádidī, tráditum	to hand over
	tráhō, tráhere (3), tráxī, tráctum	to drag, pull
	trēs, trēs, tría	three
	tū (acc. tē)	you (sing.)
	túlī (see férō)	
	tum	at that moment, then
24	tumúltus, -ūs (m)	uproar, commotion
	túnica, -ae (f)	tunic

22	túrba, -ae (f)	crowd, mob
	túus, -a, -um	your (sing.)

U

	Úbi . . . ?	Where . . . ?
	úbi	where, when
17	Únde . . . ?	Where . . . from?
22	úndique	on all sides, from all sides
	únus, -a, -um	one
	urbs, úrbis (f)	city
24	ut	as
	úxor, uxóris (f)	wife

V

18	váldē	very, exceedingly, very much
	Válē! Valéte!	Goodbye!
18	veheménter	very much, violently
	vehículum, -ī (n)	vehicle
	vélle (see vólō)	
26	vénetus, -a, -um	blue
	véniō, veníre (4), vḗnī, véntum	to come
	vérberō (1)	to beat, whip
24	verbósus, -a, -um	talkative
21	véster, véstra, véstrum	your (pl.)
25	vétō, vetáre (1), vétuī, vétitum	to forbid
	véxō (1)	to annoy
	vía, -ae (f)	road, street
	viátor, viātóris (m)	traveler
	vīcínus, -a, -um	neighboring, adjacent
26	víctor, victóris (m)	conqueror, victor
26	victória, -ae (f)	victory
	vídeō, vidére (2), vídī, vísum	to see
20	vidétur	he, she, it seems
19	vígilō (1)	to be watchful, stay awake
	vīlicus, -ī (m)	overseer, farm manager
	vīlla, -ae (f)	farmhouse
24	vínum, -ī (n)	wine
	vir, vírī (m)	man
19	Vir óptime!	Sir!
	vírga, -ae (f)	stick
22	vísitō (1)	to visit
	vītō (1)	to avoid
23	vix	scarcely, with difficulty
18	vóbīs	to you, for you
	vólō, vélle (irreg.), vóluī	to wish, want, be willing
	vōs	you (pl.)
	vōx, vócis (f)	voice